LINCOM Coursebooks
in Linguistics

full text research
abstracts of all titles
monthly updates

LINCOM webshop
www.lincom-europa.com

An Introduction to the Study of Morphology

Vit Bubenik

2003 (2nd printing)
LINCOM EUROPA

Published by LINCOM GmbH 2003 (2nd printing)
1st printing: 1999

All correspondence concerning *LINCOM Coursebooks in Linguistics* should be addressed to:

LINCOM GmbH
Freibadstr. 3
D-81543 Muenchen

LINCOM.EUROPA@t-online.de
http://home.t-online.de/home/LINCOM.EUROPA
www.lincom-europa.com

webshop: lincom.at

Printed in E.C.
Printed on chlorine-free paper

Die Deutsche Bibliothek - CIP Cataloguing-in-Publication-Data

A catalogue record for this publication is available from Die Deutsche Bibliothek (http://www.ddb.de)

PREFACE

This introductory textbook to the study of linguistic morphology is based on four previous versions of a manuscript entitled *An Introduction to the Study of Morphology*. They were published in a mimeographed form by Memorial University of Newfoundland (St. John's, Canada) in 1978, 1982, 1986 and 1997, and were used at the third-year level in the Department of Linguistics.

Its current version is designed for use as a second- or third-year university level introductory textbook to linguistic morphology. Before taking this course, students should have previously completed one or two introductory courses to the whole discipline of linguistics at their first or second year at the university.

Its argumentation is built around the major turning points in the recent history of morphology linked with European and American scholars such as C. Hockett, P. H. Matthews, J. Bybee, W. Dressler, A. Spencer, A. Carstairs-McCarthy, M. Aronoff, and others. Its primary data are taken from representative Indo-European (English, German, Spanish, Latin, Greek, Russian, Sanskrit), Afro-Asiatic (Hebrew, Arabic, Berber) and several other languages (Turkish, Chinese, Algonkian and others).

The book consists of ten chapters explicating fundamental principles of morphology by means of (numbered) examples. All chapters (with the exception of the last one) are equipped with a number of pertinent exercises often arranged in the order of increasing difficulty. Its contents are as follows:

1. Introduction
2. Grammatical Units (words, morphemes, clitics)
3. Paradigmatic and Syntagmatic Relations
4. Inflectional and Derivational Morphology
5. Inflectional Categories Associated with Nominal Elements
6. Inflectional Categories Associated with Verbal Elements
7. Morphosyntactic Properties and their Exponents
8. Morpheme and Allomorph
9. Derivational Morphology (derivation and compounding)
10. Theoretical Models of Morphology

For pedagogical purposes it is necessary to deal with subject matters in individual chapters as consisting of several units (indicated by subheadings). Recommended Readings at the end of each chapter should provide further ammunition to both instructors and students of this course.

During my twenty years of introducing the subject of linguistic morphology to third-year students of linguistics, languages, psychology, anthropology, sociology and other disciplines of Humanities and Social Sciences I benefitted enormously from various comments and suggestions made on the intermediate versions of the present textbook by my colleagues and students. At this point I want to acknowledge advice of and many helpful comments by the following scholars: Dr. A. Bartoněk (University of Brno), Dr. A. Erhart (University of Brno), Dr. J. Hewson (Memorial University of Newfoundland), Dr. B. Joseph (State University of Ohio), Dr. Stanislav Segert (University of California at Los Angeles), Dr. K. Strunk (University of Munich), Dr. H. Paddock (Memorial University of Newfoundland), Dr. H. Petersmann (University of Heidelberg), Dr. L. Zgusta (University of Illinois).

Many of my students during the 80's and 90's made a number of observations and suggestions on the style of the four previous versions, the clarity of their exposé and the level of difficulty of some of the exercises: Julie Brittain, Audrey Dawe, Barbara O'Dea, Kathy Francis, Margot French, Bernard Kavanagh, Angela Kotsopoulos, Dorothy Liberakis, Christa Lietz, Snezana Milovanovich, Sarah Rose, Donna Starks, Margot Stuart, and others. Many thanks for focusing my attention on the student point of view in composing this textbook.

And finally, I am grateful to three graduate students who formatted the fourth edition (1997) of the manuscript: Henry Muzale, Natasha Squires and Valeri Vassiliev. My special thanks are due to my research assistant Lawrence Greening who has been involved in editing, final text formatting, indexing and preparing a camera-ready copy for publication by Lincom Europa.

St. John's, April 1999

Vit Bubenik
Department of Linguistics
Memorial University of Newfoundland

CONTENTS

PRELIMINARIES

Morphology in this book will be defined as that subdiscipline of linguistics whose subject matter is (i) grammatical **units** (morphemes and lexemes) and (ii) grammatical **categories**. The latter are traditionally divided into **primary** grammatical categories (i.e., 'parts of speech' such as nouns, verbs, pronouns, adjectives, adverbs) and **secondary** grammatical categories (such as nominal categories of gender, number and case, and verbal categories of person, number, tense, mood, aspect and voice). **Morphemes** are traditionally defined as the smallest meaningful elements in a language.

In the seventies the transformational-generative view of morphology as a section of syntax with its emphasis on relational aspects of language led to a neglect of the study of grammatical units and categories qua **forms**. However, it should be made clear that all the above mentioned grammatical units and categories can be studied most legitimately in three manners: morphological (or 'formal'), functional, and syntactic (or 'positional'). Any attempts to disregard formal aspects of language by overemphasizing functional or syntactic aspects are detrimental.

Inspection of various introductory books on linguistics will reveal another aspect of the current neglect of morphology. Given the fact that the English morphological system is rather poor compared with that of, say, Spanish or Latin, these books concentrate on the phonemic aspect of morphology (phonological conditioning of allomorphs). Of course, it is important to discuss such facts as the allomorphy of the 3rd Sg Pres /s/ ~ /z/ ~ /əz/ in English (in *he walks, loves* and *poaches*); this, however, should not detract our attention from the morphological aspects of the categories of person and number in Spanish, which display six different inflectional forms for three persons and two numbers (*amo, amas, ama, amamos, amais, aman*). Thus for Spanish, our task will be to account for accentual shift (*ámo ~ amámos*) in terms of morphological categories such as **stem** and **thematic vowel** (and phonological categories such as **penultimate syllable**). Furthermore, it is necessary to consider any linguistic structure as possessing two aspects, namely **syntagmatic** and **paradigmatic**. It is the latter aspect which was completely discarded by transformational-generative grammar, but which nevertheless is a proper domain of morphology. In the following chapters we will spend a lot of time on analyzing and constructing paradigmatic sets for the above mentioned grammatical units and categories. This approach to morphology is known as the **Word and Paradigm Model** (cf. Hockett 1954, Robins 1959) and this model is especially suitable for the analysis of inflectional languages which are morphologically complicated in that they do not always display a one-to-one relationship between morpheme and sememe (polysemy and polymorphy). The other morpheme-based approach, known as **Item and Arrangement Model**, is suitable to the analysis of agglutinating and polysynthetic

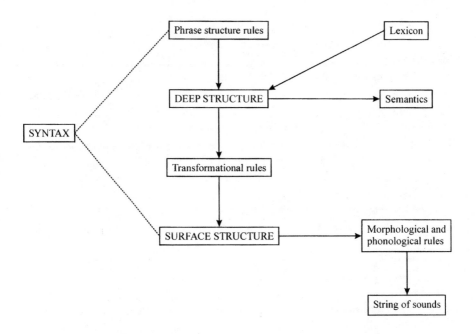

Fig. 0.1 An earlier Transformational Model of language

languages. In these languages the segmentation of words does not present any major problems, since the morphemes and sememes are mostly in one-to-one relationship.

It should be mentioned that the earlier **Transformational Model** of language did not make any provision for the formal study of primary and secondary grammatical categories. These entities were taken for granted and the emphasis was laid on the study of transformational processes. Morphology was thus viewed only as a 'surface syntactic information', as shown in Figure 0.1.

In the eighties, with de-emphasis on the transformational component the place was made for meaning-based approaches to morphology. Linguists returned to a more traditional concept of morphology as a study whose domain is the relation between meaning (semantics) and form (morphology proper). Among the earlier studies along these lines, J. Bybee's *Morphology* (1985) has the lasting merit of freeing the morphological theorizing from genetic and areal biases (her hypotheses about inflectional morphology are based on a sample of fifty languages). In the eighties another approach to morphology gained prominence under the title of **Natural Morphology** in imitation of the title **Natural Phonology** (Hooper's *An Introduction to Natural Generative Grammar*, 1976). It was developed in Germany and Austria by W. Dressler and his co-workers, and is available in the collection of their articles entitled *Leitmotifs in Natural Morphology* (1987). Dressler operates with several explanatory principles (universals, typology, system-dependency, paradigmatic structure and naturalness). The relationship between expression and meaning (Saussure's *signifiant* and *signifié*) remains the main concern. In addition, Dressler emphasizes the role of linguistic types as mediating between universal principles and language-particular behavior (universal principles of naturalness vs. system-dependent naturalness). One of the central concerns is the nature and organization of inflectional classes (the 'conjugations' and 'declensions' familiar from the traditional descriptions of many languages).

The influence of these ideas changed the study of formal syntax which in the eighties avoided the treatment of purely morphological phenomena and focused instead on the so-called interface questions such as the relation between morphology and syntax or that between morphology and phonology. To follow this change of mind one may consult Jensen (1990), Spencer (1991), Carstairs-McCarthy (1992), Aronoff (1993). Aronoff's pragmatic title, *Morphology by Itself*, marks the complete turn-about in the attitude of Generative Grammar towards morphology in that the latter is now considered not merely as an appendage of syntax and phonology; rather the author insists that linguistic theory must allow a separate and autonomous morphological component.

The reader of this manual might be surprised by the wealth of data included. This has been done on purpose, since I share Bybee's conviction (1985) that morphological universals cannot be fruitfully investigated unless we are willing to examine parallel areas of the grammars of individual languages. Morphology, of course, represents the biggest challenge to universalists' hypotheses since it is precisely here where languages differ most. Thus an important aspect of any course in morphology should be a practical and theoretical experience of analyzing phenomena which are foreign to English. Previous knowledge of the languages to be discussed is not presupposed, but the author hopes that this course will foster interest in their study.

Given the recent history of morphology, it is no surprise that there are only a few textbooks introducing linguistic morphology. The studies quoted above are not suitable for a second or a third year university course. Among earlier studies Matthews' *Morphology* (1974) has the merit of having been unique in pursuing word-based morphology independently of the generative concerns of the seventies. More recently, Bauer (1988) attempted a synthesis in the light of the influence of Natural Morphology on the field. Bauer's monograph provides both the general background to a number of morphological studies and various details of several theoretical approaches.

Neither Matthews (1974) nor Bauer (1988) contain any exercises which are essential to further progress in this field.

RECOMMENDED READINGS

Aronoff, Mark. 1993. *Morphology by Itself: Stems and Inflexional Classes.* Cambridge, Mass.: MIT Press.

Bauer, Laurie. 1988. *Introducing Linguistic Morphology.* Edinburgh: Edinburgh University Press.

Bybee, Joan. 1985. *Morphology: A Study of the Relation Between Meaning and Form.* Amsterdam: Benjamins.

Carstairs-McCarthy, Andrew. 1992. *Current Morphology.* London: Routledge.

Dressler, Wolfgang U., W. Mayerthaler, O. Panagl & W. U. Wurzel, eds. 1987. *Leitmotifs in Natural Morphology.* Amsterdam: Benjamins.

Hockett, Charles F. 1954. "Two models of grammatical description". *Word* 10.210–231.

Hooper, Joan B. 1976. *An Introduction to Natural Generative Phonology.* New York: Academic Press.

Jensen, J. 1990. *Morphology.* Amsterdam: Benjamins.

Matthews, Peter H. 1974. *Morphology: An Introduction to the Theory of Word-Structure.* Cambridge: Cambridge University Press.

Robins, Robert H. 1959. "In defense of WP". *Transactions of the Philological Society* 57.116–144.

Spencer, Andrew. 1991. *Morphological Theory: An Introduction to Word Structure in Generative Grammar.* Oxford: Blackwell.

CHAPTER ONE
INTRODUCTION

1.1 *Language and its Units*

Human language is a particular kind of sign system which bridges two areas of the nonlinguistic universe: non-linguistic real (or imagined) world, i.e. the things we talk about, on the one side, and physical speech sounds produced by human speech organs, on the other. Put differently, language is a mechanism that connects meaning with sound.

Various linguistic schools differ in the number of language levels (subsystems) they posit. Even the number of units assigned by various linguistic schools to each linguistic level is far from being agreed upon. Since the purpose of this book is not to argue for any particular linguistic school, we will simply enumerate and briefly characterize the concepts which appear in most European and American writings. Most linguists, no matter of what persuasion, recognize the following units: **distinctive features, (allo)phones, phonemes, morphophonemes, (allo)morphs, morphemes, lexemes** (words), **(allo)semes** and **sememes**. The first three may be called phonological units; morphs, morphemes and lexemes may be called grammatical units; sememes represent 'semological' or commonly semantic units.

(1)　　　Language Levels (Subsystems) Units
    (i)　　phonology　　　　　　　　distinctive features, phones, phonemes
    (ii)　　morphology　　　　　　　morphs, morphemes
    (iii)　lexicology　　　　　　　　lexemes
    (iv)　semantics ('semology')　　sememes

The phoneme has been defined as a family (class) of sounds in a given language that function as one and to which the speakers react as one sound. The members of this class are (allo)phones, which occur in mutually exclusive phonetic environments, and which share at least one phonetic feature. Phonetic features are building blocks of phones (e.g., /g/ is a 'bundle' of closure, velarity and voice). Two phones are said to be in contrast if they occupy analogous slots in two different morphemes or lexemes, i.e., if they occur in paradigmatic distribution, such as *fine* vs. *vine*. On the other hand, this opposition does not necessarily hold on the morphophonemic level, e.g., *knife* vs. *knive-s*. Here the allomorphs /najf/ ~ /najv/ belong to the same morpheme {najf} and the same lexeme *knife* whereas /fajn/ and /vajn/ are two different morphemes {fajn} and {vajn} and two different lexemes *fine* and *vine*. Thus allomorphs are not only held together by **morphophonemes**, implemented by phonemes, but they are also linked to the same semantic unit: **sememe**. Morphemes are the universal units of grammatical analysis and they are established on a semantic and distributional basis. For instance, *go* and *wen-(t)* are usually grouped together into one morpheme {go} because both mean "go", and distributionally they behave in exactly the same way as *sleep* and *slep-(t)*. However, there is no regular morphophonemic tie between the former pair whereas there is one in the latter case in the sense that there are more examples of the alternation /i/ ~ /ɛ/ as in *weep* and *wep-(t)*; consequently, /go/ and /wɛn/ should not belong to the same morpheme {go}. Here we witness that two different morphemes {go} and {wɛn} can represent the same semantic unit. This fairly well-known phenomenon, neglected by earlier theoretical treatments of morphology, is called **suppletion** or **polymorphy**. The opposite phenomenon is called **polysemy**. These phenomena are shown in Figure 1.1. For instance, in English the morpheme {s} (= /s/ ~ /z/ ~ /əz/) represents the 3rd Pers Sg of verbs, and the possessive and plural on nouns. In Arabic the same **discontinuous morpheme** /i–ā/ may represent the singular in *kitāb* "book" and plural in *kilāb* "dogs" (singular *kalb*). In other words, morphology and semantics are independent of each other even if they were collapsed in many introductory textbooks to linguistics. What is of particular interest in the study of morphology is the nature of the link-up between morpheme and sememe in the linguistic sign; it may be one-to-one but also two-to-one or one-to-two. This is illustrated in Figure 1.2. It should be emphasized that systematic confrontation of **morphemes** and **sememes** (the smallest elements of the semantic content of language) was done mostly by structuralist linguistic schools, whereas it was neglected by generativists, who concentrated more on relational aspects of language and tended to disregard units in favor of rules. Also it should be mentioned that the background for distinguishing morphology from semantics was provided a long time ago by the work of linguists dealing with typology of languages. In one type of language, commonly denoted as **agglutinating** (e.g., Turkish) each sememe is expressed by a separate morpheme, while in another type, called **inflectional** (e.g., Latin), one morpheme can express more than one sememe. Consider the inflectional forms of the word for "man" in Latin and Turkish given in (2):

(2)	Latin	Spelling	Turkish	Spelling
	vir "man"		adam "man"	
	vir - ī	virī	adam - Ø - ın	adamın
	Sg/Gen		Sg Gen	
	vir - ōrum	virōrum	adam - lar - ın	adamların
	Pl/Gen		Pl Gen	

In the Latin form *vir-ī*, *-ī* expresses two sememes (grammatical meanings) namely the singular and the genitive case; *-ōrum* expresses the plural and the genitive case. Here the relationship between morphology and 'semology' is one-to-two. On the other hand, in Turkish, each sememe is expressed by a separate morpheme: *-Ø* (zero) expresses the singular, *-lar* the plural and *-ın* the genitive case. The relationship between morphology and 'semology' is here one-to-one.

Fig. 1.1 Polymorphy and polysemy

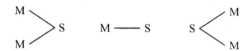

Fig. 1.2 Morpheme and sememe in linguistic sign

The distinctive features of sound have been studied extensively since Trubetzkoy's and Jakobson's pioneer work in the thirties. They are relatively easy to study because they are only a few (between twelve to seventeen in most languages). The **distinctive features** of meaning are parallel to phonetic distinctive features, but they are much more numerous and consequently much more difficult to study. Nevertheless, much has been accomplished at the level of semantics by so-called **componential analysis** limited to a few areas of lexicon, such as kinship terminology, animals, colors, etc.; there are many more semantic areas which are notoriously difficult to decompose into their semantic features. Consider, for instance, how the semantic features [+male], [+female], and [+young] combine with generic meanings of animal species, as shown in (3).

(3)	Generic Meaning	Male	Female	Young
	horse	stallion	mare	foal
	goose	gander	goose	gosling
	dog	dog	bitch	puppy
	cat	tom-cat	cat	kitten
	man	man	woman	child

The independence of morphology and semantics becomes quite clear in that the same form can represent two meanings: generic and male (*dog*, *man*), generic and female (*goose*, *cat*).

1.2 *Units and Rules*

It should be kept in mind that linguistic units cannot exist in language without rules governing their distribution. Both units and rules (or 'items' and their 'arrangements') are equally important in any serious attempt to describe the functioning of language. Their mutual relationship is of a complementary nature, i.e., it is misleading and detrimental to try to order them hierarchically, or to over-inflate either the entitative component (unit) or process component (rule) in linguistic descriptions. The study of phonotactic rules (constraints on phonological sequences) is a domain of phonology; the study of syntactic rules (**lexotactics** or rules governing distribution of words in sentences) is a domain of syntax. In morphology we will be dealing with **morphotactics**, rules of word formation. **Derivational morphology** (derivation proper and compounding) is currently treated with a strong bias towards morphophonemics; it will be shown that the semantic aspects of word formation are equally important and interesting.

1.3 *Language and its Symbolic Aspect*

We may start this section by examining one of the many problem-ridden definitions of language (Wardhaugh 1972:3):

A language is a system of arbitrary vocal symbols used for human communication.

In view of our discussion above it is preferable to view language as a 'system of (sub)systems' (with 'levels' such as phonology, morphology, lexology, semantics). The above definition makes no provision for the societal and cultural aspects of language. The term vocal in the definition over-emphasizes the fact that the primary medium of language is sound and that writing is only a secondary representation of the primary speech. Let us now examine the remaining term **arbitrary symbols** which brings us back to the Saussurean concept of the **linguistic sign**. According to Saussure the linguistic **sign** is made up of **signifier** and **signified**: *signe* = *signifiant* + *signifié*. It may be remarked that the Saussurean dichotomy continues a respectable tradition of semantics starting in Ancient Greece with the Stoics that had an identical dichotomy σημαῖνον /sēmaînon/ plus σημαινόμενον /sēmainómenon/ (σημαίνειν /sēmaínein/ "signify"). The basic assumption here is the *word* (i.e., the basic unit of syntax and semantics) as a linguistic sign composed of two parts: the *form* of the word (signifier) and what is meant (signified), or its *meaning* (concept). It will be shown in chapters dealing with inflectional morphology that the form of a word must be distinguished from its inflected ('accidental') forms which the word assumes when it functions in the sentence. It must also be mentioned that this terminology can be confusing since the 'form' of a word (signifier) could be taken to 'signify' both the 'concept' (mental image) and the 'thing' itself (referent). As is well-known, there exists extensive scholastic literature bearing on the relationship between 'concepts' and 'things', but all this is only of marginal interest to linguists. However, we have to keep in mind that the domain of linguistic meaning does not include the referent. Obviously, we can deal with 'things' themselves only by means of 'concepts', as expressed by the scholastic dictum *voces significant mediantibus conceptibus* "words signify by means of concepts". Hence the line between **form** (signifier) and **referent** (thing) in the famous 'semiotic' triangle reproduced in Figure 1.3 is only dotted.

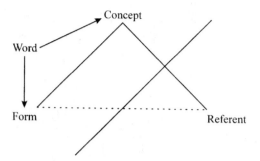

Fig. 1.3 Semiotic triangle

The relationship which holds between words (as units of linguistic meaning) and things (i.e., their referents) is the relationship of **reference**. Linguistically, words can be viewed as forms signifying **concepts**, extralinguistically (i.e., referentially) as linguistic signs referring to, or naming, extralinguistic things.

In explaining the nature of the sign, Saussure states that it is arbitrary in that one signified will have different signifiers in different languages, and almost all these signifiers were 'chosen' arbitrarily. Linguistic signs or symbols have to be learned when one acquires one's language, since they are based on a learned conventional relation; in most cases, the names we give to things are conventional, not of natural origin. However, there are two other types of linguistic signs (as defined by linguists working in semiotics), namely **icons** (literally 'pictures') and **indexes** which have to be defined referentially. **Icons** express mainly formal, factual similarity between the meaning and the form; in icons, there is physical resemblance between the shape of the sign and its referent (here, the line between form and referent is solid rather than dotted). Onomatopoeic words like *bang, thump, roar,* etc. are examples from English for this phenomenon of direct representational connection between a word and something in the 'real' world. As is well known, all languages possess highly iconic words by which speakers try to imitate the sounds of nature. **Indexes** express mainly factual, existential contiguity between meaning and form. The indexical features of language include relational concepts of place and time such as *here - there, now - then, I - you - he, this - that.* Their reference is multiple (e.g., *you* can theoretically refer to millions of addresses) and only other linguistic elements in discourse can disambiguate their meaning.

1.4 *Iconic Tendency of Language*

Onomatopoeic words are only one subcategory of icons, those sometimes called **images**. Linguists working in **semiotics** (the study of signs and sign systems) distinguish two more subclasses, namely **diagrams** and **metaphors**. **Diagrams** are characterized by a similarity between form and meaning that is constituted by the relations of their parts. A classical example of an icon of relation is **proportional analogy**. An infantile speaker of language who creates a new form **brung* (instead of *brought*) completes the following diagram (or proportion):

(4) $\dfrac{\text{ring}}{\text{rung}} = \dfrac{\text{bring}}{\text{X}}$

Metaphor is the semantic transfer through a similarity of sense perception and is based on a perception of a functional resemblance between two objects. Its full discussion belongs to semantics. Thus linguistic signs may be classified and hierarchized in the manner shown in Figure 1.4. The insistence of many linguists on the iconic tendency of language (whereby semantic sameness is reflected in formal sameness) may come as a surprise to many students of linguistics who have learned about the arbitrariness of language vs. the iconicity of certain systems of animal communication. Linguists claim, for instance, that a bee dance is iconic (rather than arbitrary) since it directly represents its subject matter (i.e., there is a direct connection between the dance itself and the source of nectar in the number and direction of the gyrations); on the other hand, it is assumed that there is almost never any connection between linguistic sign and referent — the only counter-examples being onomatopoeic words (= 'images'). However, in morphology it is comparatively very easy to find iconic correlates between linguistic signs and their referents. For instance, in English, Latin and Arabic the positive, comparative and superlative degrees of adjectives show a gradual increase in their morphological 'flesh' corresponding to the increase (or decrease) on the part of their referent, as shown in (5).

(5) | English | Latin | Arabic | |
|---|---|---|---|
| high | alt-us | kabīr | Positive |
| high-er | alt-ior | ʔakbar | Comparative |
| high-est | alt-issimus | ʔal-ʔakbar | Superlative |
| | "deep, high" | "big, great" | |

In Latin the comparative is longer than the positive and the superlative is longer than the comparative not only by sound count but also by syllable count (2 - 3 - 4); in English both comparative and superlative have the same number of syllables but the relationship holds in sound count (3 - 5 - 6) taking the diphthong as two sounds. Also, the Arabic **elative** (Arabic does not distinguish the comparative and superlative inflectionally; the superlative takes the definite article *ʔal-* while the comparative does not) is longer only by sound count than the positive. However, it is possible to find languages which show less iconicity in this respect or even where this relationship does not hold. Greek, German and Czech may be used to exemplify these two possibilities, as illustrated in (6).

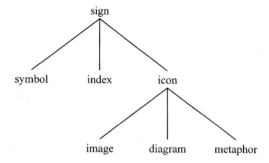

Fig. 1.4 Classification of linguistic signs

(6) Greek   German   Czech
    hupsēlós   hoch /ho:x/   vysoký   Positive
    hupsēlóteros höher /hø:ər/   vyšší   Comparative
    hupsēlótatos höchst /hø:xst/ nejvyšší   Superlative
    "high"   "high"   "high"

In German the relationship holds in sound count (3 - 4 - 5), but not in syllable count (1 - 2 - 1); in Czech the comparative is shorter by both syllable and sound count than its positive, but the superlative is longer than the comparative; and in Greek the comparative and superlative have the same number of both sounds and syllables (but both are longer than the positive).

Another frequently used example of iconicity is **reduplication** of the linguistic sign which indicates material increase on the part of referent. The subject of reduplication is practically inexhaustible with classical examples coming from languages where this linguistic strategy is grammatically less marginal than in English. For instance, in Malay *orang* means "man" and *orang-orang* means "people"; here the multiplication on the semantic side has its counterpart in the reduplication of the linguistic sign. It may be said that this type of pluralization is more iconic than the usual pluralization by means of grammatical morphology found in a variety of languages such as Indo-European or Semitic. There are situations where we are dealing with repetitive actions on the referential side; one could say that nothing would be more appropriate than reduplication on the linguistic side. Hence "daily" is expressed most 'naturally' (i.e., iconically) by reduplicating in many languages, for instance, Hebrew *yōm-yōm*, Hindi *din-din*, Malay *hari-hari* (cf. English *day by day*).

It seems that we have to assume that various languages would rank differently on the **scale of iconicity**. Latin proved to be more iconic in comparison than Czech, and Malay more iconic in pluralization than English. Of course, to make an exhaustive statement is next to impossible because it would mean contrasting the full systemic potentials of two languages and linguists are still far from being able to do that. Nevertheless, the conclusion of this section should be rather simple; earlier statements such as "any search for ... iconicity in language will reveal language to be almost entirely noniconic" (Wardhaugh 1972:25) will not stand up to the cross-language evidence as indicated above. Wardhaugh argued that "the English number system proceeds as follows: *one, two, three, four, ... ten ... thousand*, and so on, not *one, one-one, one-one-one, one-one-one-one, ...* and so on. *Four* is not four times as long as *one*". However, if we look at writing systems of various languages (add 'written' symbols to the above definitions of language), it will appear that this is a rather misleading argumentation. For instance, in the Arabic writing system *four* ٤ (four strokes) is four times as long as *one* ١ (one stroke); in Akkadian cuneiform *five* wedges is five times as long as *one* wedge), cf. Figure 1.5; similarly in Roman, Chinese and Japanese writing systems. Currently, the area of writing is not considered as secondary to linguistics; writing as the study of graphic signs (and their systems) is not essentially different from the linguistic study of vocal signs (and their systems) — both are simply subdisciplines of **semiotics**.

It is of interest to note that the clearest examples of iconicity come from grammatical morphology whereas lexical morphology is based largely on unmotivated arbitrary signs (see however 9.4 for iconicity of compounds). Grammatical morphemes are easily diagrammatizable (see the various diagrams displaying grammatical categories in this book) and they occupy fixed positions within the word (the classical example being BASE + Derivational Suffix + Inflectional suffix in Indo-European languages). Furthermore, grammatical morphemes differ from lexical morphemes by a restricted use of the sound units. For instance, in the Hebrew consonantal pattern the inflectional and derivational suffixes are realized by nasals (*m, n*), glides (*w, j*), dental stop (*t*) and glottal sounds (*h, ʔ*) whereas the lexical morphemes are built from 19 obstruents. In the Russian consonantal pattern only four obstruents (*v, t, š, x*) of the twenty-four function in inflectional suffixes. In English, the inflectional suffixes are represented by alveolar stops (*t, d*), alveolar fricatives (*s, z*), and their combination (*st*).

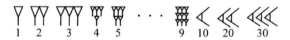

Fig. 1.5 Writing numerals in Akkadian cuneiform

RECOMMENDED READINGS

Brekle, Herbert E. 1972. *Semantik. Eine Einführung in die sprachwissenschaftliche Bedeutungslehre.* München: Fink.

Lyons, John. 1977. *Semantics.* Volume 1. Cambridge: Cambridge University Press.

Ogden, Charles K. & I. A. Richards. 1946. *The Meaning of Meaning.* 8th Edition. London: Routledge & Kegan Paul. (First edition 1923.)

Peirce, Charles S. 1955. *Philosophical Writings of Peirce* ed. by Justus Buchler. New York: Dover.

de Saussure, Ferdinand. 1955. *Cours de linguistique générale.* 5th Edition. Paris: Payot. (English translation by Wade Baskin, *Course in General Linguistics.* New York: Philosophical Library, 1959).

Wardhaugh, Ronald. 1972. *Introduction to Linguistics.* New York: McGraw-Hill.

EXERCISES

1. Analyze the paradigm of the verb "to be" in Latin, Spanish and French from the viewpoint of polymorphy (suppletion), polysemy and allomorphy. Identify first the root, stem and personal suffixes where possible. French data have to be phonemicized.

			Latin	Spanish	French
Present	Sg	1	sum	soy	suis
Indicative		2	es	eres	es
		3	est	es	est
	Pl	1	sumus	somos	sommes
		2	estis	sois	êtes
		3	sunt	son	sont
Present	Sg	1	sim	séa	sois
Subjunctive		2	sīs	séas	sois
		3	sit	séa	soit
	Pl	1	sīmus	seámos	soyons
		2	sītis	seáis	soyez
		3	sint	séan	soient

2. Analyze the paradigm of the verb "to be" in Sanskrit, Avestan (Old Persian), and Farsi (Modern Persian) from the point of view of polymorphy (suppletion) and allomorphy. As in Exercise 1, identify first the root and personal suffixes. Note: The forms of the 1st Sg and the 2nd Pl Imperfect in Avestan are not documented.

			Sanskrit	Avestan	Farsi
Present	Sg	1	ásmi	áhmi	hástam
Indicative		2	ási	áhi	hástī
		3	ásti	ásti	hást
	Pl	1	smáḥ	máhi	hástīm
		2	sthá	stā́	hástīd
		3	sánti	hə́nti	hástand
Imperfect	Sg	1	ā́sam	?	bū́dam
Indicative		2	ā́sīḥ	ás	bū́dī
		3	ā́sīt	ā́s	bū́d
	Pl	1	ā́sma	ə́hmā	bū́dīm
		2	ā́sta	?	bū́dīd
		3	ā́san	hə́n	bū́dand

3. Discuss the paradigm of the verb "to go" in Latin, Spanish and French from the point of view of polymorphy (suppletion), polysemy and allomorphy. Identify first the root, stem and personal suffixes where possible. French data have to be phonemicized.

			Latin	Spanish	French
Present	Sg	1	eō	voy	vais
Indicative		2	īs	vas	vas
		3	it	va	va
	Pl	1	ímus	vamos	allons
		2	ítis	vais	allez
		3	éunt	van	vont
Imperfect	Sg	1	íbam	iba	allais
Indicative		2	íbās	ibas	allais
		3	íbat	iba	allait
	Pl	1	ībámus	ibamos	allions
		2	ībátis	ibais	alliez
		3	íbant	iban	allaient

CHAPTER TWO
GRAMMATICAL UNITS

2.1 *The Word*

2.1.1 *Identification and Definition*

This chapter will deal with the identification and definition of lexical units, their structure, and their relationship to smaller grammatical units, namely **morphemes** (2.2) and **roots, stems** and **affixes** (2.3). The attempts at defining the two primary units of grammatical analysis, the word and the morpheme, are essentially of a circular nature, since we must presuppose the knowledge of the morpheme if we want to define the word, and vice versa. Furthermore, we have to keep in mind that lexical and morphological analysis of a language is intimately connected with its syntactic and phonological analysis, i.e., the lexical units are governed by the syntactic rules when they are combined in sentences and morphological units cannot be discussed without paying due attention to their phonological substance. Conversely, working in the realm of phonology or syntax, it would be impossible to state a number of significant generalizations without reference to the notion of the word. It is customary to include both lexical decomposition of sentences into words, and morphological decomposition of words into morphemes under the label of grammatical analysis. The word is simply the unit *par excellence* of the grammatical analysis as a final point in syntax and as a starting point in morphology.

The centrality of the concept of word will be even more obvious if we think of the grammatical analysis as the central linguistic activity flanked by discourse analysis (decomposition of texts into sentences), and phonological analysis (decomposition of morphemes into phonemes and words into syllables), as in Figure 2.1.

Word thus appears to be a unit intermediate in rank between the sentence and the morpheme. It is worth mentioning that this unit is recognized by the conventions of various writing systems (with some notable exceptions such as that of Sanskrit). Furthermore, traditional grammatical lore deals with word forms, not with morphemes.

Paying due attention to all the three aspects of wordhood (i.e., phonological, grammatical and semantic) we may adopt a 'traditional' definition of the word: word may be defined as the union of a particular meaning with a particular complex of sounds capable of a particular grammatical employment. This definition may strike us as somewhat pedantic but it is important to realize that neither one of these three aspects should be overemphasized or omitted if one wants to shorten this definition. This error was committed even by Leonard Bloomfield in his influential book *Language* (1935). His definition of word excels in Pāṇinian brevity: the word according to Bloomfield was a "minimum free form". The terms 'free' and 'bound' are more commonly used in classifying morphemes (typically, the grammatical ones such as -*s* in the plural are bound).

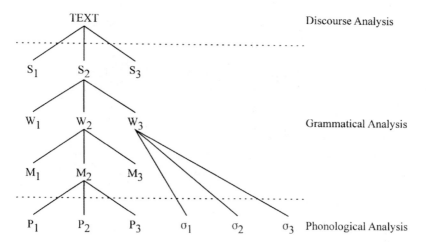

Fig. 2.1 Linguistic decomposition

Looking at the higher level, forms which occur as sentences are free forms; a free form which consists entirely of two or more lesser free forms (e.g., *poor John*) is a phrase; and, finally, a free form which is not a phrase is a word. According to Bloomfield (1935:178), "a word is a free form which does not consist entirely of (two or more) lesser free forms; in brief, a word is a minimum free form". All the units of the ranks lower than words (i.e., morphemes and phonemes) are then bound since they never occur alone as sentences. Bloomfield himself was aware of various difficulties connected with this definition. For instance, the articles *the* and *a*, though rarely spoken alone, play the same part in the English language as the forms *this* and *that*, which freely occur as sentences. Hence the traditional classification of the articles as words. Bloomfield was preoccupied more with words under their phonological aspect than their grammatical and lexical properties. These terms will be discussed in the next section.

2.1.2 *Phonological, Grammatical and Lexical Words*

As we saw in the preceding section, the term **word** turned out to be surprisingly problematic when it came to its definition. We may wish to approach the whole problem from a different angle and say that the word is a basic unit at the level of lexical analysis (lexology) called **lexeme**. Lexeme can be thought of as an abstract unit which occurs in different inflectional forms; e.g., the lexeme WRITE can be realized according to the morphosyntactic rules as *writes* (3rd Sg Present), *write* (all other persons Present), *wrote* (the past tense of *write*) and *written* (the past participle of *write*). The four inflectional forms of the lexeme WRITE may in their turn be referred to as four different **grammatical words**. The fact that these four grammatical words have to be realized at the phonological and orthographical level of the language brings us to the phonological and orthographical aspects of the word. For instance, the **phonological word** /rajts/

and its orthographic counterpart *writes* represent a particular grammatical word which can be categorized as the third person singular present indicative. Needless to say, the relationship between phonological and grammatical words need not be one-to-one. The phonological word /rʌn/ represents two different grammatical words: the present tense of *run* and the past participle of *run* (i.e., two different inflectional forms of the lexeme RUN); the phonological word /hɪt/ represents three grammatical words (plus the past tense of *hit*), etc.

2.1.3 *Internal Cohesion of the Word*

One of the characteristics of the word is that it tends to be internally stable, i.e., that the morphemes constituting a complex lexical item occur in a fixed order. The internal cohesion of the word contrasts with its **positional mobility** in the framework of the sentence. For instance, we may topicalize the sentence

(1)   His carelessness was astonishing
       1   2   3   4

by beginning with the complement *astonishing*:

(2)   Astonishing was his carelessness
       4   3   1   2

The permutation 4 3 1 2 yields an acceptable English sentence. However, the three morphemes of *carelessness* (*care* + *less* + *ness*) cannot be permuted. Similarly in Latin the sentence of three words may be permuted by topicalization in at least four ways, as shown in (3).

(3)   Ignis carnem coquet   "The fire cooks the meat"
       1   2   3
       Ignis coquet carnem
       1   3   2
       Carnem ignis coquet
       2   1   3
       Carnem coquet ignis
       2   3   1

However, the two morphemes of either the nouns *ignis* and *carnem* or the verb *coquet* cannot be permuted (**isign* or **etcoqu* are impossible). It appears that the positional mobility of meaningful elements is found at the level of phrase (and sentence), whereas the lower level of word shows the internal positional mobility only exceptionally. For instance, in the sequence of several inflectional suffixes variations sometimes may occur. In Turkish the phenomenon of positional mobility between the grammatical morphemes of the plural and past is actually quite common (and meaningful), as shown in (4).

(4) alı   -   yor   -   lar   -   dı
     take   -   PROGRESSIVE   -   PLURAL   -   PAST
     "they were taking"

or

     alı   -   yor   -   du   -   lar
     take   -   PROGRESSIVE   -   PAST   -   PLURAL
     "they were taking"

For further discussion see 4.2.

2.1.4 *Phonological Correlations*

Phonological criteria may be used for the segmentation of phonetic strings, since in many languages the word is phonologically marked in some way. Of course, the use of phonological criteria for segmenting the phonetic strings presupposes some knowledge of the phonological system of the examined language; on the other hand, the phonological analysis of the language in question can advance only after a sufficient number of word and morpheme boundaries have been established. This fact demonstrates nicely the interdependence of grammatical and phonological analyses in that linguists cannot hope to complete first the grammatical analysis and then move on to phonology, or vice versa.

Several kinds of phonological evidence are relevant in segmenting the phonetic strings in words. For instance, a great number of languages have the so-called **word accent**, which means that most words (with the exception of clitics, cf. 2.4) are accented on one and only one syllable (the accent may be of dynamic or melodic nature). In French the accent can fall only on the last pronounced syllable of a word (with the exception of the reduced schwa [ə]); knowing this one may conclude that there is a word boundary somewhere before the next unaccented vowel. Analyzing Czech data, where the accent falls on the initial syllable of the word, it may be assumed that the following phonetic string contains at least four words:

(5) Jánúdeřilpsákláckem.
     "John hit the dog with the stick"

A more complicated situation arises in languages where the accent is fixed with reference to the end of the word by the length or weight of the last or the penultimate syllable. For instance, in Ancient Greek the accent cannot fall on the antepenultimate syllable if the ultima contains a long vowel; in Latin, on the other hand, the antepenultimate syllable can be accented provided the penultimate syllable is light (i.e., open and containing a short vowel). Analyzing Latin data it may be assumed that the following phonetic string contains at least three words:

(6)   Amíkuslúpumnekăvit
      "The friend killed the wolf"

It may be of interest to consider orthographical correlates of the phonological criteria since some writing systems employ **graphemes** which display different forms for initial, medial and final position in the word. For instance, in Biblical Hebrew the fricatives [β ɣ x f θ] do not occur initially unless the preceding word ends in a vowel and these two words are in close connection, e.g. בָּבֶל /bāβel/ "Babel" but בִּבְבֶל /bəβāβel/ "in Babel" and וּבְבֶל /uβəβāβel/ "and in Babel"; the plosives in initial position are indicated by the dot placed inside the letter. The Arabic system of graphemes is made up of four **allographs** (or only two in some cases) used for the three positions mentioned above plus the allograph when the grapheme is to be realized in isolation. Students of Greek will be reminded of the letter σ (sigma) which has the allograph ς when occurring in final position in the word.

2.2 The Morpheme

2.2.1 Identification and Definition

Morphemes are traditionally defined as the smallest meaningful elements in a language. Grammatical analysis (i.e., analysis dealing with meaningful elements) of any language has to stop here since the units of lower ranks, namely syllables and phonemes, are non-meaningful. It should be emphasized that defining the morpheme as the minimal unit of grammatical (i.e., meaningful) analysis is conditioned by some explicit or implicit reference to the word as a grammatical unit of next higher rank (2.1.1). Morphemes are simply the units of lowest rank out of which words are composed. To use as an example one of the longest words in English:

anti + dis + establish + ment + ari + an + ism

It may be said that each one of the seven constituting parts of this word is associated with a particular meaning and that we are dealing with seven morphemes. Each one of them has a particular distribution and also a particular phonological (and orthographical) shape.

In the era of American structuralism it was customary to segment sentences transcribed phonetically into strings of morphemes and thus by-pass the level of word. This procedure was developed when working on languages of agglutinative and polysynthetic typologies; the results are strange for flective languages such as English. For instance, Fromkin and Rodman in their introductory textbook to linguistics (1974:103) proposed to analyze the sentence *The boys tossed Mary's hat over the fence* in this fashion:

(7) The + boy + s + toss + ed + Mary + s + hat + over + the + fence.

The level of word is by-passed and we reach the level of sentence directly from the level of morpheme. Despite the fact that some words in this sentence consist of only one morpheme we have to introduce word boundaries (#) to avoid the confusing of the lexical and grammatical morphemes.

(8) The # boy + s # toss + ed # Mary + s # hat # over # the # fence.

2.2.2 Segmentability of Words

It is important to realize that whether a word can be divided into smaller meaningful elements is only a matter of degree. Of course, typical examples from a number of flective languages are those which are determinate with respect to segmentation, where the identification of morpheme boundary simply consists of putting the plus sign between two segments: *hat + s, walk + ed*, etc. But there are quite a few English nouns and verbs which cannot be analyzed in this way. For instance, the irregular plurals *men, geese, mice* have to be analyzed in terms of process which replaces the vowel occurring in the singular form /æ, u, aw/ by another vowel which is appropriate in the plural form /ɛ, i, aj/. If the vast majority of English nouns are pluralized segmentally (i.e., by adding the morpheme *-s*), there are some exceptional cases where the pluralization is a matter of morphological processes, such as æ → ɛ (*man*), u → i (*goose*), aw → aj (*mouse*), etc. Similarly, the vast majority of English verbs form their past tense segmentally by adding the morpheme {ed}. But there are about a hundred of the strong verbs which form their past tense irregularly by a morphological process which replaces the vowel occurring in the singular form by another vowel which is appropriate in the plural form:

(9) aj → ow   (ride → rode)
     u → ow   (choose → chose)
     aj → aw   (find → found)

Thus in all these instances we are not dealing with the addition of segments but with replacing one segment by another one, hence the use of the arrow. Some linguists call these processes rather misleadingly **process morphemes** (confusing units and processes). Of course, it can be maintained that the addition of segments represents replacive processes in that the so-called zero morpheme (Ø) of the unmarked form is replaced by the real morpheme of the marked form:

(10) Ø → s   (hat → hats)
      æ → ɛ   (man → men)

Intuitively, however, we feel that these two strategies (adding the segments and replacing one segment by another) are sufficiently distinct to justify the introduction of the terms **external** versus **internal inflection**. External inflection consists of adding segments whereas internal inflection is realized through the modification of the phonological shape by replacing one of the internal segments by another one. In English there are examples of both external and internal inflection taking place in one word: *child - children* (where /aj/ is replaced by /ɪ/ and /rən/ is added) and *keep - kept* (where /i/ is replaced by /ɛ/ and /t/ is added). To demonstrate that internal inflection may be central to the nominal and verbal sub-systems we may look at Arabic, which distinguishes about twenty productive patterns of internal inflection. For instance, the plural of *kitāb* "book" is *kutub*, *jabal* "mountain" *jibāl*, *nasr* "vulture", *nusūr,* etc. The replacive processes in Arabic are more complicated than in English, as can be seen. Indeed, it is necessary to talk about the **consonantal root** ('trilitteral') into which various **vocalic patterns** are interdigitated:

(11)

root	K T B		J B L		N S R	
singular	i	ā	a	a	a	Ø
plural	u	u	i	ā	u	a

The replacive processes in the verbal system are equally complex, e.g., *kataba* "he wrote", *kutiba* "it was written", *yaktubu* "he writes", *yuktabu* "it is written":

(12)

	K T B			Y K T B	
past active	a	a	present active	a	u
past passive	u	i	present passive	u	u

(*-a* in *katab-a* and *-u* in *yaktub-u* are suffixes).

Finally, it is possible to find so-called **suppletive** words which are indeterminate with respect to segmentation: *go* vs. *went*, *bad* vs. *worse*, French *œil* "eye" vs. *yeux*, Berber *tit* "eye" vs. *aln*. Undoubtedly, *went* stands in the same grammatical relationship to *go* as *walked* is to *walk*, but whereas there is phonological resemblance between the members of the latter pair there is none whatever between *went* and *go*. Similar examples could be provided from any language. Students of Greek will be reminded of their difficulties with learning the heavily suppletive morphology of the aorist (for instance, *élipon* "I left" stands in the same grammatical relationship to *leipō* "I leave" as *eîdon* "I saw" to *horô̄* "I see").

We have to conclude that in many languages there are words which cannot be segmented into parts and that the morpheme does not always have to be an identifiable segment of the word. Still, we would maintain that all the above unsegmentable words enter into a proposition of grammatical equivalence with the segmentable words:

(13) <u>hat</u>   = <u>man</u>   = <u>goose</u>
      hats   men   geese

      <u>walk</u>   = <u>write</u>   = <u>find</u>
      walked   wrote   found

Clearly, in these equations we may replace the lexemes by arbitrary symbols (using capital letters) and the exponents of the grammatical meaning (number, tense) by another set of arbitrary symbols (using small letters):

(14) $\dfrac{A\,x}{A\,y}$ = $\dfrac{B\,x}{B\,y}$ = $\dfrac{C\,x}{C\,y}$

      $\dfrac{P\,m}{P\,n}$ = $\dfrac{R\,m}{R\,n}$ = $\dfrac{S\,m}{S\,n}$

In (14), each word is analyzed into two components — its lexical and its grammatical meaning (singular = x, plural = y, present = m, past = n). All the nouns on the top line of the equation have the component x (singular), on the bottom line y (plural); all the verbs on the top have the component m (present), and on the bottom n (past). Thus it can be maintained, as Lyons (1968:183) puts it, that "the morpheme is not a segment of the word at all ... but merely its 'factorial function'". What is distributed in the word are sememes rather than morphemes, or, its lexical and grammatical meaning. It is only when the lexical and grammatical meaning are matchable with distinct segments, i.e., when the word is segmentable into parts that these can be referred to as morphs. The word *wrote,* which cannot be segmented into two morphs, still represents the combination of two sememes: *write* (lexical meaning) + Past (grammatical meaning). On the other hand, the word *walked* is segmentable into two morphs *walk* + *ed* and, of course, these are exponents of two sememes: *walk* (lexical meaning) + Past (grammatical meaning). It will be argued correctly that the morph /t/ occurring in *walked* (or /d/ occurring in *begged*) are indicative of the phonic substance of the morpheme {d}. However, we should avoid segmenting *wrote* in this manner: *write* + *ed*, since here the grammatical meaning of the past is expressed by the process of replacing /aj/ with /ow/ (see further discussion in 8.2); see Figure 2.2.

2.2.3 *Allomorphs*

In the preceding section we noticed that the regular past tense morpheme {d} can be realized by two different **allomorphs** /t/ and /d/ in two different contexts: the former after voiceless consonants and /d/ elsewhere. If we examined further examples (such as *petted, padded)* we would discover that there is a third allomorph /əd/ occurring after /t/ and /d/. This is summarized in (15).

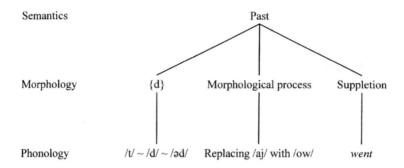

Fig. 2.2 Morphological units and processes

(15) (i)   /əd/ after /t/, /d/
      (ii)   /t/ after voiceless consonants other than /t/
      (iii) /d/ elsewhere

It is customary to call these three alternative representations of the same morpheme allomorphs. For instance, the regular past tense morpheme in English, which may be referred to as {d}, is regularly represented by three allomorphs /əd/, /t/ and /d/. It is important to realize that all these three allomorphs are **phonologically conditioned**, which simply means that the selection of one of them is determined by the phonological shape of the preceding segment: the voiceless consonant selects /t/, the voiced one /d/, and in the case of the homorganic /t/ and /d/ at the end the third allomorph /əd/ is selected. Using the same procedure we would be able to establish that the plural morpheme {z} is realized by three allomorphs, namely /z/, /s/ and /əz/. (See the analysis under 8.1). These three allomorphs are again phonologically conditioned, in the sense that the latter is selected after sibilants and affricates, and the former two after voiced and voiceless segments, respectively. (The voiceless allomorph /s/ is not selected after voiceless sibilants and affricates since this is the environment where /əz/ is selected). So far, all these alternations in the phonological shape of these two morphemes were explicable in purely phonological terms without reference to the notions of morphology. We may wish to add other pluralizing elements to the list of the three regular allomorphs of the plural morpheme: {en} as in *oxen* and *brethren*, {Ø} as in *deer* and *sheep*, {a} as in *data* and *criteria*, etc. (See their complete list in 8.2). Examining the suffix *-en* in *oxen* we obviously cannot say that /ən/ is a phonologically conditioned variant of the morpheme {z}. First of all, /z/ and /n/ are not phonologically similar enough (the only feature they have in common is voice); second, similar words such as *box* select the regular allomorph /əz/. Similarly, it is equally easy to argue against /ə/ in *data* being an allomorph of the regular morpheme. When some morphs are distributed in this manner we have to acknowledge the fact that they are not **conditioned** phonologically but

lexically, in the sense that the word *ox* selects the pluralizing morpheme {n} and the word *datum* keeps the Latin pluralizing morpheme *-a* /ə/. See the more detailed discussion in 8.2.

2.3 *Analysis into Roots, Stems and Affixes*

Inflectional and derivational morphemes (cf. 4.1) are traditionally classified by their position with regard to the **root** (or the **base**). If they precede the root they are called **prefixes**; if they follow the root **suffixes**; and if they are placed inside the root **infixes**. In the word *cats*, for instance, *cat* is the root and *-s* is an inflectional suffix. In the word *careless, care* is the root (or the derivational base) and *-less* is a derivational suffix. Since English does not have inflectional prefixes, we may look at Arabic where in *yaktubu* "he writes" *ya-* is an inflectional prefix (meaning 3rd person), *KTuB* is the root (note that the root in Arabic is a discontinuous morpheme), and *-u* is an inflectional suffix (meaning singular and indicative). In the word *bemoan, moan* is the root (or the derivational base) and *be-* is a derivational prefix. To exemplify infixes we may look at Latin or Arabic. For instance, in Latin the morpheme *-n-* which appears in the present *tangō* "I touch" is an infix; notice that the perfect of the same verb *tetigī* "I have touched" does not show it. The root is then said to be discontinuous *ta-n-g*. In Arabic the infix *-t-* derives reflexive or passive forms from the transitive verbs: *FaHiM* "understand" vs. *[i]F-t-aHaM* "comprehend". The root *FHM* is again discontinuous: *F-t-aHaM*. 'Interdigitated' vocalic patterns in Arabic roots are sometimes called **transfixes** (double or triple infixes): *šaʕīR* "poet" vs. *šuʕaRāʔ* "poets". Another type of a double affix is called **circumfix**; for instance in Berber the circumfix *t-t* (prefix and suffix added simultaneously) derives feminine nouns from their masculine counterparts: *amdakul* "friend" → *t-amdakul-t* "friend (Fem)". A less fitting example would be the German passive participle, e.g. *ge-schlag-en* "hit" because here the prefix and suffix do not display the same morpheme. And finally there is also a so-called **interfix** seen in compounds such as English *hunt-s-man* or German *Tag-e-buch* or *Tag-es-buch* "diary" (lit. day-INTERFIX-book). The interfix should not be confused with an infix which by definition splits the lexical root in two segments.

Sanskrit and other flective languages such as Latin and Greek have additional kinds of affixes, which are added to the roots, and inflectional affixes are then added to the complex form. This additional affix is known as a **thematic vowel** and the resulting complex form as a **stem**. For instance, in the Latin accusative singular *puellam, puell-* is the root, the added vowel *-a* is a thematic vowel, and *-m* is the inflectional suffix marking the accusative singular. (It may be noted that a traditional school analysis keeps the ending *-am* unanalyzed). In the Latin form *laudāmus* "we praise", *laud-* is the root, the added vowel *-ā* is a thematic vowel and *-mus* is the inflectional suffix marking the 1st person plural. This is shown schematically in Figure 2.3. The stem can be formed even by prefixing stem-forming elements, for instance, in Arabic *yankatibu* "it is written", where *KaTiB* is the root to which the stem-forming prefix *n* (accompanied by the transfix *a-i*) is added (*ya* is an inflectional prefix meaning 3rd person and *u* is an inflectional suffix meaning singular and indicative). This is shown in Fig. 2.4. From these examples it appears that there is

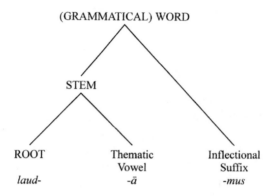

Fig. 2.3 Grammatical word in Latin

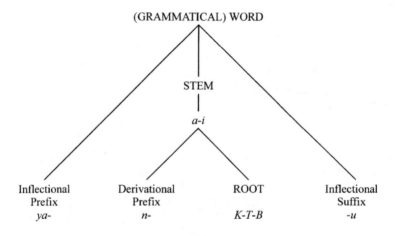

Fig. 2.4 Grammatical word in Arabic

a universal tendency for derivational affixes (prefixes and suffixes) to occur closer to the root than inflectional affixes (prefixes and suffixes); derivational elements tend to be central and inflectional elements peripheral. The root and derivational affixes (if any) constitute the stem, and the inflectional affixes are prefixed or suffixed to it (see the discussion in 4.2 for some controversial examples). Figure 2.5 visualizes this.

At this point we have to distinguish more clearly between inflectional and derivational affixes. Inflectional affixes are those that mark **secondary grammatical categories**: gender, number, case with nouns (cf. 5.2), and person, tense, aspect, mood, voice with verbs (cf. 6.3). Defining negatively, it may be said that derivational affixes are those that are non-inflectional.

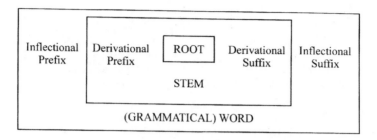

Fig. 2.5 Inflectional and derivational affixes

Derivational affixes have the potential to change the membership in the group of **primary grammatical categories** (see under 5.1 and 6.1). For instance, the addition of the derivational suffix *-ic* to the noun *democrat* results in an adjective; the addition of the derivational suffix *-ize* results in a verb. On the other hand, the verb *democratize* inflected for the past tense remains a verb, or an adjective inflected for gender, number and case to agree with its head noun (in Latin) remains an adjective.

The distinction between inflection and derivation may be blurred in some cases. For instance, the nasal infix of Latin mentioned above is a derivational rather than inflectional affix even if it serves to mark the secondary grammatical category of aspect (i.e., its presence does not change the grammatical class — both the present *tangō* "I touch" and the perfect *tetigī-* "I have touched" are only grammatical forms of the same verb). Perhaps the best we can do is to recall the traditional grammatical theory according to which inflection was considered to be any change made in the form of a word to express its relation to other words in the sentence. Hence all the grammars of flective languages include lengthy sections describing the **declensions** of nouns, adjectives, and pronouns, and the **conjugations** of verbs, according to selected models of formations, called **paradigms**. Shorter sections would be devoted to the study of various derivational processes, by which new words are formed from existing words (or roots) — verbs from nouns, nouns from verbs, etc. (See the discussion under 4.1).

2.4 *Clitics*

At this point a mention must be made of certain word classes (parts of speech) which traditionally are viewed as falling between full-fledged words and grammatical affixes. They are referred to by the term **clitics** or **grammatical words** (not to be confused with grammatical words discussed in 2.1.2). Full-fledged words (nouns, verbs, adjectives, and adverbs) carry lexical accent and their lexical meaning is of symbolic nature; on the other hand, adpositions (prepositions and postpositions), articles, particles and pronouns do not (usually) carry accent and their lexical meaning is of indexical nature (cf. 1.3).

The absence of their own lexical accent makes them clitics in that they have to 'lean' against full-fledged words (from Ancient Greek ἐγκλινόμενα /enklīnómena/ "(words) leaning against").

For instance, the definite article in English is a proclitic *the=mán* while its counterpart in Rumanian is an enclitic *óm=ul*. Upon closer examination we may classify the English article as more 'word-like' than the Rumanian one, because of its ability to be separated from its noun by an adjective: *the good man*; in Rumanian, the article behaves almost as a suffix in being always attached to the noun or the adjective (both phonologically and orthographically): *óm-ul bun ~ bún-ul om*. Other languages may repeat the article in the noun phrase, e.g. Biblical Hebrew *hā-ʔīš haṭ-ṭōβ* or Ancient Greek *ho anḕr ho agathós* (but also *ho agathòs anḕr*).

Typical examples of clitics are short pronominal forms as in Ancient Greek *moi* "me" and *soi* "you" (vs. full form *emoí* "to me" and *soí* "to you"); contrast *dós moi* "give me (it)" or "gimme (it)" with *dós X emoí* "give X to me"; similarly, *aréskei moi*, lit. it pleases me "I like it" vs. *emoì aréskei*, lit. it pleases ME (not someone else) "I (emphasized) like it".

Their intermediate status between full words and affixes is also reflected in varying spelling conventions of various languages; for instance, French hyphenates pronominal clitics in the imperative *donnez-nous-la* "give her to us" whereas Spanish spells them together with their verb *damelo* "give me it" (not **da me lo*). However, both French and Spanish spell their pronominal clitics as full words in preverbal position: *je le vois* and *lo veo* "I see him", respectively. On the other hand, Semitic languages spell their pronominal clitics always as clitics. The same is true of the conjunction "and" and various prepositions which are always spelled as proclitics in Arabic and Hebrew. On the Indo-European side, in Latin the conjunction *que* "and" is spelled as an enclitic (e.g. *pater materque* "father and mother") but not the other copulative conjunction: *pater et mater*. In the same language, the postposition *cum* "with" is spelled as an enclitic with pronouns: *mēcum* "with me" but as a full word with nouns: *cum patre* "with the father".

To express the intermediate status of clitics between full words and affixes it is customary to place the equation sign (=) between the word and the clitic, e.g. *the=man*; **morpheme boundary** is specified by +; and **word boundary** by #, e.g. *the=good#friend+s*. As far as the accentual properties of clitics and affixes are concerned, it is usually claimed that, unlike full words, they do not possess any accent. Of course, there are all sorts of counter-examples (e.g. Ancient Greek *lógos=tis* "a certain word" vs. *lógoi=tinés* "certain words"; Latin *láud+ō* "I praise" but *laud-ā́+mus*; Ancient Greek *paideu+tós* "educated"; etc.) But, on the whole, the above statement may be used as a first approximation in their identification.

2.5 *Basic Approaches to Morphology*

There are three basic approaches to morphology: Item and Arrangement Model (IA), Word and Paradigm Model (WP), and Item and Process Model (IP).

2.5.1 *Item and Arrangement Model*

The **Item and Arrangement Model** is a purely linear model which seeks to split each word (more specifically, each phonological form of a word) into a number of independently functioning segments (morphemes). This model operates with

(i)   a set of morphemes
(ii) a set of phonemes
(iii) a relation of sequence.

This model is successful in the description of agglutinative and polysynthetic languages where the phenomena of suppletion and discontinuity (see under 2.5.2) are non-existent, or are only very marginal. For instance, Cree verbal forms *niwāpamaw* "I see him" and *niwāpamik"* he sees me" would be analyzed as follows:

(16) ni   +   wāp   +   am   +   aw   "I see him"
     1SG   see   3SG   1 → 3

     ni   +   wāp   +   am   +   ik   "He sees me"
     1SG   see   3SG   3 → 1 (*-ik* = inversion marker)

In this model morphemes and sememes are paired in an exhaustive one-to-one correspondence. In the past this model was overused to the detriment of the useful distinction between morphological and syntactic structure, i.e. word vs. phrase/clause/sentence. If transferred from the analysis of the agglutinative and polysynthetic languages to that of flective languages, one may become oblivious of a crucial role played by the word in most grammatical theories. In practical terms, one has to operate with two types of boundaries: + morpheme boundary and # word boundary, in the analysis of inflecting languages. Contrast

(17) Cree: ni + wāp + am + ik   Polysynthetic
     English: he # see + s # me   Inflecting

It would be wrong to analyze English * *he + see + s + me*.

2.5.2 *Word and Paradigm Model*

The **Word and Paradigm Model** is a hierarchical (vertical) model which assigns a central role to the word as well as to its constitutive elements (morphemes). This model is successful in the description of inflecting (flective) and introflecting languages where the phenomena of infixation and transfixation create so-called **discontinuous morphemes**. Examine the following set of data from Latin:

(18) rumpō   "I break"   rūpī   "I have broken"
     relinquō   "I leave"   relīquī   "I have left"
     fundō   "I pour"   fūdī   "I have poured"

In the left column all the forms have one thing in common vis-à-vis their counterparts in the right column: they display a **nasal infix** before the final consonant of the root. Contrast $ru + m + p$ with *rūp* etc. However, to acknowledge the fact that there is a nasal infix in *rumpō* in terms of sequencing (so far the IA model) is not enough. One has to specify its meaning and this can only be done by contrasting the forms in the left and right columns. The conclusion based on the examination of English glosses would be that the nasal infix marks non-perfect forms or, to express it in negative terms, its absence marks perfect forms. This is the essence of the WP model: to come up with a grammatical solution one has to juxtapose, or rather superimpose, two related forms:

(19)   aquam $\begin{Bmatrix} \text{fundō} \\ \text{fūdī} \end{Bmatrix}$ = $\begin{Bmatrix} \text{"I pour} \\ \text{"I have poured} \end{Bmatrix}$ the water"

Another aspect of the WP model which is totally absent from the IA model is its preoccupation with irregular and suppletive morphology; **suppletion** is the phenomenon where totally different forms may belong to the same paradigm, e.g., English *go - went, be - was* (cf. 2.2.2). To stay with Latin verbal morphology examine additional data with non-perfect vs. perfect contrast:

(20)   rumpō   "I break"   rūpī   "I have broken"
         tangō   "I touch"   tetigī   "I have touched"
         laudō   "I praise"   laudāvī   "I have praised"
         dūcō   "I lead"   dūxī   "I have led"
         ferrō   "I carry"   tulī   "I have carried"

Morphological irregularities of inflecting languages are captured by allocating forms with similar irregularities to different morphological paradigms. In our data *laudā-v-ī* which forms the perfect by attaching the suffix *-v* belongs to Conjugation I, whereas *dūk-s-ī* (spelled *dūxī*) which forms the perfect by the suffix *-s* belongs to Conjugation III. The verbs which form their perfect by removing the nasal infix from the root (*te-tig-ī* with partial reduplication and vocalic change) belong also to Conjugation III. In the last example, however, there is no resemblance whatever between the root *fer-* and its counterpart in the perfect, *tul-*.

Transfixation found in **introflecting** languages such as Arabic splits not only the verbal or nominal root but also creates discontinuous grammatical morphemes. Examine the following set of Arabic plural forms with their lexical roots capitalized:

(21)   K i T ā B   "book"   K u T u B   "books"
         J̇ a B a L   "mountain"   J̇ i B ā L   "mountains"
         Ḥ i M ā R   "donkey"   Ḥ a M ī R   "donkeys"

The transfixed (interdigitated) grammatical morpheme *i-ā* is discontinuous, and so is the lexical consonantal root *K-T-B*). To come up with its grammatical analysis one has to apply the WP model, i.e. one has to juxtapose, or superimpose, the singular and plural forms. The solution is that *i-ā* marks singular in "book" and "donkey" but plural in "mountain"; hence the need to classify Arabic nouns into declensional paradigms (cf. 2.2.2).

2.5.3 *Item and Process Model*

While the IA and WP models are diametrically opposed (horizontal syntagmatic versus vertical paradigmatic model) the concerns of the **Item and Process Model** are endemic to both IA and WP models. Its main concern are the morphological processes undergone by both lexical and grammatical morphemes. For instance, when contrasting the plural formation processes of inflectional vs. agglutinating languages one may profitably draw on this model. Examine the following sets of Latin and Turkish data:

(22) Latin   Turkish

amīc-us	amīc-ī	dost	dost-lar	"friend" - "friends"
pater	patr-ēs	baba	baba-lar	"father" - "fathers"
cas-a	cas-ae	ev	ev-ler	"house" - "houses"
vīc-us	vīc-ī	köy	köy-ler	"village" - "villages"

In Latin one will notice morphophonemic change in the root *pater* versus *patr-ēs*; in Turkish the plural suffix {-lar} undergoes the process of vowel harmony /-lar/ ~ /-ler/, cf. 8.3.

RECOMMENDED READINGS

Bloomfield, Leonard. 1935. *Language*. London: Allen and Unwin. (Revised edition.) (Chapters 13–16).

Fromkin, Victoria & Robert Rodman. 1974. *An Introduction to Language*. New York: Holt, Rinehart and Winston.

Gleason, Henry A. 1961. *An Introduction to Descriptive Linguistics*. New York: Holt, Rinehart and Winston. (Revised Edition.) (Chapters 5 and 6).

Harris, Zelig S. 1951. *Methods in Structural Linguistics*. Chicago: University of Chicago Press.

Hockett, Charles F. 1958. *A Course in Modern Linguistics*. New York: The Macmillan Company. (Chapters 14, 15, 19, 20).

Klavans, Judy. 1985. "The independence of syntax and phonology in cliticization". *Language* 61.95–120.

Krámský, Jiří. 1969. *The Word as a Linguistic Unit*. The Hague: Mouton.

Lyons, John. 1968. *Introduction to Theoretical Linguistics*. Cambridge: Cambridge University Press. (Sections 3.2 and 5.3).

Nida, Eugene A. 1949. *Morphology: A Descriptive Analysis of Words*. 2nd Edition. Ann Arbor, Mich.: University of Michigan Press.

EXERCISES

(A) Identification of words

1. Latin is a language that permits many variations in word order. Positional mobility is therefore highly relevant to the location of word boundaries in Latin sentences. Use the accentual criteria discussed in 2.1.4 in isolating the words in the sentences below and giving their grammatical meanings.

(1) Rēgínamágnafēminaerŏsamdédit.
"The great queen gave a rose to the woman".

(2) Fēminaedéditrŏsamrēgínamágna.
"The great queen gave a rose to the woman".

(3) Pátersápiēnsfílióepístulammísit.
"The wise father sent a letter to the son".

(4) Epístulamsápiēnspátermísitfílió.
"The wise father sent a letter to the son".

(5) Mágnusrēxgládiumfíliódédit.
"The great king gave a sword to the son".

(6) Fíliómísitepístulamrēxsápiēns.
"The wise king sent a letter to the son".

(7) Gládiummílesmágnusrēgídédit.
"The great soldier gave a sword to the king".

(8) Rēxsápiēnsmágnaerēgínaerŏsamdédit.
"The wise king gave a rose to the great queen".

(9) Sapiéntīpátrīepístulamfíliusmísit.
"The son sent a letter to the wise father".

(10) Mágnarēgínarēgīsapiéntīgládiumdédit.
"The great queen gave a sword to the wise king".

2. Isolate the following words in the Russian sentences below and state their meaning. Your analysis should assign every phonological segment in Russian to a certain English word. There should be no residues.

(a) here	(d) mother	(g) was	(j) sick
(b) friend	(e) father	(h) my	
(c) dog	(f) will come	(i) tomorrow	

(1)	býlzdésʲdrúg	"(A) friend was here".
(2)	sʌbákəbylábʌlʲná	"(The) dog was sick".
(3)	drúgbýlbólen	"(The) friend was sick".
(4)	sʌbákəbylázdésʲ	"(The) dog was here".
(5)	mójʌtétspridʲótzáftrə	"My father will come tomorrow".
(6)	mʌjámátʲbʌlʲná.	"My mother is sick".
(7)	záftrəpridʲótmʌjámátʲ	"My mother will come tomorrow".
(8)	mójʌtétsbólʲen	"My father is sick".

3.   Isolate the words in the following Czech sentences and state their meanings. Your analysis should assign every phonological segment of every sentence to some word. There should be no residues.

I.

(a)	here	(d)	sick	
(b)	man	(e)	was	
(c)	cat			

(1)	bíltučlóvʲek	"(A) man was here".
(2)	kóčkabílanémocnā	"(The) cat was sick".
(3)	člóvʲekbílnémocen	"(The) man was sick".
(4)	bílatukóčka	"(The) cat was here".

II.

(a)	tomorrow	(d)	father	
(b)	mother	(e)	is	
(c)	my	(f)	sick	

(1)	mūjótecpříjdezítra	"My father will come tomorrow".
(2)	mojemátkajenémocnā	"My mother is sick".
(3)	zítrapříjdemojemátka	"My mother will come tomorrow".
(4)	mūjótecjenémocen	"My father is sick".

4.   The make-up of a word in Turkish differs crucially from its make-up in Latin. Discuss this statement with regard to (a) phonological and (b) grammatical criteria for wordhood. You can use the following data for (b):

Turkish

(1)　Ankara　　　　ve　　Izmire　　　　gidccegim

(lit)　Ankara+NOM　and = Izmir+DAT　go+PROGR+1SG

　　　"I am going to Ankara and Izmir".

(2)　uzun　yol　　　　uzun　yollar

(lit)　long　road　　　long　roads

　　　"the long road"　"the long roads"

Latin

(3)　Ancyram　　　　Smyrnam-que　　eō

(lit)　Ankara+ACC　　Izmir+ACC = and　go+1SG

　　　"I am going to Ankara and Izmir".

(4)　via longa　　　　viae longae

　　　"the long road"　"the long roads"

(B) Identification of morphemes and morphological processes

5.　One of the characteristic features of Swahili (and Bantu languages in general) is the existence of noun classes. There are specific singular and plural prefixes that occur with the nouns in each class. In the following sentences, two of these classes are included:

(1)　mtoto amefika　　　　　"The child has arrived".
(2)　vitabu vitaanguka　　　"The books will fall".
(3)　mtu amelala　　　　　 "The person has slept".
(4)　visu vitaanguka　　　　"The knives will fall".
(5)　mtoto anafika　　　　　"The child is arriving".
(6)　vikapu vinaanguka　　 "The baskets are falling".
(7)　visu vimeanguka　　　 "The knives have fallen".
(8)　watu wamelala　　　　"The people have slept".
(9)　watoto watafika　　　 "The children will arrive".
(10)　kitabu kimeanguka　　"The book has fallen".
(11)　kisu kinaanguka　　　 "The knife is falling".
(12)　watoto wanalala　　　 "The children are sleeping".

(a)　Identify all the lexical and grammatical morphemes you can detect and specify their meaning.

(b) How is the verb constructed? That is, what kinds of morphemes are strung together and in what order?

(c) How would you say in Swahili:

(13) The men are falling.
(14) The books have arrived.
(15) The children will sleep.
(16) The basket will fall.

6. Describe the morphological process found in the following data from Classical Arabic. Try to specify its meaning(s).

(1)	kataba	"he wrote"	kattaba	"he dictated"
(2)	šarufa	"he was noble"	šarrafa	"he honored"
(3)	fahima	"he understood"	fahhama	"he explained"
(4)	kabura	"he was old"	kabbara	"he magnified"
(5)	šakka	"he was doubtful"	šakkaka	"he filled him with doubt"
(6)	ʕazza	"he was strong"	ʕazzaza	"he reinforced"
(7)	fasara	"he discovered"	fassara	"he explained"
(8)	qāma	"he got up"	qawwama	"he set upright"

7. Using the IP and WP models identify and construct the paradigms for the formation of plural of nouns (and adjectives) in Biblical Hebrew. Start by separating them into two groups: those which form their plural by a suffix vs. those which form their plural by a suffix accompanied by a morphological processes. Hebrew distinguishes two genders, masculine and feminine, marked by -Ø and -ā, respectively.

Note: Fricative counterparts of /b, d, g, p, t, k/ resulting from postvocalic lenition are transcribed /β, ð, γ, f, θ, x/. Stress is always on the last syllable, unless marked on the penult.

(1)	sūs	"horse"	sūsīm
(2)	ḥōq	"law"	ḥuqqīm
(3)	ʔurwā	"manger"	ʔurāwōθ
(4)	ʔōṣār	"treasure"	ʔōṣārōθ
(5)	māʕōz	"fortress"	məʕuzzīm
(6)	ḥerpā	"shame"	ḥərāfōθ
(7)	kōxāβ	"star"	kōxāβīm
(8)	lēβ	"heart"	libbīm
(9)	ʔahβā	"love"	ʔəhāβōθ

(10)	rōʕē	"shepherd"	rōʕīm
(11)	yārōq	"green"	yəruqqīm
(12)	māšīaḥ	"Mesiah"	məšīḥīm
(13)	śāḏe	"field"	śāḏōθ
(14)	báyiθ	"house"	bātīm
(15)	nāβī	"prophet"	nəβīʔīm
(16)	māqōm	"place"	məqōmōθ
(17)	sūsā	"mare"	sūsōθ
(18)	máweθ	"death"	mōθīm
(19)	ʕēṣ	"tree"	ʕēṣīm
(20)	śāfā	"lip"	śāfōθ
(21)	dōβ	"bear"	dubbīm
(22)	rōfē	"physician"	rōfəʔīm
(23)	raβ	"many"	rabbīm
(24)	ṣəḏāqā	"justice"	ṣəḏāqōθ
(25)	ʔōyēβ	"enemy"	ʔōyəβīm
(26)	ləβēnā	"brick"	ləβēnīm
(27)	zāqēn	"old man"	zəqēnīm
(28)	yōšəβā	"inhabitant" (F)	yōšəβōθ
(29)	ʔīš	"man"	ʔənāšīm
(30)	pe	"mouth"	pīfiyyōθ
(31)	ḥāxām	"wise man"	ḥəxāmīm
(32)	malkā	"queen"	məlāxōθ
(33)	ʔāmā	"maid"	ʔəmāhōθ
(34)	ʕēnāβ	"grape"	ʕənāβīm
(35)	ḥorbā	"ruin"	ḥorāβōθ
(36)	rōš	"head"	rāšīm
(37)	mélex	"king"	məlāxīm
(38)	ʔəxuzzā	"property"	ʔəxuzzōθ
(39)	kāḥōl	"blue"	kəḥullīm
(40)	séfer	"book"	səfārīm
(41)	ʕiβrī	"Hebrew"	ʕiβrīm
(42)	kóaḥ	"chameleon"	kōḥīm
(43)	qóḏeš	"holiness"	qoḏāšīm
(44)	ʔāβ	"father"	ʔāβōθ
(45)	déleθ	"door"	dəlāθōθ
(46)	ʔēm	"mother"	ʔimmōθ
(47)	təhillā	"psalm"	təhillīm
(48)	ʕīr	"city"	ʕārīm

(49)	ʔiššā	"woman"	nāšīm
(50)	yōnā	"pigeon"	yōnīm
(51)	kéleβ	"dog"	kəlāβīm
(52)	bēṣā	"egg"	bēṣīm
(53)	ʕippārōn	"pencil"	ʕefrōnōθ
(54)	baθ	"daughter"	bānōθ
(55)	ben	"son"	bānīm
(56)	šāhōr	"black"	šəhōrīm
(57)	ʔī	"island"	ʔiyyīm
(58)	ʔādōm	"red	ʔədummīm
(59)	ʔéreṣ	"earth"	ʔərāṣōθ
(60)	lāβān	"white"	ləβānīm

(C) Definitions

8. Define and exemplify the following morphological processes:

(a)	vowel change	(e)	tonal modification	(i)	stress change
(b)	interfixation	(f)	subtraction	(j)	infixation
(c)	suppletion	(g)	partial reduplication	(k)	complete
(d)	transfixation	(h)	circumfixation		reduplication

9. Define and exemplify the following terms:

(a)	simple root	(d)	derivational stem
(b)	complex root	(e)	inflectional stem
(c)	inflectional prefix	(f)	thematic vowel

10. The morpheme has been defined as "the minimal unit of grammatical analysis" (Lyons, 1968:181). However, in some languages there are words which cannot be segmented into morphemes although these words belong to the same grammatical class as other words which are segmentable. Discuss this problem.

11. There are various problems connected with defining 'word'. It is usually claimed that the word should be simultaneously a semantic, a phonological (orthographical), and a grammatical unit. Discuss these three aspects of 'wordhood'.

CHAPTER THREE
PARADIGMATIC AND SYNTAGMATIC RELATIONS

3.1 *The Notion of Distribution*

Every linguistic unit (i.e., phoneme, morpheme, lexeme and to a certain degree even sentence) has a characteristic **distribution**. There are basically four types of distribution:

(i)   Distributional equivalence
(ii)   Complementary distribution
(iii) Distributional inclusion
(iv) Overlapping distribution

Two units are said to be **distributionally equivalent** if they occur in the same range of contexts; on the other hand, if they do not have any contexts in common they are said to be in **complementary distribution**. These two terms cover the familiar distinction between phonemes, morphemes and sememes (**contrastive units**) on the one side, and allophones, allomorphs and allosemes (**complementary units**) on the other. Examples of total distributional equivalence can be found most easily in phonology. For instance, phonemes /p/ and /b/ seem to be distributionally equivalent as a glance at the following range of contexts may demonstrate:

(1)   Initial Position   Final Position
       pin - bin   lope - lobe
       pic - buy   rip - rib
       pain - bane   sip - sib
       poor - boor   cop - cob
       pat - bat   cap - cab

On the other hand, phonemes /p/ and /h/ are not distributionally equivalent since the range of contexts of /h/ does not include the final position (i.e., /h/ is phonotactically inadmissible in final position in native English words):

(2)   Initial Position
       pit - hit
       pike - hike
       pail - hail

Similarly, the phonemes /n/ and /ŋ/ are not distributionally equivalent since there are no **minimal pairs** (phonologically identical morphemes or lexemes with a single segmental difference) for the initial position (i.e., /ŋ/ is phonotactically inadmissible in initial position in native English words):

(3)   Final Position
      kin - king
      ban - bang
      run - rung

Hence some linguists might be inclined to label phonemes /h/ and /ŋ/ as **subphonemes**. But it can easily be shown that even full-fledged phonemes such as /p/ and /b/ are not completely distributionally equivalent; thus there is no word **reab* to match *reap* or **fip* to match *fib* etc. Obviously, an exhaustive distributional analysis would be a tedious business and it seems that at a certain point it would become a meaningless exercise, e.g., looking for an exhaustive description of contrasts in middle position. Of course, all these difficulties would multiply at higher linguistic levels where we are dealing with hundreds and thousands of units.

Between these two extremes of distributional equivalence and complementary distribution we must distinguish two more types of distribution. **Distributional inclusion** is found between two linguistic units if one of them (x) occurs in all contexts in which the other one (y) occurs and there are also contexts in which only (y) occurs, cf. Figure 3.1. As an example of distributional inclusion at the level of morphology we may use the Modern Greek aorist and perfect. Here the range of contexts of the aorist *y* includes that of the perfect *x*. Put differently, it is always possible to use the aorist in narrating past events (perfective or imperfective) whereas the perfect can be used only if the speaker wishes to express unambiguously that the past perfective event results in the present state (cf. 6.3.3). **Overlapping distribution** is found between two linguistic units if they have some contexts in common but each unit has contexts in which the other does not occur, cf. Figure 3.2. French or Latin subjunctive and indicative may be used as an example of this type of distribution. In French we have to use the indicative in the context such as *Je crois (qu'il vient)* but the subjunctive if the main clause contains a negative verb *Je ne crois pas (qu'il vienne)*. We use the indicative in *Il est probable (qu'il viendra)* but the subjunctive in *Il est possible (qu'il vienne)* depending on whether there is *probable* vs. *possible* in the main clause. Here the question of the contrast between indicative and subjunctive does not arise; however there are various contexts in which the indicative and subjunctive are interchangeable, i.e., where they are distributionally equivalent. There are minimal pairs of sentences such as *On cherche une secrétaire qui sait le russe* (expressing confidence about finding such a person) and *On cherche une secrétaire qui sache le russe* (expressing doubts about finding such a person). Similarly in Latin the question of the contrast between indicative and subjunctive only in certain limited

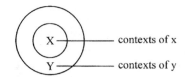

Fig. 3.1 Distributional inclusion

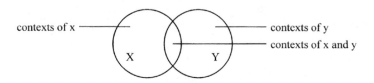

Fig. 3.2 Overlapping distribution

contexts, for instance, in reporting the events from somebody else's point of view. Contrast the following minimal pair of sentences:

(4)   Caesar mīlitēs punīvit quod malē pugnāverant.
       "Caesar punished the soldiers because they had fought badly"
       Caesar mīlitēs punīvit quod malē pugnāvissent.
       "Caesar punished the soldiers for having fought badly"

In the latter sentence the narrator, by using the subjunctive, implies what was in Caesar's mind when he punished the soldiers (i.e., he gives an alleged reason), whereas the former sentence presents the event as a plain fact. Similar pairs show nicely that meaningfulness implies 'choice' (to use Halliday's terminology) and furthermore that it is impossible for two linguistic units to be in meaningful contrast unless they are at least partially equivalent in their distribution.

3.2 *Paradigmatics and Syntagmatics*

According to Saussure, every linguistic unit enters into relations of two different kinds: those called **paradigmatic** and those called **syntagmatic**. **Paradigmatic relations** are those in which a particular unit can be replaced by another unit or contrasts with another unit. To use a familiar example from phonology, the phonological unit /p/ contrasts with the phonological unit /b/ in the context of /-ɪt/. The replacement of /p/ by /b/ in this context, of course, entails change of meaning (i.e., the morpheme {pɪt} does not mean the same as the morpheme {bɪt}). **Syntagmatic relations** are those which are entered into by a particular linguistic unit with the other units of the same level with which it co-occurs and which may be said to constitute its context. Thus phonological units /p/ and /ɪt/ (or /p/ and /ɪ/ and /t/) stand in syntagmatic relationships to one another. Obviously, paradigmatic and syntagmatic relationships are interdependent: we may consider them as two dimensions (vertical and horizontal) characterizing each linguistic unit and placing it in its network of relationships, cf. Figure 3.3.

Syntagmatic relations have to do with the linear character of language, the necessary sequencing of linguistic units in time, whereas paradigmatic relations may be said to work *in absentia* in that each linguistic unit derives its meaning from the potentiality of its occurrence in opposition to another linguistic unit (i.e., from the paradigmatic contrast).

Paradigmatic and syntagmatic relationships are relevant at all linguistic levels: phonology, morphology, and syntax. For instance, in Latin the grammatical morpheme *-ī* by virtue of its potentiality of occurrence in such contexts as *domin-* contracts paradigmatic relations with other grammatical morphemes such as *-ō* and *-um* etc. and a syntagmatic relation with a lexical morpheme *domin-* "lord". On the level of syntax, the inflected form *Rōmam* (Acc) contracts paradigmatic relations with the forms such as *Rōmā* (Abl) in contexts such as *eō* "I go", and syntagmatic relations with *eō*: *Rōmam eō* "I am going to Rome" vs. *Rōmā eō* "I am going from Rome", cf. Figure 3.4. It is customary to talk about **phonotactics** (syntagmatics at the level of phonology) and **morphotactics** (syntagmatics at the level of morphology). Phonotactics deals with patterns of permissible and impermissible groupings of phonemes. For instance, in English the initial cluster of three consonantal phonemes can contain only *s* - voiceless stops - liquids or glides. Morphotactics deals with patterns of permissible and impermissible groupings of morphemes. For instance, in English we cannot say **ed+work* for *work+ed*, whereas Turkish morphotactics permit both sequences *alı-yor-lar-dı* take+PROGRESSIVE+PLURAL+PAST and *alı-yor-du-lar* take+PROGRESSIVE+PAST+PLURAL "they were taking". Syntagmatics at the level of lexology, i.e., **lexotactics**, would then correspond to syntax — at least, in the traditional view of functioning of language where grammaticalized lexemes are put together to form higher units called sentences. We may push this reasoning further and talk about paradigmatics and syntagmatics at the level of syntax. Syntagmatics would deal with the linking of syntactic units (sentences) into higher units (texts) and paradigmatics would deal with minimal pairs of sentences such as the above mentioned contexts in French where the indicative and subjunctive contrast:

(5) On cherche une secrétaire $\begin{cases} \text{qui sait le russe} \\ \text{qui sache le russe} \end{cases}$

It is of interest to note that under this assumption syntax should be redefined as **discourse analysis** where construction of larger units than sentence would be studied.

Paradigmatics and syntagmatics are quite often interpreted as 'code' and 'message'; in other words, as the distinction between an 'inventory' of items and the 'strings' of items constituting the message. Particularly fitting are Halliday's terms: 'choice' for paradigmatics and 'chain' for syntagmatics. Thus in the French example above the speaker has a choice of using the indicative or the subjunctive, i.e. the speaker can draw from the inventory of verbal forms depending on

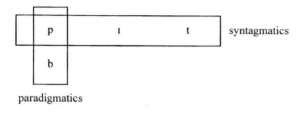

Fig. 3.3 Paradigmatics and syntagmatics in phonology

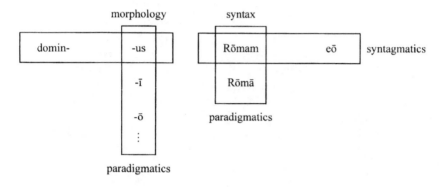

Fig. 3.4 Paradigmatics and syntagmatics in morphology and syntax

whether he wants to express confidence or doubts about finding a Russian speaking secretary. In answering the question *What happened to Mary?* the speaker has a choice between the active *John kissed her* or the passive construction *She was kissed by John* depending on whether he wants to foreground the event of *kissing* or its instigator.

Paradigmatics and syntagmatics may also be interpreted in terms of the Saussurean dichotomy of *langue* and *parole*. As pointed out above, paradigmatic relationships work *in absentia* which means that a particular linguistic sign is opposed to other signs (phonemes, morphemes, lexemes) not because they are in the message but because they belong to *langue*, and thus according to many structuralists, paradigmatics reflects the essential characteristic of *langue* (system). On the other hand, the reality of syntagmatic relationships contracted by a particular linguistic sign with those before or after should be relegated to *parole*.

Under this assumption, only the study of linguistic units (phonemes, morphemes, lexemes and sememes) and their paradigmatic relationships would belong to the study of *langue*, whereas their syntagmatic relationships would belong to the study of *parole*. Hence some structural linguistic schools do not treat syntax as the proper object of linguistic description since syntax (i.e., lexotactics) does not belong to *langue*. However, we cannot say that phonotactics and morphotactics do not belong to *langue* (the former implements morphemes and the latter lexemes) and it is necessary to give syntagmatic relationships their due place in the study of *langue.*

3.3 *Markedness*

Where two or more linguistic units (e.g., perfective versus imperfective) are in contrast, it is often the case that one member of the opposition is positive, or **marked**, while the other is neutral, or **unmarked**. The marked member of the opposition is intuitively felt to be less usual, less normal, or, on the other hand, more specific, more notionally complex. The commonest understanding of markedness may be exemplified by the plural in English. Most English nouns have a plural form which is related to a singular form *dogs - dog*; *chairs - chair*; etc. The plural form may be said to be positively marked by the final *-s,* whereas the singular form is unmarked (or marked by the Ø-suffix). Here the markedness relates simply to the presence of a particular marker (morpheme) in contrast with its absence; the criterion of markedness is of a morphological nature. However, there are other types of markedness; most notably those based on criteria of a semantic, statistical and contextual nature. That these categories are logically independent of one another may be shown by way of contrasting pluralization in Arabic and English. Consider the following data from Egyptian Arabic:

(6) šagar   "trees"   (a group of trees)
     šagar-a   "tree"   (a single tree)
     hagar   "stones"   (a pile of stones)
     hagar-a   "stone"   (a single stone)

In Egyptian Arabic the morphological marking in these cases seems to be opposite of that in English. The unmarked Arabic forms (which have to be translated as plurals "trees", "stones") represent the category of **collectives** (a group of trees, a pile of stones). To denote a single specimen of this category Arabic has to **singularize**, i.e., to form a **singulative** by suffixing *-a*. However, to say, in semantic terms, that the plural in English and the singulative in Arabic are notionally more complex because they are morphologically marked by the presence of a marker would be misleading. We have to admit that morphological markedness and semantic markedness do not have to agree in one-to-one relationship and that they can run their separate courses. After all, semantics is independent of morphology. Ascertaining that Arabic collectives are grammatically singular, we have to think of them as **internal plurals**, cf. Fig 3.5. It is more difficult to demonstrate this morphology-semantics disagreement for English since there is no overt morphological process of singularizing (contrasts such as *hair* collective vs. *a hair* 'singulative' are implemented by the grammatical word *a*). Morphologically, English pluralizes whereas Arabic singularizes and, of course, also pluralizes. We may think of natural collectives such as generic terms denoting an indefinite number of animals, e.g., "cattle" as opposed to a single representative "a cow". (cf. Egyptian Arabic *baʔar* "cattle" vs. *baʔar-a* "cow"). Obviously,

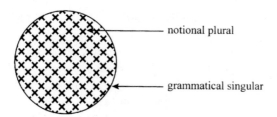

notional plural

grammatical singular

Fig. 3.5 Internal plural

in English, the discussion of notional complexity of either collective *cattle* or singular *cow* cannot rely on morphological markedness since we are dealing with **heteronymy** (lexical difference), whereas in Arabic we have to do with a productive derivational process. We have to keep in mind that it is not at all necessarily the case that all oppositions will have an unmarked member and a marked member (or members). It is possible for some oppositions to have all members equally marked. If we use Latin instead of English for the discussion of pluralization it is obviously impossible to attribute a positive value to the plural solely on the basis of morphological markedness (i.e., the presence of a morpheme). In Latin and many other inflectional languages both singular and plural may have distinctive markers and there is no easy way to decide which one is 'weightier' on purely morphological grounds. Contrast Latin and English:

(7) Latin   English
     taur-us   taur-ī   bull   bull-s
     can-is   can-ēs   dog   dog-s

Startling as these conclusions may appear, there is no reason to reject them. Let us remind ourselves that the situation in morphology parallels that in phonology. Here the oppositions with all members equally marked are called **equipollent**, and those binary oppositions with an unmarked and marked member are called **privative**, using terms introduced by Trubetzkoy (1939). As an example of an equipollent opposition in phonology we may use that of the place of articulation (bilabial - dental - alveolar - retroflex - palatal - velar - uvular - pharyngeal - glottal) or height (high - mid - low). Examples of privative oppositions are numerous, e.g., nasal vs. non-nasal, round vs. non-round, syllabic vs. non-syllabic etc. Ladefoged (1975) maintains that even such a seemingly privative opposition as that of voice is actually equipollent (i.e., multivalued in his terminology), i.e., the simple binary opposition voiced - voiceless is replaced in his system by a number of members: glottal stop - laryngealized - voiced - murmured - voiceless. Thus we have to keep in mind that markedness is not just a matter of simple-minded **binarism**, i.e., a black or white choice (marked vs. unmarked). Furthermore, there are oppositions where the markedness differences between the members are great, and oppositions where the differences are small — consequently, we have to acknowledge that there can be various **degrees of markedness**.

One of the most important and decisive criteria of markedness is that of **distribution**. In many cases, the meaning of the unmarked category encompasses that of its marked counterpart (so-called **distributional inclusion**); this is illustrated in Figure 3.6. For instance, the word *dog* is semantically unmarked or less specific than its female counterpart *bitch*, which is marked for sex. There are numerous cases when overt expression of the meaning of the marked category is optional, i.e., when the unmarked category can replace the marked one. For instance, in Modern Greek the perfect is a marked category as opposed to the aorist (the former denotes the past perfective events which result in the present state, whereas the aorist denotes past events which can be both perfective or imperfective; the aorist simply narrates past events without relating them to the present state). This is shown in Figure 3.7. Thus in Modern Greek even in a situation where the use of the perfect (marked category) would be appropriate it is possible to use the aorist (unmarked category), as (8) illustrates.

(8)   tóra éxo fái (Perfect) ðén pinó piá
       "I have eaten, I am not hungry any more"

Here, the semantic category of **resultative** (cf. Irish English *I am after eating*) is marked overtly by the perfect *éxo fái*. However, it is equally possible to leave this category unmarked by using the aorist *éfaya*. Similarly, in Spanish the **progressive** form *estoy escribiendo* "I am writing" can always be replaced by the non-progressive *escribo* "I write" and the category of progressive remains unmarked (i.e., the progressive meaning is not excluded but it is not overtly marked). However, the application of the criterion of distributional inclusion is connected with all kinds of difficulties having to do mainly with the strait-jacket of binarism. It is apparently more insightful to treat Modern Greek categories of aorist and perfect (and imperfect) as equally marked members of an equipollent opposition; the same would be true of the Spanish example and other examples from other languages (see further discussion in 6.3.3).

Let us examine some of the morphological peculiarities which tend to correlate with the marked - unmarked opposition. It is well-known that unmarked categories tend to have less morphological 'flesh' than their marked counterparts. For instance, English progressive (*be* V+*ing*) or perfect (*have* V+*en*) are morphologically more complex than their unmarked non-past counterpart; similarly, Spanish progressive (*ser* V+*ando*) or perfect (*haber* V+*ado*) are morphologically more complex than their present tense counterpart; similar examples could be multiplied from a variety of languages. On the other hand, morphology (i.e., increase in morphological complexity) correlates less perfectly with markedness in Slavic or Semitic languages. For instance, in Czech and Russian it is possible to form perfective counterparts from imperfective verbs (primarily by prefixation), and also to form imperfective counterparts from perfective verbs (by suffixation). Consider the following derivational processes in Czech in (9).

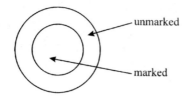

Fig. 3.6 Distributional inclusion

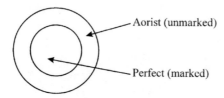

Fig. 3.7 Distributional inclusion and aspect

(9) Imperfective   Perfective   Imperfective
     mřít "be dying"   →   umřít "have died"
                           umřít   →   umírat "be dying"

     bít "beat"   →   zabít "kill"
                           zabít   →   zabíjet "be killing"

It is equally difficult to use the criterion of morphological complexity in discussing markedness in Semitic languages. Classical Arabic conjugates its perfective (past) forms by means of suffixes and imperfective (present) forms by means of prefixes. Which category is marked? Or more marked?

(10)   Perfective   Imperfective
     Sg 3   kataba   "he wrote"   yaktubu "he writes"
         2   katabta "you wrote"   taktubu "you write"
         1   katabtu "I wrote"   ʔaktubu "I write"

Another morphological criterion for markedness is the greater likelihood of morphological irregularity in unmarked forms. In Ancient Greek the category of the aorist is morphologically extremely irregular (suppletive), whereas the marked category of the imperfect (vis-à-vis the present) is usually predictable from the present stem of the verb. Consider the following data:

(11) Present   Imperfect   Aorist
      phérō   "I carry"   épheron   ēnenkon
      trékhō   "I run"   étrekhon   édramon
      dáknō   "I bite"   édaknon   édakon
      leípō   "I leave"   éleipon   élipon

See further discussion in 6.3.3.

Another morphological criterion for markedness is that of so-called **syncretism** (morphological identity) of forms. It can be observed that frequently there is syncretism of forms in the marked category, while these forms are kept apart in the unmarked category. For instance, in Russian there is a three-way tense distinction (Past - Present - Future) in the unmarked aspectual category of the imperfective, while the marked category of the perfective allows only for a two-way distinction (Past - non-Past, where non-Past refers to future time).

(12)   Imperfective   Perfective
      Past   nosíl   "used to carry"   prinʲós   "brought in"
      Present   nošú   "I carry (habitually)"   prinesú   "I will bring in"
      Future   búdu nosít' "I will carry"

RECOMMENDED READINGS

Anderson, Stephen R. 1985. "Inflectional morphology". *Language Typology and Syntactic Description.* Volume 3 ed. by T. Shopen, 150–201. Cambridge: Cambridge University Press.

Comrie, Bernard. 1976. *Aspect: An Introduction to the Study of Verbal Aspect.* Cambridge: Cambridge University Press. (Chapter 6).

Halliday, Michael A. K. 1967. "Notes on transitivity and theme in English, Part I". *Journal of Linguistics* 3.37–81.

Ladefoged, Peter. 1975. *A Course in Phonetics.* New York: Harcourt Brace Jovanovich.

Lyons, John. 1968. *Introduction to Theoretical Linguistics.* Cambridge: Cambridge University Press (Section 2.3).

——. 1977. *Semantics,* Volume 2. Cambridge University Press. (Chapter 8.)

Mitchell, Terence F. 1962. *Colloquial Arabic.* London: The English Universities Press.

de Saussure, Ferdinand. 1955. *Cours de linguistique générale.* 5th Edition. Paris: Payot. (Part 2, Chapter 5).

Trubetzkoy, Nikolai S. 1939. *Grundzüge der Phonologie. Travaux du cercle linguistique de Prague* 7. (English translation by C. A. M. Baltaxe, Berkeley/Los Angeles: University of California Press, 1969).

EXERCISES

1. Discuss and exemplify the four basic types of distribution of linguistic units.

2. According to Saussure paradigmatic and syntagmatic relationships are relevant at every level of linguistic description. Explain this statement and supply some good examples for each level (sounds, morphemes, words and sentences).

3. The notion of markedness is extremely important at all levels of language structure. Discuss the following aspects of markedness and provide some convincing examples:

   (a)   distribution
   (b)   notional complexity
   (c)   overt morphology
   (d)   privative vs. equipollent opposition

4. A large proportion of Arabic nouns are pluralized by changing the base pattern, e.g., *kalb* "dog", Pl. *klāb* "dogs"; *ktāb* "book", Pl. *kətob* "books". There are many different pluralizing patterns and frequently it is not possible to deduce the plural patern from the singular (or vice versa) with any high degree of certainty. Various traditional grammars of Arabic claim that the plurals of most nouns must be memorized individually.

   Discover and describe as many plural patterns as you can in the following data taken from Syrian Arabic (Damascus dialect):

(1)	mʕallem	"teacher"	mʕallmīn
(2)	ḍabʕ	"hyena"	dbāʕ
(3)	šaxṣ	"person"	ʔašxāṣ
(4)	ʔaṣl	"origin"	ʔṣūl
(5)	bank	"bank"	bnūk
(6)	ktāb	"book"	kətob
(7)	waʔt	"time"	wʔāt
(8)	bṣāṭ	"rug"	bəṣoṭ
(9)	raʔīs	"chief"	rəʔasa
(10)	šahr	"month"	ʔəšhor
(11)	ḥṣān	"horse"	ʔḥṣne
(12)	tāžer	"merchant"	təžžār
(13)	ʔamīṣ	"shirt"	ʔəmṣān
(14)	ʔahl	"family"	ʔahāli

(15)	šāreʕ	"street"	šawāreʕ	
(16)	nažžār	"carpenter"	nažžārīn	
(17)	tōr	"bull, ox"	twār	
(18)	māl	"wealth"	ʔamwāl	
(19)	suʔāl	"question"	ʔasʔile	
(20)	ʕāmel	"worker"	ʕəmmāl	
(21)	fallāḥ	"peasant"	fallāḥīn	
(22)	blād	"country"	bəldān	
(23)	ʔəsm	"name"	ʔasāmi	
(24)	knīse	"church"	kanāyes	
(25)	žāmeʕ	"mosque"	žawāmeʕ	
(26)	dəkkān	"shop"	dakakīn	
(27)	madfaʕ	"cannon"	madāfeʕ	
(28)	mallāk	"proprietor"	mallākīn	
(29)	baḥḥār	"sailor"	baḥḥāra	"crew"
(30)	səkkīn	"knife"	sakakīn	
(31)	xūri	"priest"	xawārne	
(32)	ṣayyād	"hunter"	ṣayyādīn	
(33)	dahhān	"painter"	dahhāne	
(34)	lōn	"color"	ʔalwān	
(35)	ʕīd	"holiday"	ʔaʕyād	
(36)	sənn	"tooth"	snān	
(37)	baḥr	"sea"	bḥūr	
(38)	safīne	"ship"	səfn	
(39)	rasūl	"apostle"	rəsol	
(40)	šərīk	"partner"	šəraka	
(41)	nahr	"river"	ʔənhor	
(42)	ḥarf	"letter"	ʔaḥrof	
(43)	ʔimām	"imam"	ʔaʔimme	
(44)	ḥāyck	"weaver"	ḥiyyāk	
(45)	xalīž	"gulf"	xəlžān	
(46)	ʔarḍ	"land"	ʔarāḍi	
(47)	bāʕes	"motive"	bawāʕes	
(48)	tārīx	"date"	tawārīx	
(49)	šəbbāk	"window"	šababīk	
(50)	doktōr	"doctor"	dakātra	
(51)	ʕaṣfūr	"birdie"	ʕaṣafīr	
(52)	banna	"builder"	bannāyīn	
(53)	ʕattāl	"porter"	ʕattāle	"a group of porters"

(54)	ħāl	"situation"	ʔħwāl
(55)	žabal	"mountain"	žbāl
(56)	bāb	"door"	bwāb
(57)	žəfn	"eyelid"	žfūn
(58)	nəsr	"vulture"	nsūr
(59)	madīne	"city"	mədon
(60)	ṣūra	"picture"	ṣuwar
(61)	xēme	"tent"	xiyam
(62)	baxīl	"miser"	bəxala
(63)	nafs	"person"	ʔənfos
(64)	niẓām	"system"	ʔanẓime
(65)	rākeb	"passenger"	rəkkāb
(66)	ṣabi	"boy"	ṣəbyān
(67)	ʔahwe	"coffee"	ʔahāwi
(68)	ʔəsʔof	"bishop"	ʔasāʔfe
(69)	žəsr	"bridge"	žsūr
(70)	sabīl	"way"	səbol
(71)	zalame	"man"	zəlm
(72)	ʕēn	"eye"	ʕyūn
(73)	xabīr	"expert"	xəbara
(74)	žnēne	"garden"	žanāyen
(75)	bāxra	"steamship"	bawāxer
(76)	žākēt	"jacket"	žawākīt
(77)	kabbūt	"coat"	kababīt
(78)	sbūʕ	"week"	ʔasābīʕ
(79)	fəlfol	"pepper"	falāfel
(80)	ʔəstāz	"professor"	ʔasātze
(81)	baṭrak	"patriarch"	baṭārke
(82)	balkōn	"balcony"	balakīn
(83)	ṣarrāf	"moneychanger"	ṣarrāfe
(84)	zərr	"button"	zrār
(85)	ṣāħeb	"friend"	ṣħāb
(86)	sabab	"cause"	ʔasbāb
(87)	žēbe	"pocket"	žyūb
(88)	tēs	"billy goat"	tyūs
(89)	walad	"boy"	wəld
(90)	ṭarīʔ	"road"	ṭəroʔ
(91)	ʔūḍa	"room"	ʔuwaḍ
(92)	šōke	"fork"	šuwak

(93)	šāʕer	"poet"	šəʕara
(94)	lsān	"tongue"	ʔəlson
(95)	wisām	"medal"	ʔawsime
(96)	nāʔeb	"representative"	nuwwāb
(97)	ġūl	"ghoul"	ġīlān
(98)	haʔīʔa	"truth"	haʔāyeʔ
(99)	məṭrān	"archbishop"	maṭārne
(100)	kazzāb	"liar"	kazzābīn

5. A certain proportion of Arabic nouns are pluralized by suffixes but a large proportion are pluralized internally by changing the vocalic pattern of the noun (infixation and transfixation). There are many different pluralizing patterns and frequently it is not possible to deduce the plural pattern from the singular (or vice versa) with any high degree of certainty. Discover and describe as many plural patterns as you can in the following data taken from Modern Literary Arabic:

(1)	sinn	"tooth"	asnān
(2)	lawn	"color"	alwān
(3)	ʕīd	"holiday"	aʕayād
(4)	māl	"wealth"	amwāl
(5)	θawr	"bull"	aθwār
(6)	najjār	"carpenter"	najjārūn
(7)	šāriʕ	"street"	šawāriʕ
(8)	tājir	"merchant"	tujjār
(9)	hiṣān	"horse"	ahṣina
(10)	šahr	"month"	ašhur
(11)	raʔīs	"chief"	ruʔasāʔ
(12)	kitāb	"book"	kutub
(13)	bank	"bank"	bunūk
(14)	ʔaṣl	"origin"	ʔuṣūl
(15)	muʕallim	"teacher"	muʕallimūn
(16)	suʔāl	"question"	asʔila
(17)	ʕāmil	"worker"	ʕumalāʔ
(18)	fallāh	"peasant"	fallāhūn
(19)	bilād	"country"	buldān
(20)	kanīsa	"church"	kanāʔis
(21)	jāmiʕa	"mosque"	jawāmiʕ
(22)	imraʔa	"woman"	marʔāt
(23)	dukkān	"shop"	dakakīn

(24)	mallāk	"owner"	mallākūn
(25)	baḥḥār	"sailor"	bāḥḥāra	"crew"
(26)	baḥr	"sea"	buḥūr
(27)	safīna	"ship"	sufun
(28)	rasūl	"apostle"	rusul
(29)	šarīk	"partner"	šurakāʔ
(30)	nahr	"river"	anhur
(31)	ḥarf	"letter"	ḥurūf
(32)	ʔimām	"imam"	aʔimma
(33)	xalīj	"gulf"	xuljān
(34)	ʕattāl	"porter"	ʕattāla	"a group of porters"
(35)	qarīna	"wife"	qarīnāt
(36)	ḥāl	"situation"	aḥwāl
(37)	jabal	"mountain"	jibāl
(38)	bāb	"door"	abwāb
(39)	madīna	"city"	mudun
(40)	ṣūra	"picture"	ṣuwar
(41)	nāʔib	"representative"	nuwwāb
(42)	madad	"help"	amdād
(43)	mādda	"stuff"	mawādd
(44)	maks	"tax"	mukūs
(45)	baxīl	"miser"	buxalāʔ
(46)	nafs	"person"	anfus
(47)	jisr	"bridge"	jusūr
(48)	sabīl	"way"	subul
(49)	ʕayn	"eye"	ʕuyūn
(50)	xabīr	"expert"	xubarāʔ
(51)	kabbūt	"coat"	kababīt
(52)	balkōn	"balcony"	balakīn
(53)	sabab	"cause"	asbāb
(54)	tays	"billy goat"	tuyūs
(55)	walad	"boy"	awlād
(56)	ṭarīq	"road"	ṭuruq
(57)	šāʕir	"poet"	šuʕarāʔ
(58)	sayf	"sword"	suyūf
(59)	zawja	"wife"	zawjāt
(60)	ʕaqaba	"obstacle"	ʕiqāb
(61)	ʕāqiba	"end"	ʕawāqib
(62)	ġadīr	"pond"	ġudur

(63)	qiṭṭa	"cat"	qiṭaṭ
(64)	lisān	"tongue"	alsun
(65)	ḥaqīqa	"truth"	ḥaqāʔiq
(66)	ġūl	"ghoul"	ġīlān
(67)	nāzila	"misfortune"	nazāʔil
(68)	nūr	"light"	anwār
(69)	haram	"pyramid"	ahrām
(70)	wiθāq	"chain"	wuθuq
(71)	dīk	"rooster"	diyaka ~ duyūk ~ adyāk
(72)	dīwān	"council"	dawāwīn
(73)	zalzala	"earthquake"	zalāzil
(74)	firʕawn	"pharaoh"	farāʕina
(75)	maʕ(a)z	"goat"	amʕuz ~ maʕīz
(76)	kahf	"cave"	kuhūf
(77)	nīr	"yoke"	anyār ~ nīrān
(78)	farīsa	"prey"	farāʔis
(79)	hirr	"tomcat"	hirara
(80)	hirra	"cat"	hirar
(81)	hilāl	"crescent"	ahilla ~ ahālīl
(82)	hāmma	"reptile"	hawāmm
(83)	wakr	"(bird"s) nest"	awkār ~ awkur
(84)	kubša	"hook"	kubaš
(85)	nīšān	"target"	nayāšīn
(86)	tāj	"crown"	tījān
(87)	būq	"trumpet"	abwāq
(88)	būsa	"kiss"	būsāt
(89)	uwār	"heat"	ūr
(90)	zaʕafrān	"saffron"	zaʕāfir
(91)	xātūn	"lady"	xawātīn
(92)	mōda	"fashion"	mōdāt
(93)	lakan	"basin"	alkān
(94)	qanaṭ	"despair"	qunūṭ
(95)	buʔra	"focus"	buʔar
(96)	ʕuḍw	"limb"	aʕḍāʔ
(97)	ʕirzāl	"lion's den"	ʕrāzīl
(98)	walīma	"banquet"	walāʔim
(99)	kursūʕ	"wristbone"	karāsīʕ
(100)	ḍayʕa	"village"	ḍiyaʕ ~ ḍiyāʕ

CHAPTER FOUR
INFLECTIONAL AND DERIVATIONAL MORPHOLOGY

4.1 *The Scope of Inflection and Derivation*

Traditionally, **inflection** (spelled also **inflexion**) is defined as a change in the form of a word to express its relation to other words in the sentence; **derivation**, on the other hand, deals with various processes whereby new words are formed from existing words (or bases). In English, for instance, verbs may be modified by the addition of a suffix in the 3rd Person Singular Present: *(he) chooses;* by changing the vowel in the root in the stem in the Past: *(he) chose;* by the addition of a suffix in the Past Participle: *chosen*; and by the addition of a suffix in the Gerund: *choosing.* We may say that morphologically English verbs consist of paradigmatic sets of five forms:

(i)   Infinitive ('base')
(ii)   3rd Sg Pres
(iii) Past
(iv)   Past Participle
(v)   Gerund (or Present Participle)

A full-fledged five-member paradigm, such as that of *choose, see,* etc., is exceptional. Actually, these verbs are classified as irregular. The majority of English regular verbs have typically the same form for (iii) Past and (iv) Past Participle, e.g., *worked.* There are various types of **morphological identity (syncretism)** in that some verbs such as *run* have the same form in (i) Infinitive and (iv) Past Participle; in regional English (i) Infinitive and (iii) Past may have the same form (*I give it to him* = Standard *I gave it to him*). We may say that the structural framework of grammatical relationships ('systems') gives a grammatical meaning to each element of the system. However, semantics and morphology do not have to be in one-to-one relationship, and as it happens in English, all the five underlying meanings mentioned above are only exceptionally realized by overt morphology:

(1) | Grammatical Meaning | Morphology | | |
|---|---|---|---|
| Infinitive | choose | work | run |
| 3rd Sg Pres | chooses | works | runs |
| Past | chose | worked | ran |
| Past Participle | chosen | worked (Past) | run (Infinitive) |
| Gerund | choosing | working | running |

What is an essential characteristic of inflection is the fact that all the five (or less) forms qualify as verbs; put differently, inflectional processes do NOT change the membership in the class of primary grammatical categories (= parts of speech). What they do is they express (i.e., grammaticalize) the lexical notion to which they are attached: *-s* marks the secondary grammatical categories of person and number, *-ed* the category of tense, etc.

Derivational morphemes, on the other hand, may derive one part of speech from another; in other words, derivational processes usually change the membership in the classes of primary grammatical categories. Consider the following derivational set (derivational paradigm) with arrows showing derivational processes:

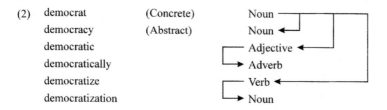

(2)   democrat   (Concrete)   Noun
      democracy   (Abstract)   Noun
      democratic   Adjective
      democratically   Adverb
      democratize   Verb
      democratization   Noun

The suffix {-ɪk} derives adjectives from nouns: *democrat → democratic*; the suffix {-li} derives adverbs from adjectives: *democratic → democratically*; the suffix {-ajz} derives verbs from nouns: *democrat → democratize* ('denominal' verb); the suffix {-cšn} derives nouns from verbs: *democratize → democratization* ('deverbal' noun). It is more difficult to establish the derivational relationship, if any, between *democrat* and *democracy*. Here we have to account precisely for the allomorphy of /démɔkræt/ and /dɔmákrɔsi/; these two alternants which are held together by the morphophonemic alternations /ɛ ~ ɔ/ and /ɔ ~ a/; furthermore, *democrat* and *democracy* are also linked to the same semantic unit which is usually called a **derivational base**. However, the problem with a derivational base lies in the degree of abstractness. Champions of abstract phonology do not hesitate to postulate an unaccented derivational base and a number of morphological rules which are necessary for the derivation of surface forms. To account for /dɔmákrɔsi/ from underlying /dɛmɔkræt + i/ we would need vowel-reduction rules conditioned by the preceding or following stress (ɛ → ɔ /— V́ and æ → ɔ / V́—) and a morphophonemic rule with a **morphological conditioning**: *t → s*/— derivational suffix *-y* (/i/). Note that this rule is NOT **conditioned phonologically**, i.e., the change *t → s* has nothing to do with phonological properties of /i/, since there are forms such as *democratic*. For this and other reasons this solution is unacceptable to many linguists and we may consider an alternative less abstract solution, namely two accented derivational bases: /démɔkræt/ (→ *democrat, democratic*) /dɔmákrɔt-/ (→ *democratize*). Those who are unwilling to write abstract phonological rules with morphological conditioning have to consider the alternation *t ~ s* in /dɔmákrɔt-/ ~ /dɔmákrɔs-/ 'exceptional' and rely for its 'explanation' on parallel paradigmatic sets:

(3) democrat   aristocrat   autocrat
     democratic   aristocratic   autocratic
     democracy   aristocracy   autocracy

Those synchronic linguists who do not hesitate to open the Oxford English Dictionary will discover that *democrat* and *aristocrat* are popular formations of the French Revolution (formed around 1790), whereas the other two forms are borrowed from Greek via Latin. In other words, the rule *t* → *s* postulated above is nothing else but a historical palatalization of Old French (in those times, of course, it was a purely phonological rule) which has been putatively morphologized in Modern French. This, of course, is another way of saying that the palatalization rule of Old French is dead. If we try to avoid postulating an abstract derivational base, we may be inclined to postulate a derivational relationship between *democrat* and *democratic* — i.e., the former formed from the latter by clipping (which is most likely what happened historically). At this point, it would be preferable to leave the issue of **morpheme-based** or **lexeme-based derivational morphology** open; however, it is worth emphasizing that the construction of far-reaching systems of derivational rules is only one aspect (the dynamic aspect) of the whole problem; the other aspect has to do with paradigmatics (the static aspect) discussed in Chapter Three. Obviously, any speaker of English stores the paradigmatic set such as *democrat*, *democratic* and *democracy* in his/her memory — the controversy among various linguistic schools starts when we try to account for the 'inner' form of his/her grammar in terms of rules.

4.2 *Some Universal Tendencies of Inflection and Derivation*

As mentioned under 2.3, there is a universal tendency for inflectional affixes to occur on the periphery of words, whereas derivational affixes occur closer to the root. The assumption is that only when derivational morphemes have been added to derive nouns, adjectives or verbs, can inflectional elements be subsequently added to grammaticalize the lexical content. For instance, in Latin the derivational base *cogit-* "think" might be followed by a verbal inflectional suffix such as *-ō* (1st Pers Sg Pres Indic) *cogitō* "I think": or by a derivational suffix *-ātiōn* yielding a deverbal noun *cogitātiō* "thinking". The latter suffix may be followed by any of the six case endings to grammaticalize the lexical content of "thinking":

(4) cogitātiōnis   cogit-ātiōn-is   Genitive
     cogitātiōnī   -ī   Dative
     cogitātiōnem   -em   Accusative

There are some rare and doubtful counter-examples. Consider the following German inflectional and derivational forms of (*das*) *Kind* "child":

(5)   Kind   "child"
(Plural of *Kind*)   Kind-er   "children"
(Diminutive of *Kind*)   Kind-chen   "baby"
(Plural of *Kind-chen*)   Kind-er-chen   'babies'

Here instead of expected *Kind-chen-er* (Base - Diminutivizing Suffix - Plural Suffix) we obtain *Kind-er-chen* (Base - Plural Suffix - Diminutivizing Suffix). However, here it seems that we are not dealing with a real plural suffix but with a **stem-forming element** (*Stammbildungselement*). This will become obvious if we compare the above forms with pluralized and diminutivized forms of *(der) Bruder* "brother":

(6)   Kind   "child"   Bruder   "brother"
      Kind-er   "children"   Brüder   "brothers"
      Kind-chen   "baby"   Brüder-chen   "little brother"
      Kind-er-chen   "babies"   Brüder-chen   "little brothers"

We observe that there is no morpheme boundary in *Brud-er* (*brud-* is not a meaningful element in German); the plural has been formed by means of a productive process of vowel change $u \rightarrow \ddot{u}$ [y] (called **mutation** or **umlaut**); the diminutive has been formed by adding the usual diminutive suffix; and finally the diminutivized form has been pluralized by a Ø-suffix (the formation of plural by Ø-suffix is one of the possibilities of German, e.g., *der Lehrer* "teacher", *die Lehrer* "teachers"; the article is inflected and shows unambiguously that the following noun is in the plural). Consequently, we may assume that the first morpheme boundary in *Kind-er-chen* is rather illusory and that the correct morpheme break-down should look as follows:

(7)   Kinder-chen-Ø
      Base - Diminutivizing Suffix - Inflectional Suffix

Note that this decision could be developed as an argument in favor of lexeme-based derivational morphology.

The correctness of this solution (or more generally, universality of the sequence Base-Derivation-Inflection) may be confirmed by looking at languages with higher index of synthesis (Greenberg 1966) such as Czech or Latin:

(8)   German   Czech   Latin
                 Bruder   bratr   fräter
      Diminutive   Brüder-chen   bratř-īk   fräter-cul-us
      Plural   Brüder-chen-Ø   bratř-īc-i   fräter-cul-ī

In the latter two languages, the plural suffix unmistakably follows the diminutivizing suffix. Only in Latin is there an inflectional suffix marking the nominative in the singular, while both German and Czech have a Ø-suffix here. Thus to avoid any misunderstanding in this type of cross-language comparison the chart in (8) should be constructed as shown in (9):

(9)   German   Czech   Latin
                 der Bruder   bratr   fräter
    Diminutive   das Brüder-chen-Ø brati̯-ìk-Ø   fräter-cul-us
    Plural   die Brüder-chen-Ø brati̯-ìc-i   fräter-cul-ì

It might be of interest to ascertain what happens when we have the sequence of base and several inflectional or several derivational suffixes. In the sequence of several inflectional suffixes, variations sometimes occur. This phenomenon may be regarded as a minor piece of counter evidence to the internal cohesion of the word (discussed under 2.1.3), but it is significant that examples appear to come only from agglutinative languages such as Turkish. Thus, whereas in English it is impossible to say *they *ed-love* (or in Old English *hìe *luf-on-od* instead of *luf-od-on*), in Turkish it is quite common to find examples of positional mobility such as the following:

(10) alı-yor-lar-dı   al-ıyor-du-lar
      take-PROGRESSIVE-PLURAL-PAST   take-PROGRESSIVE-PAST-PLURAL
      "they were taking"

      al-ır-lar-dı   al-ır-dı-lar
      take-AORIST-PLURAL-PAST   take-AORIST-PAST-PLURAL
      "they took"

In these Turkish verbal forms the suffixes marking tense (Past) and number (Plural) are positionally interchangeable, but they must follow the suffix marking verbal aspect (Progressive, Aorist). There are no similar examples of positional mobility in derivational affixation. Derivatives are internally stable because derivation changes the membership in the class of primary grammatical categories; consequently, it is not possible to say **democrat-ation-ize* if we want to form a deverbal noun *democrat-ize-ation*. The same seems to be true of compounds, but admittedly to a lesser degree. In word composition, the respective order of elements may be variable in certain areas of the lexicon. For instance, in Standard English we say only *twenty-five* (*five-and-twenty* is dialectal and archaic), in German only *fünfundzwanzig* but in Czech it is possible to say both: *dvacetpět* and *pětadvacet*. The explanation seems to be a loan influence (calquing) of German on Czech, i.e., *pět-a-dvacet* "five-and-twenty" is modelled on the pattern of German *fünf-und-zwanzig* whereas *dvacet-pět* is the native formation. Thus we may conclude this section by assuming that with the possible exception of **copulative compounds** such as higher numerals, the order of elements in compounds is stable.

4.3 *Analysis of Inflections*

The following grammatical categories may be inflected in English: nouns (for gender, number and case), adjectives (for comparison, i.e., comparative and superlative), adverbs (for comparison), pronouns (for gender, number and case), and verbs (for person, number, tense, and partly mood). The three other verbal categories (aspect, mood and voice) are realized syntactically (by means of auxiliaries). A striking characteristic of English, in comparison with other Indo-European languages such as Spanish, Latin or Russian, is its paucity of inflections. Excluding for a while adjectives, adverbs and pronouns, one may almost say that English manages with one inflectional suffix, namely -*s*, which is used to mark all nominal and verbal categories (with the exception of tense, marked by -*ed*, present participle, marked by -*ing*, and past participle, marked regularly by -*ed*, and irregularly by -*en* and/or **ablaut**). Historically, however, even English was highly inflectional. Old English shows inflections for four cases (five with pronouns), three numbers (singular, dual and plural) and three genders with nouns, pronouns and adjectives; for three persons with verbs (in the singular only) and pronouns; for tense and mood (subjunctive) with verbs; and for strong and weak nouns, adjectives and verbs. Almost all of this morphology was lost during the Middle English period (1150–1500). To exemplify some of the above forms we may look at **strong** and **weak nominal declensions** in Old English:

(11) Strong Declensions

		Masculine	Neuter		Feminine	
			(short root)	(long root)	(short root)	(long root)
		"stone"	"ship"	"house"	"gift"	"teaching"
Sg.	Nom	stān	scip	hūs	giefu	lār
	Acc	stān	scip	hūs	giefe	lāre
	Gen	stānes	scipes	hūses	giefe	lāre
	Dat	stāne	scipe	hūse	giefe	lāre
Pl.	Nom/Acc	stānas	scipu	hūs	giefa,-e	lāra, -e
	Gen	stāna	scipa	hūsa	giefena	lārena
	Dat	stānum	scipum	hūsum	giefum	lārum

(12) Weak Declensions

		Masculine	Neuter	Feminine
		"name"	"eye"	"sun"
Sg.	Nom	nama	ēage	sunne
	Acc	naman	ēage	sunnan
	Gen	naman	ēagan	sunnan

Dat	naman	ēagan	sunnan
Pl. Nom	-an		
Acc	-an		
Gen	-ena	(all plurals)	
Dat	-um		

This system is remarkably similar to that of Modern German (which has preserved its earlier morphology in much better condition than English). Compare, for instance, the following forms:

(13)

		Old English		Modern German	
		Strong	Weak	Strong	Weak
Sg	Nom	stān	nama	Stein	Name
	Gen	stānes	naman	Steines	Namens
Pl	Nom	stānas	naman	Steine	Namen
	Dat	stānum	namum	Steinen	Namen

It may be observed that -s in weak German *Namens* (Gen Sg) is analogical with strong *Steines*. The category **strong** (vs. **weak**) will be discussed in the following chapter (under Gender, 5.2.1) and in the meantime we may look at an even more formal classification of nouns based on the **thematic vowel** (cf. 2.3) as it exists in various archaic Indo-European languages such as Sanskrit, Greek or Latin. In the latter language, the nouns are classified into five declensions according to the five types of stems: *a-*, *o-*, C(onsonant)- and *i-*, *u-* and *e*-stems. The five Latin declensions are usually displayed in the following manner:

(14) Five Latin Declensions

		I	II	III	IV	V
		a-stems	*o*-stems	C-stems	*i*-stems	*u*-stems	*e*-stems
Sg	Nom	puella	servus (< os)	rūmor	ignis	manus	rēs
	Gen	ae (< āī)	ī	is	is	ūs	eī
	Dat	ae	ō	ī	ī	uī	eī
	Acc	am	um (< om)	em	em	um	em
	Abl	ā	ō	e	e	ū	ē
Pl	Nom	ae (< āī)	ī	ēs	ēs	ūs	ēs
	Gen	ārum	ōrum	um	ium	uum	ērum
	Dat/Abl	īs	īs	ibus	ibus	u/ibus	ēbus
	Acc	ās	ōs	ēs	ēs/īs	ūs	ēs

The traditional teaching of Latin was based on the memorization of this battery of endings. Linguists maintain that these inflectional suffixes are segmentable in a more abstract analysis operating with the notion of thematic vowel. However, they can be segmented only at the price of a certain arbitrariness and inconsistency and only some of them are analyzable. Working with the older Latin form *servos* (occurring in Plautus) we may discover the following pattern for the formation of the nominative, accusative and ablative:

(15)

	a-stems	*o*-stems	*u*-stems
Nom	puell-a-Ø	serv-o-s	man-u-s
Acc	-a-m	-o-m	-u-m
Abl	-a-: (length)	-o-: (length)	-u-: (length)

Even monosyllabic *i*-stems, e.g., *vīs*, *vim*, *vī* "force" and *e*-stems fit this pattern, but the problem would be to account for the length in the nominative. Consequently, we may try to reformulate the traditional statement (-*a* marks the Nom Sg of *a*-stems and -*os* marks the Nom Sg of *o*-stems etc.) by identifying case markers with post-thematic elements: -Ø would mark the Nom Sg of *a*-stems and -*s* the Nom Sg of all other stems. Then, we would need some morphophonemic rules to account for *rūmor* "rumor" and *honōs* "honor" from 'underlying' representations **rūmor-s*, **honor-s* cf. **dent-s > dēns*); -*m* would mark the Acc Sg everywhere (*rūmōrem* would be derived from **rūmor-m*); and the Abl Sg would be formed by the lengthening of the thematic vowel. As far as the thematic vowel is concerned, it might be tempting to identify it with markers of gender: -*a* feminine, -*o* masculine (and neuter). *U*-stems are mostly masculine and *e*-stems feminine; unfortunately, *i*-stems are both masculine and feminine. Whoever is interested in this analysis may proceed along these lines. Actually, this analysis was proposed at the end of the 19th c. by the Neogrammarians who maintained that a good many of the Latin inflections could be explained as being due to the coalescence of a once distinct morphology.

The best we can do for Latin is to assume that its inflections are not synchronically analyzable into morphemes. Hence, undoubtedly, the traditional handling of Latin declensions by memorizing and this is why classical grammarians did not establish morphophonemic rules, but merely patterns of formation (i.e., paradigms). This problem will be discussed again from a different angle in Chapter Seven; for the time being we can make a significant observation that Latin inflectional endings show a considerable degree of **cumulation** (or **fusion**) of significates. Latin is simply a typical example of a fusional linguistic type (other well-known examples are Sanskrit, Greek, Lithuanian, Russian, Czech, Polish, Serbian).

Diametrically opposed are so-called **agglutinating languages** in which inflectional suffixes are typically composed of a sequence of morphemes with each morpheme representing one grammatical meaning. Turkish, or any other Altaic language, may be taken as an example of this linguistic type. Consider the data in (16) from Latin and Turkish.

(16)

		Latin	Turkish
Sg	Nom	vir	adam
	Acc	vir-um	adam-ı
	Gen	vir-ī	adam-ın
Pl	Nom	vir-ī	adam-lar
	Acc	vir-ōs	adam-lar-ı
	Gen	vir-ōrum	adam-lar-ın

The plural in Turkish is marked with the suffix -*lar* (the singular with the Ø-suffix) and the case is marked with distinct suffixes added after the plural suffix. Assuming that the nominative (or rather **absolutive**, see under 5.2.3) is marked with the Ø-suffix we may elaborate the following tripartite analysis for the whole Turkish paradigm:

(17)

		Stem	Number	Case
Sg	Nom	adam	Ø	Ø
	Acc	adam	Ø	ı
	Gen	adam	Ø	ın
Pl	Nom	adam	lar	Ø
	Acc	adam	lar	ı
	Gen	adam	lar	ın

As we have seen above an analysis along these lines proved to be possible only for some cases and only for some stems in Latin:

(18)

		Root	Gender	Case
Masc	Nom	serv	o	s
	Acc	serv	o	m
	Abl	serv	o	: (length)
Fem	Nom	puell	a	Ø
	Acc	puell	a	m
	Abl	puell	a	: (length)

This type of analysis would certainly be enormously difficult for the number and case of *vir*-; actually, we should analyze Latin endings for three categories: gender, number and case (Turkish, as a 'genderless' language has only number and case). For instance, we may entertain the idea that the plural is marked by the lengthening of the thematic vowel (the long thematic vowel in the singular was analyzed above as Gender Case) and we would end up with the following tripartite analysis of some Latin endings:

(19)

			Root	Gender	Number	Case
Fem	Sg	Nom	puell	a	Ø	Ø
		Gen	puell	a	:	ī
		Acc	puell	a	Ø	m
		Abl	puell	a	Ø	:
	Pl	Nom	puell	a	:	ī
		Gen	puell	a	:	rum
		Acc	puell	a	:	s
Masc	Sg	Nom	serv	o	Ø	s
		Gen	serv	o	Ø	ī
		Acc	serv	o	Ø	m
		Abl	serv	o	Ø	:
	Pl	Nom	serv	o	:	ī
		Gen	serv	o	:	rum
		Acc	serv	o	:	s

It is obvious that all this is still far from Turkish determinacy with respect to segmentation into morphemes (one-to-one correspondence between morpheme and grammatical meaning). First, we analyzed only some of the o- and a-stems. Second, many problems remain. For instance, the Fem Sg Gen shows a long thematic vowel; the Masc Sg Gen is homophonous with Masc Pl Nom -ī but in this type of analysis the former has underlying -o -Ø -ī the latter o-:-ī (plus the fact that we have to write a phonological rule for o + ī → ī. Furthermore, we still do not escape the issue of polysemy (multiple meaning) of grammatical morphemes. For instance, in the above tripartite analysis -s marks not only the nominative (Sg Masc) but also the accusative (Pl) and genitive elsewhere. Thus we have to conclude that whereas Turkish is a typical example of an agglutinating language in that it shows a one-to-one correspondence between morphemes and grammatical meaning, Latin is **fusional** in this respect, even if there are some traces of agglutination. However, as with all typological distinctions, we are dealing with a continuum and it might be instructive to examine a language which may be classified as **semi-agglutinative** (or **semi-fusional**). In contrast with Latin, Classical Arabic is more successful in keeping plural markers from fusing with gender markers. These are the instances referred to as **broken plurals** e.g., *rajul-un* "man", pluralized *rijāl-un* (-u indicates nominative and -n corresponds to the indefinite article of English). Consider the following paradigmatic sets (Classical Arabic has only three cases and two genders):

(20)

		Masculine	Feminine
Sg	Nom	rajulun "a man"	ʔimraʔatun "a woman"
	Acc	rajulan	ʔimraʔatan
	Gen	rajulin	ʔimraʔatin

Pl	Nom	rijālun	?imra?ātun
	Acc	rijālan	?imra?ātin
	Gen	rijālin	?imra?ātin

Sg	Nom	mudarrisun "a teacher (M)"	mudarrisatun "a teacher (F)"
	Acc	mudarrisan	mudarrisatan
	Gen	mudarrisin	mudarrisatin
Pl	Nom	mudarrisūna	mudarrisātun
	Acc/Gen	mudarrisīna	mudarrisātin

Clear cut examples of agglutination come from the inflection of feminine nouns. Assuming that the masculine gender is marked with the Ø-suffix (versus feminine -*at*) we may propose the following tripartite analysis of the endings of externally inflected nouns (length is marked with a colon (:)).

(21)

			Stem	Gender	Number	Case (+Indef)
Masc	Sg	Nom	mudarris	Ø	Ø	un
		Acc	mudarris	Ø	Ø	an
		Gen	mudarris	Ø	Ø	in
Fem	Sg	Nom	mudarris	at	Ø	un
		Acc	mudarris	at	Ø	an
		Gen	mudarris	at	Ø	in
Masc	Pl	Nom	mudarris	Ø	:	una
		Acc	mudarris	Ø	:	ina
		Gen	mudarris	Ø	:	ina
Fem	Pl	Nom	mudarris	at	:	un
		Acc	mudarris	at	:	in
		Gen	mudarris	at	:	in

The case endings of masculine nouns inflected externally in the plural are not identical with those in the singular. However, they are identical if the noun is inflected internally (*a-u* → *i-ā*):

(22)

		Root+Number	Gender	Case
Masc Sg	Nom	RaǰuL	Ø	un
	Acc	RaǰuL	Ø	an
	Gen	RaǰuL	Ø	in
Masc Pl	Nom	RiǰāL	Ø	un
	Acc	RiǰāL	Ø	an
	Gen	RiǰāL	Ø	in

Summarily, in Classical Arabic we may find clear cut examples of agglutination but these are counterbalanced by examples of fusion, especially by a rather unusual fusion of lexical and grammatical morphemes (somewhat reminiscent of ablaut in Indo-European languages). It may also be noted that we have to assume that number is expressed by the lengthening of the gender marker of feminine nouns but by the lengthening of the case marker of masculine nouns, cf. *mudarrisātin* vs. *mudarrisīna* in (21).

RECOMMENDED READINGS

Applegate, Joseph R. 1958. *An Outline of the Structure of Shilḥa*. New York: American Council of Learned Societies.

Campbell, A. 1959. *Old English Grammar*. Oxford: Clarendon Press.

Greenberg, Joseph. 1966. *Language Universals with Special Reference to Feature Hierarchies*. The Hague: Mouton.

Kuryłowicz, Jerzy. 1964. *Inflectional Categories of Indo-European*. Heidelberg: Carl Winter.

Lewis, Geoffrey L. 1967. *Turkish Grammar*. Oxford: Clarendon Press.

Moreland, Floyd L. & Rita M. Fleischer. 1973. *Latin: An Intensive Course*. Berkeley: University of California Press.

Wright, W. 1896–1898. *A Grammar of the Arabic Language*. Volumes 1 and 2. Cambridge: Cambridge University Press.

EXERCISES

1. Identity the following morphological categories in Tašelhit, the Berber dialect spoken in southwest Morocco as described by Applegate (1958):

   (a) Verbal roots and their lexical meaning.
   (b) Derivational verbal affixes and their lexico-grammatical meaning.
   (c) Inflectional verbal affixes and their grammatical meaning.
   (d) Describe morphological processes expressing the past tense.
   (e) Construct paradigmatic sets for

      (i) Subject affixes
      (ii) Direct object affixes
      (iii) Indirect object affixes

   Describe their distribution within words with respect to the roots in various inflectional categories.

   Use the following data. Notice that the examples are in phonemic transcription (i.e., do not try to pronounce them):

   (1) tdīt   "you went"
   (2) dānt   "they (F) went"
   (3) ifaiast   "he gave it to him/her"
   (4) urasntfint   "they (F) did not give it to them (M)"
   (5) tramt   "ye (F) wanted"
   (6) umzɣt   "I took him/it"
   (7) raiiamz   "he will take me"
   (8) išfirtt   "he stole her"
   (9) fanasntt   "they (M) gave it to them (F)"
   (10) ndā   "we went"
   (11) tšfirmt   "ye (F) stole"
   (12) ramtfiɣ   "I will give it to you (F)"
   (13) fiɣast   "I gave it to him/her"
   (14) tkaɣast   "I used to give it to him/her"
   (15) uramtifi   "he did not give it to you (F)"
   (16) urakzriɣ   "I will not see you (M)"
   (17) izrai   "he saw me"
   (18) rakmiamz   "he will take you (F)"

(19) raiitifa   "he will give it to me"
(20) urrastfin   "they (M) will not give it to him/her"
(21) tbnunt   "they (F) used to build"
(22) tbnutt   "you built it"
(23) raktbnuɣ   "I will build it for you (M)"
(24) fantaunt   "they (F) gave it to you (M Pl)"
(25) urraunttʃint   "they (F) will not give it to ye (F Pl)"
(26) itʃfar   "he used to steal"
(27) tʃfirt   "you stole"
(28) nird   "we were clean"
(29) tsirdmt   "ye (F) washed"
(30) sirdn   "they (M) washed"
(31) rakuntizra   "he will see you (F Pl)"
(32) urkunizri   "he did not see you (M Pl)"
(33) tzraɣtnt   "I used to see them (F)"
(34) itdū   "he used to go"
(35) tkant   "they (F) used to give"
(36) ntamz   "we used to take"
(37) ifaiamt   "he gave it to you (F)"
(38) fantast   "they (F) gave it to him/her"
(39) riɣ   "I wanted"
(40) urttriɣ   "I did not want her"
(41) rattizra   "he will see her"
(42) tbint   "they (F) used to cross"
(43) ttbit   "you used to cross"
(44) rabiɣ   "I will cross"
(45) tzrati   "you saw me"
(46) ifaiit   "he gave it to me"
(47) tʃitast   "you gave it to him/her"
(48) tfamtasnt   "ye (M) gave him/it to them (F)"
(49) dīɣ   "I went"
(50) tdām   "ye (M) went"

2. Segment the words of Latin, Classical Arabic and Turkish given below into morphemes, and discuss the correspondence between morphemes and grammatical meaning.

		Latin	Classical Arabic	Turkish
Sg.	Nom.	vir "man"	raǰulun	adam
	Acc.	virum	raǰulan	adamı
	Gen.	virī	raǰulin	adamın
Pl.	Nom.	virī	riǰālun	adamlar
	Acc.	virōs	riǰālan	adamları
	Gen.	virōrum	riǰālin	adamların
Sg.	Nom.	fēmina "woman"	imraʔatun	kadın
	Acc.	fēminam	imraʔatan	kadını
	Gen.	fēminae	imraʔatin	kadının
Pl.	Nom.	fēminae	imraʔātun	kadınlar
	Acc.	fēminās	imraʔātin	kadınları
	Gen.	fēminārum	imraʔātin	kadınların

3. It was shown in 4.3 that Latin is fusional with respect to inflection of nouns. However, the inflectional suffixes of Latin are segmentable in a more abstract analysis operating with notions such as a short and long thematic vowel, zero suffix and morphophonemic rules. Attempt to reduce along these lines the variety of the five traditional declensions displayed in (15).

4. Identify the following morphological categories of Classical Arabic:
   (a) Verbal roots and their lexical meaning.
   (b) Derivational affixes and processes and their lexico-grammatical meaning.
   (c) Construct paradigmatic sets of inflectional suffixes expressing subject and direct object.
   (d) Predict the following forms: "ye (M)" and "you (F)".

Use the following data:

(1)	katabahū	"he wrote it"
(2)	fahimathā	"she understood her"
(3)	iktatabta	"you (M) subscribed"
(4)	iftahamtinī	"you (F) comprehended me"
(5)	kutiba	"it was destined"
(6)	aktabnāhū	"we dictated it"
(7)	afhamtunna	"ye (F) instructed"
(8)	istafhamna	"they (F) inquired"
(9)	tafāhamū	"they (M) understood one another"

(10)	takātabna	"they (F) wrote to each other"
(11)	qutilat	"she was killed"
(12)	taqātalnā	"we fought with one another"
(13)	istaqtalti	"you (F) risked your life"
(14)	tadāxalti	"you (F) interfered"
(15)	adxaltunnahā	"ye (F) introduced her"
(16)	adxalatki	"she introduced you (F)"
(17)	fahimaka	"he understood you"
(18)	adxalnākunna	"we introduced you (F Pl)"
(19)	xaraj̈tu	"I left"
(20)	axrajnākum	"we dismissed you (M Pl)"
(21)	istaxraj̈ūhum	"they (M) exploited them (M)"

Translate the following sentences into Classical Arabic:

(22) "they (F) left"
(23) "she was dismissed"
(24) "we understood one another"
(25) "ye (F) inquired"
(26) "they (F) introduced you (M Pl)"

5. The following table displays the battery of 60 inflectional suffixes of Sanskrit as presented in various traditional grammars. Prove that their number may be reduced considerably in a more abstract analysis which operates with the following notions:

(a) thematic vowel
(b) suffix
(c) morphophonemic rules of ablaut (gradation)

Hint: Consider /ē/ and /ō/ as diphthongs /ai/ and /au/ in the underlying form (IP model).

		ā-stems "daughter"	*a*-stems "son"	C-stems "friend"	*i*-stems "fire"	*u*-stems "sun"
Sg	Nom	sutā	sutas	suhrd	agnis	bhānus
	Acc	ām	am	am	im	um
	Instr	ayā	ēna	ā	inā	unā
	Dat	āyai	āya	ē	ayē	avē
	Abl	āyās	āt	as	ēs	ōs
	Gen	āyās	asya	as	ēs	ōs
	Loc	āyām	ē	i	āu	āu
Pl	Nom	ās	ās	as	ayas	āvas
	Acc	ās	ān	as	īn	ūn
	Instr	ābhis	ais	bhis	ibhis	ubhis
	Dat	ābhyas	ēbhyas	bhyas	ibhyas	ubhyas
	Abl	ābhyas	ēbhyas	bhyas	ibhyas	ubhyas
	Gen	ānām	ānām	ām	īnām	ūnām
	Loc	āsu	ēṣu	su	iṣu	uṣu

CHAPTER FIVE
INFLECTIONAL CATEGORIES ASSOCIATED WITH NOMINAL ELEMENTS

5.1 *Primary Nominal Categories*

5.1.1 *Nouns and Adjectives*

Classical **parts of speech** have been limited to a few broad classes: **noun, verb, adjective, adverb, pronoun, preposition, interjection, numeral, conjunction**, and possibly **article** and **particle**. In traditional grammatical theory the parts of speech were defined in notional terms. **Noun** was defined as the name of any person, place, animal and thing (**concrete nouns**) and the name of any property, action and state (**abstract noun**). **Adjective** was defined as an **attribute** (**property**) of any person, place, animal or thing denoted by a noun. Properties of substances expressed by adjectives are of a static nature; on the other hand, properties of substances expressed by **verbs** are of a dynamic nature, or, more commonly, **verbs** denote **actions**, **states** and **changes of state** of the subject. (Discussion of subjectless sentences belongs to syntax). Grammatical redefinition of these three notional categories would establish a basic dichotomy of noun and verb. Noun (and adjective) would be defined as a primary grammatical category the domain of which includes sub-categories of **gender**, **number** and **case** (plus **comparison** with the adjective); the verb would be defined as a primary grammatical category the domain of which includes subcategories of **person, number, tense, aspect, mood**, and **voice**. It may be noted in passing that this dichotomy became the first axiom of Transformational Grammar (S → NP VP). In other words, the definition of the major grammatical classes of noun and verb cannot be made independently of syntactic and logical considerations (noun-verb, subject-predicate, agent-action). Plato (429–347 B.C.), who was the first to distinguish explicitly between **nouns** and **verbs**, used the term ῥῆμα /rhêma/ for the latter category — the word *rhêma* means both 'verb' and 'predicate'. It is significant that in this classification verbs and adjectives were put together in the same class. This may seem surprising on grammatical grounds since adjectives have the same sub-categories of gender, number and case as nouns do, but, on notional grounds, it makes perfect sense since both verbs and adjectives may be characterized as features on substances (dynamic and static). In this connection, it is of interest to note that later Greek grammarians abandoned the Platonic dichotomy of noun - (verb - adjective) and replaced it by another dichotomy of (noun - adjective) - verb, where nouns and adjectives were brought together in one class. If the Platonic dichotomy was of a notional nature, the later dichotomy was of a grammatical nature (i.e., the emphasis was on nominal subcategories shared by nouns and adjectives). The tripartite distinction of nouns, adjectives and verbs, or the compromise between notional and grammatical criteria, was made later on in medieval times and since those times it has survived in our school grammars. The emphasis on a tripartite distinction was born in dealing with Classical languages (Latin and

Greek) which are heavily flective and where the adjective shows the same sub-categories as the noun does. However, if we look elsewhere, we realize that this situation is far from being universal. For instance, in English and Turkish attributively used adjectives are not inflected for gender and number, whereas in Latin and French they are. Put differently, the nominal sub-categories of gender, number and case are inherent in nouns, but they are only secondary in adjectives; marking for nominal sub-categories with adjectives by **agreement** or **congruence** was claimed to be only a matter of 'surface' grammar. Consider the following data:

(1)   English   Turkish   Latin
   a good man   iyi bir adam   vir bonus
   a good woman   iyi bir kadın   fēmina bona
      good men   iyi adamlar   virī bonī
      good women   iyi kadınlar   fēminae bonae

The Latin adjective shows complete agreement with its noun in gender, number and case (*vir bonus* = Nominative, *virī bonī* = Genitive Sg or Nominative Pl, etc.). On the other hand, we cannot say **good-s men* in English or **iyi-ler adam-lar* in Turkish. Neither will the case be shown in the latter two languages, thus versus Latin *virōrum bonōrum* (Genitive Plural) we find English *good men's* and Turkish *iyi adam-lar-ın*. Of course, in both English and Turkish, adjectives can be nominalized. For instance, *young* is an adjective used as a nominal in the English sentence: *What can one expect from the young?*. Observe, however, that we still cannot pluralize; **from the youngs* is not grammatical. On the other hand, in Turkish, nominalized adjectives behave like nouns in that they may take the plural, case and personal suffixes after them, or the indefinite article *bir* before them; consider: *büyük* "big, old", *büyük-ler-im* "my elders"; *hasta* "ill", *bir hasta* "a sick person"; *genç* "young", *genç-ler-in* "of the young".

If we take as the criterion of an adjective the permissibility of forming the comparative and superlative, nouns will be excluded. For instance, in English we may say *The rich live on the bay* or *The richest live on the bay*, but nothing similar can be done with *The man lives on the bay*. In other words, although most adjectives are nominalizable (i.e., can be used as nouns), the converse is not true (adjectivals, such as *bus* in *bus stop* cannot form the comparative or superlative). Note also that the 'noun-ness' of the adjective can be a matter of degree. From the discussion above it appears that adjectives in Turkish are more noun-like than adjectives in English; we cannot say **The riches live on the bay*, i.e. to treat the adjective *rich* as a noun in respect to pluralization, but we can in Turkish. However, even in Turkish, and perhaps in all languages, we have to draw a dividing line between noun and adjective when it comes to the specific adjectival category of comparison.

Latin and Greek adjectives are not formally different from nouns. As was shown in (1), we cannot talk about specific adjectival inflection. The adjective, as far as the categories of gender, number and case are concerned, is inflected nominally. Nevertheless, the Germanic and Balto-

Slavic families of the Indo-European phylum created what may be called a specific **adjectival inflection**. Let us consider Old English as a representative of the Germanic family. The so-called **strong declension** of adjectives displays endings which differ from those of nouns but which are almost identical with those of pronouns. Consider the following data:

(2)

		Noun (Masc) Strong "stone"	Adjective (Masc) Strong "good"	Demonstrative Pronoun (Masc) "this"
Sg	Nom	stān	gōd	θes
	Acc	stān	gōd-ne	θis-ne
	Gen	stān-es	gōd-es	θiss-es
	Dat	stān-e	gōd-um	θiss-um
	Instr		gōd-e	θȳs

However, the so-called **weak declension** of adjectives is identical with that of weak nouns:

(3)

		Noun (Masc) Weak "name"	Adjective (Masc) Weak "good"
Sg	Nom	nama	gōda
	Acc	naman	gōdan
	Gen	naman	gōdan
	Dat	naman	gōdan

Baltic and Slavic languages have two types of adjectives: **simple** (or indefinite) and **complex** (or definite). The simple forms are inflected, with some exceptions, identically with nouns. Consider the following data from Lithuanian:

(4)

		Noun (Masc) "man"	Simple Adjective (Masc) "good"
Sg	Nom	výras	gĕras
	Gen	výro	gĕro
	Dat	výrui	gerám
	Acc	výrą	gĕrą
	Loc	výre	geramè
	Instr	výru	gerù

The endings of complex forms betray their pronominal origin, as is obvious from their juxtaposition to personal pronouns of the 3rd person, cf. (5).

(5)

		Complex Adjective (Masc) "good"	Personal Pronoun (Masc) "he"
Sg	Nom	geràsis	jìs
	Gen	gĕrojo	jõ
	Dat	gerájam	jám
	Acc	gĕraji̇	jī̇
	Loc	gerãjame	jamè
	Instr	gerúoju	juõ

5.1.2 *Pronouns*

Expressed traditionally, **pronouns** do not 'name' persons, animals and things but 'replace' them (the Latin term *pronomen* was calqued on Greek ἀντωνυμία /antōnymíā/ "instead of the noun"). On the one hand, pronouns resemble nouns in that they are inflected for number, case and, to a limited degree, for gender; on the other hand, pronouns share the category of person with verbs. Furthermore, pronouns are a small **closed** (grammatical) **class**, whereas nouns are a large **open** (lexical) **class** to which we may freely add new ones.

To analyze personal pronouns we have to introduce the notion of **deixis** (derived from Greek δείκνυμι /deíknūmi/ "I point, indicate"). We may say that personal pronouns are only one class of the so-called deictic elements, which include also adverbials of place: *here* and *there* ('close to the speaker' vs. 'not close to the speaker') and time: *now* and *then* ('at the time of speaking' vs. 'not at the time of speaking'). The deictic category of **proximity** is not too common with personal pronouns of the 3rd Pers but examples may be found in more 'exotic' languages. For instance, Hindi pronouns of the 3rd Pers show this contrast: *yē* 'he/she close to the speaker' vs. *hō* 'he/she not close to the speaker'. Obviously, the deictic category of proximity is irrelevant with pronouns of the 1st and 2nd Pers since the speaker and the addressee are always (disregarding conversations on the telephone, etc.) in the same spatiotemporal situation. This circumstance may explain why marking for gender is rather unusual in the 2nd Person, and even less common with the 1st Person. The situation in English is typical of many languages. Here, the personal pronouns of the 1st and 2nd Pers Sg are genderless but the pronoun of the 3rd Pers Sg shows gender distinctions (*he, she, it*). In French and Latin even their plural counterparts show gender distinctions, whereas in Germanic languages they do not.

Pronominal forms in Germanic and Romance languages are contrasted in (6).

(6)

English		German	
he		er	
she	} they	sie	} sie
it		es	

Latin		French	
is	ii	il	ils
ea	eae	elle	elles
id	ea		

Examples of gender distinctions in the 2nd Pers may be found among languages belonging to the Afro-Asiatic phylum. For instance, Classical Arabic has distinct 2nd Person forms in both singular and plural:

(7)		Singular	Plural
2nd Person	Masc	ʔanta	ʔantum
	Fem	ʔanti	ʔantunna
3rd Person	Masc	huwa	hum
	Fem	hiya	hunna

In Modern Arabic dialects the gender distinctions in the plural disappeared. The system of Syrian Arabic is as follows:

(8)		Singular	Plural
2nd Person	Masc	ʔənte	ʔəntu
	Fem	ʔənti	
3rd Person	Masc	huwwe	hənne
	Fem	hiyye	

The reasons for this simplification have to do with reference. In referring to "men and women" Classical Arabic had to use the masculine form *hum* (this form would be used even when referring to "a hundred women and one man"), whereas Modern Syrian Arabic uses the unmarked form *hənne*, which is not in conflict with natural gender. This clash between natural and grammatical gender contributed probably to the loss of dual pronominal forms. In Classical Arabic, these were formed from the masculine base: *ʔantumā* "you (two)" and *humā* "they (two)". Again, in referring to the couple of "a man and a woman" or to "two women", there was a clash between natural and grammatical gender. In these cases Modern Syrian Arabic uses plural forms *ʔəntu* and *hənne*. As an example of a language making gender distinction in the 1st Pers Sg we may mention Adeni Arabic where we find *anā* "I (Masc)" vs. *anī* "I (Fem)". "We" distinguishes gender in Spanish *nosotros* "we (Masc)" vs. *nosotras* "we (Fem)". There are also examples of gender distinction with possessive pronouns. For instance, Bedawye (Kushitic group of the Afro-Asiatic phylum) has three forms of "my" and "your" (realized as suffixes on nouns):

(9)		1ˢᵗ Sg	2ⁿᵈ Sg
		-hēb	-hōk
Masc		-hēba	-hōka
Fem		-hēbi	-hōki

The first form is unmarked for gender, the second form specifies that the 1ˢᵗ (or 2ⁿᵈ) Pers possessor is male, and the third form specifies that the possessor is female.

It may comes as a surprise to realize that truly genderless languages are genderless even in their pronominal systems. Examples are comparatively numerous and may be found among Altaic, Uralic and Amerindian languages. Turkish (Altaic family) may be used as an example:

(10)	Singular	Plural
2ⁿᵈ Person	sen	siz
3ʳᵈ Person	o	onlar

As shown in (7), Classical Arabic has two forms in each of these four slots. Or we may contrast this 'poor' system with the 'rich' systems of Latin and Czech:

(11)		Latin 3ʳᵈ Person		Czech 3ʳᵈ Person		Turkish 3ʳᵈ Person	
		Sg	Pl	Sg	Pl	Sg	Pl
Masc		is	ii	on	oni		
Fem		ea	eae	ona	ony	o	onlar
Neuter		id	ea	ono	ona		

Returning to gender-languages, it is of interest to observe that Latin and Czech show the typical Indo-European syncretism of Feminine Singular and Neuter Plural (cf. Neut Pl *verb-a* "words" and Fem Sg *fēmin-a* "woman") even with personal pronouns.

There are various problems with pronominal number distinctions in the 1ˢᵗ Person. Whereas "three tables" is "table$_1$ + table$_2$ + table$_3$" we cannot say that "we (= three of us)" is "I$_1$ + I$_2$ + I$_3$". The pronoun *we* covers basically two distinct groups which can be established on the basis of the **speaker** and **addressee** distinction:

(i) the speaker-group (= I + he$_1$ + he$_2$ ...) but NOT the listener group;

(ii) the speaker-group (= I or I + he$_1$ + he$_2$ ...) AND the listener group (= you or you and he$_1$ + he$_2$...) as well.

In both cases, one or more 3ʳᵈ Persons may or may not be included. It is of interest to note that some languages (most notably the Algonkian family) grammaticalize this distinction between two meanings of "we". Thus Cree has two 1ˢᵗ Person plural forms which keep these two basic possibilities apart:

(i)   *nīlanān* includes the speaker group but excludes the group being addressed: "I and he/they but not you." This form is called 1ˢᵗ Pers Pl **exclusive**.

(ii) *kīlanānaw* specifies that both the speaker group and the addressee-group are included: "I (and he/they) and you (and he/they)". This form is called 1ˢᵗ Pers Pl **inclusive**.

Nevertheless, there are languages which form their plural personal pronouns by the simple pluralizing of their singular counterparts. As a classical example we may quote Chinese which does not pluralize nouns, but does pluralize pronouns. The Cantonese system is as follows:

(12) ngǎw "I"   ngǎw-dā̄y "we"
      nǎy "you"   nǎy-dā̄y "you, ye"
      kŏei "he/she"   kŏei-dā̄y "they"

Even some Altaic languages could be analyzed similarly; for instance, Turkish, as shown in (13) and (14):

(13) ben "I"   biz "we"
      sen "you"   siz "ye"
      o "he/she"   onlar "they"

Here the situation is more complicated. The 3ʳᵈ Person pronoun is pluralized by the regular nominal suffix (e.g., *çocuk* "child", *çocuk-lar* "children") whereas the 1ˢᵗ and 2ⁿᵈ Person show the pronominal pluralizing suffix *-iz* which occurs typically with possessive suffixes:

(14) ev   "house"
      ev-im   "my house"   (the possessor is in the singular)
      ev-im-iz   "our house"   (the possessor is in the plural)

Turkish may be taken as an example of a linguistic type where **possessive pronouns** are realized as suffixes (bound morphemes), whereas Latin and many other Indo-European languages realize their possessive pronouns as attributive adjectives (free morphemes) which may be inflected for gender, number and case (to show agreement). Let us consider the less common Turkish system first:

(15) ev-im   "my house"   ev-ler-im   "my houses"
    -in   "your (Sg) house"   -in   "your (Sg) houses"
    -i   "his/her house"   -i   "his/her houses"
    ev-im-iz   "our house"   ev-ler-im-iz "our houses"
    -in-iz   "your (Pl) house"   -in-iz   "your (Pl) houses"
    -ler-i   "their house"   -ler-i   "their houses"

An interesting problem connected with marking for nominal and pronominal plural appears in the 3rd Pers. Here the single form *evleri* has three meanings:

(16)

$$evleri \begin{cases} \text{(i)} & \text{his/her houses} \\ \text{(ii)} & \text{their house} \\ \text{(iii)} & \text{their houses} \end{cases}$$

(i)   (ev+Pl)   Poss Sg   (ev + ler)i
(ii) (ev)   Poss Pl   (ev)ler + i
(iii) (ev+Pl)   Poss Pl   (ev + ler) ler + i

The form in (iii) **ev+ler+ler+i* is simplified into *ev+ler+i*. The curiosity of this system lies in the fact that the possessive suffix of the 3rd Pers Pl *ler+i* "their" is anomalous if compared with the 1st and 2nd Person. In these persons the pluralizing suffix is added on the right (as usual with nouns): *im* + *iz*, whereas it is added on the left in the 3rd Pers: *ler+i*. Hence the homophony of "his/her houses" (*ev+ler+i*) and "their house" (*ev+ler+i* instead of **ev+i+ler*). This clash does not exist in other languages with similar systems of possessive suffixes. For instance, Persian (which is one of the few Indo-European languages with a system of possessive suffixes) admits a pluralizing suffix on the right even in the 3rd Person. This is shown in (17):

(17) barādar-am   "my brother"   barādar-ān-am   "my brothers"
     barādar-eš   "his brother"   barādar-ān-eš   "his brothers"

     barādar-em-ān "our brother"   barādar-ān-em-ān "our brothers"
     barādar-eš-ān "their brother" barādar-ān-eš-ān "their brothers"

Systems of other Indo-European languages show the typical **heteronymy of personal pronouns** (*I - we, he - they*) even in the system of possessive pronouns. Consider the Latin data in (18).

(18) frāter meus   "my brother"   frātrēs meī   "my brothers"
     frāter noster "our brother"   frātrēs nostrī   "our brothers"

In Latin the possessive pronoun has to agree in gender, number and case with its noun, whereas Turkish simply adds the case suffixes to the grammatical word consisting of the lexeme and its possessive suffix. Contrast the following examples:

(19)

Latin	Turkish	English
fräter meus	kardeş-im	my brother
frätris meī	kardeş-im-in	my brother's
frätrēs meī	kardeş-ler-im	my brothers
frätrum meōrum	kardeş-ler-im-in	my brothers'
fräter noster	kardeş-im-iz	our brother
frätris nostrī	kardeş-im-iz-in	our brother's
frätrēs nostrī	kardeş-ler-im-iz	our brothers
frätrum nostrōrum	kardeş-ler-im-iz-in	our brothers'

The difference between these two linguistic systems may be portrayed as shown in (20).

(20)

Latin	LEXEME	Gender Number Case	POSS PRONOUN	Gender Number Case

Turkish   ((LEXEME + Number) Poss + Number) Case

Interrogative, relative and **indefinite pronouns** exhibit morphological similarities in many languages. In the flective Indo-European languages we find two sets of interrogative and indefinite pronouns: the **nominal set** has typically only two forms: one used in inquiring about animate beings (*who?*) and another one used about inanimate objects (*what?*); the **adjectival set** differentiates gender in reference to animate beings. Latin forms are given in (21).

(21)

	Nominal Set	Adjectival Set	
Masc	quis? "who?"	quī (quis)?	"which (one)?"
Fem		quae?	
Neut	quid? "what?"	quod?	

The adjectival forms are used if we demand additional information about animate beings or objects which have already been mentioned. For instance, if the discussion is about "poets" we may demand additional information by asking "Which poet is the best (one)?" or in Latin *Quī poēta est optimus?* However, if we wanted to ask 'out of the blue' about the best poet (i.e., in the case when "poet" would not be given as the topic by the context), we could use the form *quis*: *Quis est optimus poēta?* "Who is the best poet?". A full explanation of this phenomenon belongs to syntax and discourse analysis; here we have to be satisfied with observing morphological differences between nominal and adjectival interrogative pronouns. Russian data offer another example of this constraint:

(22)   Nominal Set   Adjectival Set

Masc	} kto? "who?"	kotóryj?	}
Fem		kotóraja?	"which (one)?"
Neuter	čto? "what?"	kotóroje?	

Their use corresponds to Latin or English in (21): *Kotóryj poét nailúčšij?* "Which poet is the best (one)?" versus *Któ nailúčšij poét?* "Who is the best poet?"

5.2 Secondary Nominal Categories

5.2.1 Gender

It is customary to start a discussion of grammatical gender with non-linguistic considerations and proceed from them to establishing a 'natural' semantic basis for gender in individual languages. It is clear that the non-linguistic universe can be classified in a variety of ways according to various sets of properties. One of the major distinctions is undoubtedly that of living or **animate beings** (human and animal beings) versus **inanimate things**. This is the essence of one of the most famous classifications of the universe as elaborated by the neo-Platonic philosopher Porphyry, shown in Figure 5.1.

Inorganic things (Porphyry's minerals) are inanimate and so are plants. However, the classification of animals (Porphyry's brutes) as animate beings depends crucially on the interpretation of the word animate. Etymologically this word means "provided with soul" (Latin *anima* "soul"), but in modern linguistic terminology this term means simply "living". For instance, some semantic features of *man* are [+animate], [+human] and those of *cat* are [+animate], [-human]. This type of specifying the lexis for semantic features is claimed to capture significant universal properties of human languages. Many linguists entertain the idea that the vocabularies of all human languages can be analyzed in terms of a finite set of **semantic features** or **semantic components** (such as [±animate], [±countable], [±male], etc.), which are themselves independent of the particular semantic structure of a given language. To quote Katz (1966:156) "semantic markers ... cannot be identified with the words or expressions of the language ... Rather, they are to be regarded as constructs of a linguistic theory." Currently, however, linguists are more interested in the fact that universal semantic features are intimately linked with conceptual structures of individual languages which are accessible to us through their morphological systems. Let us ascertain whether we can use the semantic 'marker' animate in analyzing the grammatical system of Sumerian (genetically isolated). The basic dichotomy of Sumerian lexis is usually referred to as a group of 'persons' versus a group of 'things' with the membership as shown in (23).

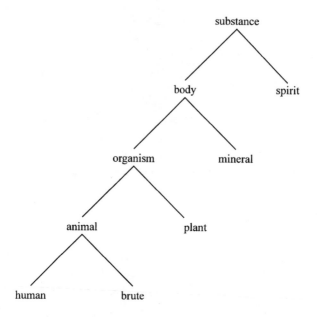

Fig. 5.1 Porphyry's classification of the universe

(23) PERSONS   THINGS
      gods   things
      heroes   abstracts
      human beings   animals

This dichotomy is imposed on lexis by grammar; for instance, only PERSONS may form their plural by the suffix *-ene*, THINGS or their determining adjectives have to be reduplicated. It might seem very strange that Sumerian grammar treats animals as THINGS; but, obviously, the Sumerian dichotomy PERSONS-THINGS is best explainable in terms of 'soul' in that divine and human beings possess a soul whereas animals do not. Consequently, we may wish to use the pair animate - inanimate in its etymological meaning [+soul] vs. [-soul] for the Sumerian PERSONS - THINGS opposition. Obviously, we cannot say that the meaning of animacy in Sumerian and, say, English is co-extensive. It is of interest to note that groups of PERSONS [+animate collective] in Sumerian may be treated as THINGS [+inanimate]. Needless to say, attempts to work with the category of animacy defined independently of a particular language would be doomed *a priori*.

It may come as a surprise that some grammatical systems do not reflect the 'natural' dichotomy of animate (human and non-human) beings into male-female. In other words, there is nothing in them which would correspond to the masculine-feminine dichotomy of many Indo-

European or Afro-Asiatic languages. Examples of such grammatical systems can be found among Altaic (Turkish) or Amerindian (Cree) and Eskimo-Aleut languages (Inuktitut). Thus in Turkish the 3rd Pers pronoun *o* is used in referring to both male and female beings and in translating from Turkish we have to use "he" or "she" (or "it") according to the context. Similarly, in Cree *wīya* expresses all "he", "she", and "it". It is of interest to note that in genderless languages **epicene** lexemes occur even in the most unexpected cases (epicene = common gender, e.g., *cat* in English may denote both *tom-cat* or *(she-)cat*). In Turkish *kardeş* may denote either "brother" or "sister"; to refer to "sister" unambiguously we have to use *kız* "girl" in apposition: *kızkardeş* (literally "female sibling"). Or in Sumerian the epicene lexeme *dumu* may denote either "son" or "daughter"; to refer to "daughter" unambiguously we have to use *mí* "woman" in apposition: *dumu mí* (literally "female offspring"). An unusual example of this nature comes from Janjero (Kushitic language, Afro-Asiatic phylum) which has an epicene lexeme *asu* denoting either "man" or "woman". These may be referred to unambiguously by using words *adk* "male" and *mašk* "female" in apposition: *adk asu* "male human being" = "man" and *mašk asu* "female human being" = "woman". The phenomenon of common gender is not limited to 'exotic' languages; epicene lexemes may be found in all natural languages. However, what is of interest from the viewpoint of anthropological linguistics, is the balance of epicenes and **heteronyms** (heteronymy is the opposite phenomenon of the common gender; e.g., *stallion* and *mare* are heteronyms since these two words cannot be related morphologically). Heteronymy is much more common in the case of domesticated animals (*ram* vs. *ewe*, *gander* vs. *goose* etc.); in the case of wild animals, various languages use epicene lexemes plus productive derivational processes *lion* ~ *lioness*, *tiger* ~ *tigress*). Turkish indicates the gender of animals by *erkek* "male" and *dişi* "female" as English does with pronouns *he* and *she*:

(24) erkek ayı   he-bear

       dişi ayı   she-bear

Similarly, Latin could specify the natural gender of animals denoted by epicene lexemes by *mās* "male" and *fēmina* "female":

(25) vulpēs mās   "fox"

       vulpēs fēmina   "vixen" or "she-fox"

       lupus   "wolf"

       lupa *or* lupus fēmina   "she-wolf"

All the nouns of many Indo-European languages can be classified into three genders masculine, feminine and neuter in order to account for several grammatical phenomena:

(i)   occurrence of specific endings (suffixes)

(ii)   adjectival concord (agreement)

(iii) pronominal reference

(iv)   correspondence to natural gender

Any discussion of gender without paying attention to all these four points would be misleading. The first point, occurrence of specific endings, is not particularly reliable. For instance, it is impossible to assign gender in Latin solely on the basis of this criterion. If we say that the noun *dominus* "lord" is grammatically masculine because it has a characteristic suffix *-us*, then we have to make some provisions to accommodate nouns like *manus* "hand" which is feminine (as shown by **adjectival concord** (ii): *manus longa* "a long hand". On the other hand, the noun *agrīcola* "peasant" is grammatically masculine even if it has the same inflectional suffix *-a* as *fēmina* "woman". As these few examples show, adjectival concord and **pronominal reference** are more reliable indicators of grammatical gender than nominal morphology (i). The criterion of adjectival concord is also a better indicator of grammatical gender than **natural gender** (iv) since this criterion is useless when it comes to inanimate things (concrete objects, parts of human body, etc.)

(26)		I	II+III	IV	
		Morphology	Adjectival Concord Pronominal Reference	Natural Gender	Grammatical Gender
dominus "lord"		-us	bon-us	male	masculine
agrīcola "peasant"		-a	bon-us	male	masculine
fēmina "woman"		-a	bon-a	female	feminine
manus "hand"		-us	long-a	—	feminine

For the purposes of Latin it was not necessary to deal with criteria (ii) and (iii) separately. However, in the Germanic languages the situation is different; here, adjectival concord is purely formal in being overridden by the morphological criterion (i). Thus in Old English the noun *wīfmann* "woman" shows the same type of adjectival concord as its masculine counterpart *mann* "man": *sē gōda wīfmann* "the good woman" and *sē gōda mann* "the good man". However, in pronominal reference the noun *wīfmann* behaved as feminine in accordance with its denoted natural gender (it was necessary to say *Gesāwest θū hīe?* "Did you see *her*?" and not *hine* "him" when referring to a woman).

What is the notional basis for gender assignment in Indo-European languages? As is well-known, the three grammatical genders masculine, feminine and neuter found in many Indo-European languages reflect the association established by the traditional grammar between **natural gender** (sex) and **grammatical gender**. However, as is equally well-known all Indo-

European languages abound in disagreements between linguistic and non-linguistic worlds. Proverbial examples come from Old English where *wīf* "wife, woman" and *mægden* "maiden" were neuter (as are their German counterparts *das Weib* and *das Mädchen*); among body parts *brēost* "breast" and *hēafod* "head" were neuter, but *wamb* "belly" and *eaxl* "shoulder" were feminine.

On the other hand, some natural feminines (nouns denoting female beings) were grammatically masculine: *wīfmann* "woman" and *mægdenmann* "virgin". Similar examples could be multiplied from all Indo-European languages. It is significant that diachronically these 'illogical' systems were everywhere 'improved' on in essentially two ways. On the one hand, the language got rid of the gender system or, on the other hand, it made the system more 'logical' by establishing more agreement between natural and grammatical gender. Standard English went in the first direction when its 'illogical' system of gender started to break down by the end of the Old English period (11th c.) and the result is the genderless typology of Modern English. The loss could be only partial, as is exemplified by French, which modified the three-way gender distinction of Latin into a two-way distinction (masculine - feminine). On the other hand, Slavic languages and Modern Greek preserved the three genders of Indo-European and consequently had to introduce various alignments of the 'illogical' relationship between natural and grammatical gender. In Czech the natural distinction male animate (human or animal) being vs. female animate being vs. 'neutral' animate being (i.e., functionally neutral young human or animal) is frequently paralleled by the three-way grammatical distinction. Consider some examples:

(27)

Masculine	Feminine	Neuter
býk	kráva	tele
"bull"	"cow"	"calf"
beran	ovce	jehně
"ram"	"ewe"	"lamb"
hřebec	klisna	hříbě
"stallion"	"mare"	"foal"
muž	žena	dítě
"man"	"woman"	"child"

Smaller adjustments on the 'illogical' gender system are numerous in dialects. For instance, Yiddish reassigned the gender of "horse"; *der Pferd* is masculine in Yiddish, whereas standard German keeps the less 'logical' neuter *das Pferd*. However, we should be careful not to push this type of reasoning too far. For instance, it would be hard to argue that Yiddish reassigned the noun *Wasser* "water" (which is neuter in Standard German *das Wasser*) to the category of feminine, *die Wasser*, for some deeper notional reasons as in the case of the "horse". In this case the most likely explanation is the interference from the Slavic adstratal languages where *voda* "water" is feminine.

To criticize 'illogical' gender systems of various languages from a universalist viewpoint that only nouns denoting animate beings could be legitimately subcategorized into masculine and feminine (and eventually neuter) would be very misleading. Linguists have to look at language specific reasons (language internal 'logic') for this subcategorization. It is exactly here that all kinds of perennial problems of linguistic semantics emerge. Let us consider some examples from Latin. The most general principles of gender assignment (not including nouns denoting animate beings) in Latin can be formulated as follows:

Masculine: names of nations, rivers, winds and months.
Feminine: names of trees, countries, islands and cities.

These semantic principles override those of morphology. For example, the river *Tiberis* "Tiber" is masculine, even if the morphologically identical noun (belonging to the same declinational pattern) *turris* "tower" is feminine. However, no rule is without exceptions; thus the river *Mātrona* "Marne" is feminine, the reason obviously being its morphology, i.e. the suffix *-a*. What is the ultimate explanation of the 'inherent masculinity' of rivers, winds and months in Latin? To take another example: the city of "Rome" *Rōma* is feminine and so is the city of "Corinth" *Corinthus*. In the second case semantic principles override again those of morphology (*Corinthus* is inflected identically with *dominus* "lord"). What is the ultimate explanation of the 'inherent femininity' of cities, trees, countries and islands? That these problems are not pseudoproblems and consequently that they have their legitimate place in any coherent exposé of linguistic systems may be proven by examining another language. Let us compare principles of gender assignment in Hebrew with those of Latin to see if there is something 'deeper' behind their seemingly illogical systems. The Hebrew principles are basically as follows:

Masculine: names of nations, rivers, mountains, seas, winds, months and metals.
Feminine: names of cities, countries, parts of human body occurring in pairs.

It appears that there is far-reaching agreement between Latin and Hebrew which cannot be due to coincidence. Various explanations have been proposed ranging from mythological to more linguistically based reasoning. Thus if female beings living in trees make part of the mythology of a certain nation, it should not be surprising to find names of trees being assigned feminine gender in the language of this nation. Countries and cities are felt to be naturally feminine for all kinds of reasons (mother and her children?), but it is worth mentioning that very frequently they are regarded as **collectives** (cf. 3.3 and 5.2.2). Evidence for collectives being somehow 'inherently feminine' may be found in a variety of languages (e.g., in Old English all the following nouns are feminine: *burg* "city", *ceaster* "military camp", *scīr* "county"). But obviously there is nothing universal on that phenomenon as can be proven by examining other languages. In German names of cities are neuter and in Czech they can belong to any gender: *Montreal* is masculine, *Praha* "Prague" is feminine, and *Toronto* is neuter; in Czech morphological criteria (suffixes -Ø, -*a*, -*o*) override those of semantics.

5.2.2 *Number*

The distinction between singular and plural, found in many languages all over the world, is the most common manifestation of the category of **number**. A logical counterpart of this linguistic category is the category of **quantity** which is based on the recognition of **unity** and **plurality** (i.e., persons, animals and objects can be enumerated as 'one' or 'many' = more than one). The distinction between 'one' and 'more than one', i.e. **countability** is far from being a straightforward notion since many entities are simply not countable. It is usually claimed that **mass nouns** are not pluralizable, which might imply that entities denoted by them are not countable. However, we have to keep in mind, that what is taken as a 'single object', 'many objects', 'group of objects' or an amorphous 'mass' depends to a considerable degree on the lexical and morphological make-up of individual languages. But there is no doubt that the semantic categories **countable**, **mass** and **collective** have to figure in our descriptions of individual languages even if the semantic categorization of the world varies from language to language. Indeed, languages differ drastically in their grammaticalization of these semantic universals. Assuming that the notion of countability is probably a universal category of all human languages, we may place it under substance in the following hierarchy of semantic features shown in Figure 5.2. It is fairly common to recategorize certain mass nouns as countable in certain contexts, such as *They drink three or four different wines at every meal*. Also some nouns can be used both as mass or countable, for instance, *Have some apple* vs. *Have an apple*.

The category of **collective** (group of objects as opposed to many objects) is not grammatic-alized in English, but it is grammaticalized in many other languages. For instance in Arabic collective nouns (nouns denoting natural groups of objects or beings) are a starting point in the derivation of **singulative nouns** (nouns denoting an individual unit of what its basic noun denotes collectively); the examples shown in (28) are from Syrian Arabic.

(28) Collective   Singulative
      ʔamērkān   "Americans"   ʔamērkān-i "an American"
      dəbbān   "flies"   dəbbān-e   "a fly"
      bēḍ   "eggs"   bēḍḍ-a   "an egg"

We have to emphasize that collectives (except for ethnic collectives) are grammatically singular. This is shown by their agreement as in the sentence *bəž-žabal bətʕīš* (the verb in singular) *d-dyāb* (the noun in internal plural) "In the mountains live wolves". It may be said that in Arabic

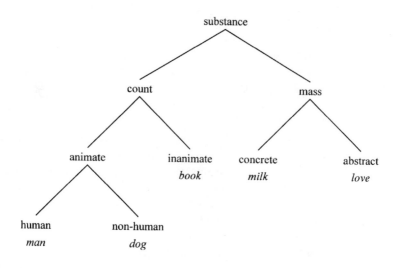

Fig. 5.2 Hierarchy of semantic features

collectives behave as mass nouns in English. In the latter language observe that hunters tend to use words denoting animals as mass nouns: *an elephant* and *a herd of elephant*; *a fish* and *a school of fish*. An interesting phenomenon in Arabic is the possibility of forming plurals of collectives. In a sense, we may talk about a double plural paraphrasable as "many/various groups", shown in Figure 5.3. Since even singulatives are pluralizable we may obtain two different plurals with many nouns. The system works as shown in (29) for Egyptian Arabic.

(29)   Singular   Plural

Singulative   samak-e "a fish"   samak-āt "many"

Collective   samak   "(a school of) fish"   ʔasmāk   "(various types of) fish, fishes"

Singulative   šagar-a "a tree"   šagar-āt "(a few) trees"

Collective   šagar   "(a lot of) trees"   ʔašgār   "(different kinds of) trees"

In similar cases the plural of a singulative (a count plural) stands in contrast to the plural of the underlying collective (which indicates abundance or variety and which is not used after numerals). In terms of morphology, the singulative *šagar-a* "a tree" is regularly related to the collective *šagar* "(a lot of) trees" or "trees" in general by the addition of the feminine suffix *-a* (or *-e*). This suffix is lengthened and *-t* added to form the so-called **plural of paucity** since forms such as *šagarāt* "(a few) trees" occur most commonly with numerals from three to ten. The 'double plural', called **plural of abundance**, is formed by a base pattern change ('broken' plural): *ŠaGaR → aŠGāR* "(different kinds of) trees".

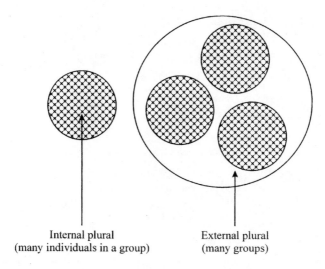

Internal plural   External plural
(many individuals in a group)   (many groups)

Fig. 5.3 Plural of collectives

Another numerical category in Arabic is **dual**. In Classical Arabic it is formed by the suffix *-āni* (Egyptian *-ēn*) added to both masculine (*rajul-āni* "two men), and feminine and singularized collective nouns (*zawj̄-at-āni*) "two wives" and *šajar-at-āni* "two trees"). It possesses only one oblique form *-ayni* (both genitive and accusative) versus two oblique forms in the singular (*-in* genitive and *-an* accusative). The plural may display two or only one oblique form (depending on whether it is formed internally or externally):

(30)

	Singular	Plural (internal)	Plural (external)	Dual
	"king"		"clerk"	
Nom	malik-un	mulūk-un	kātib-ūna	malik-āni
Gen	-in	-in	-īna	-ayni
Acc	-an	-an	-īna	-ayni

This state of affairs is paralleled by other languages possessing the category of dual (Inuktitut, Sanskrit, Ancient Greek). In terms of universal principles of markedness (cf. 3.3) one expects fewer forms in the marked categories of plural and dual. For instance in Ancient Greek masculine nouns distinguish five forms (with vocative) in the singular, four in the plural and only two in the most marked category of dual. This is shown in (31):

(31) Ancient Greek masculine nouns (*o*-stems) "man"

	Singular	Plural	Dual
Nom	ánthrōp-os	ánthrōp-oi	anthrṓp-ō
Gen	-ou	-ōn	-ōin
Dat	-ōy	-ois	-ōin
Acc	-on	-ous	-ō
Voc	-e	-oi	-ō

Given the seeming universality of the notion of countability it may come as a surprise that some languages do not have a grammatical category of number. A notorious example is Chinese, where the distinction between singular and plural can be made, if necessary, by means of a numeral but it may equally well be left unexpressed. Other means of expressing plurality in languages without morphological plural include reduplication of the lexical item or of its attribute. For instance Malay pluralizes as shown below:

(32) orang   orang-orang
     "man"   "people"
     pĕrĕmpuan   pĕrĕmpuan-pĕrĕmpuan
     "woman"   "women"

However, it should be kept in mind that the morphological process of reduplication expresses not only numerical plurality but also other notions such as indefiniteness, intensity or distribution. Examples from the same language include *tujoh orang* "seven people" (not **tujoh orang-orang*), *lama-lama dahulu* "long ago", *mata* "eye" but *mata-mata* "policeman". Reduplication of the attributive adjective is common in Sumerian: *na* "stone", *gal* "big" *na-gal-gal* "big stones". It is of interest to notice that only nouns denoting THINGS are pluralizable by reduplication; nouns denoting PERSONS have to be pluralized by the suffix *-ene*, e.g., *lugal* "king" *lugal-ene* "kings", cf. 5.2.1).

5.2.3 *Case*

It was recognized by ancient grammarians a long time ago that **case** is the most important of the inflectional categories of the noun. In a traditional display of cases, such as that familiar from textbooks of Latin, Greek, Old English or German, each case is given a label which suggests at least one of its semantic functions. Thus the **nominative** was the case associated with **naming** (or marking) the subject of the sentence, the **dative** was the case denoting the **receiver** or **beneficiary** of giving. Some linguists tend to disregard these traditional taxonomies as worthless; this attitude, however, is based on taking certain cases at their 'face value' (thus it is easy to show how 'illogical' the Latin case system is by singling out examples such as **accusative of place**, where Latin uses the same syntactic case which is appropriate with transitive verbs: *Rōmam* *videō* "I see Rome" and *Rōmam eō* "I go to Rome"). However, no traditional grammar maintains that labelling cases by their principal semantico-syntactic functions (basic meaning) exhausts the total meaning of various cases and all traditional grammars have to specify a whole array of subsidiary meanings in lengthy sections dealing with syntactic and semantic values of cases. Before discussing attempts to specify the category of case in terms of its total meaning, let us examine some of the most common semantico-syntactic properties (grammatical functions) of cases in Latin. The traditional paradigm with principal semantico-syntactic functions of individual cases is given in (33):

(33)	Case	Function	
	dominus "lord"	Nominative	subject of a sentence
	domine	Vocative	name of addressee
	dominum	Accusative	direct object of transitive verb
	dominī	Genitive	possession
	dominō	Dative	indirect object
	dominō	Ablative	(i) point of departure
			(ii) instrument

Starting with the **genitive** (the case of 'possession') it is obvious that this label is fitting in examples such as *domus meī patris* "my father's house" where "my father" is a possessor and the "house" his possession. However, we will be in trouble if we try to use the label 'possessive' in cases such as *amor patris*. This phrase is ambiguous and can be translated (i) "father's love" or (ii) "love towards father". (Transformational Grammar maintained that *amor patris* in meaning (i) is a transformation of *pater amat* "father loves [us]" and in meaning (ii) that of *amāmus patrem* "we love [our] father"). Obviously, "my father's love toward me" and "my father's house" can hardly be said to be 'possessed' in the same way. Traditional grammars recognize this fact by referring to the case in (i) as **subjective genitive** ("the father loves") and the case in (ii) as **objective genitive** ("we love the father"); in other words, they recognize the different sources of the genitive. To use another example, the genitive *decem annōrum* in a phrase *puer decem annōrum*, lit. boy of ten years, "ten year old boy" cannot be labelled 'possessive'. Its value is simply descriptive of a certain age of the boy; the genitive expresses here an attribute of the substantive (note that Russian would use an adjective in this case). If we examined a sufficient number of examples, it would appear that there is a basic dichotomy between purely **syntactic genitives** and the ones with more semantic content; the former can be subdivided into the **subjective** and **objective genitives**, the latter into a number of subtypes such as **possessive, descriptive, partitive**, etc. The last mentioned subtype of the genitive, the partitive genitive, denotes totality from which a part is taken out, e.g., *libra oleī* "a pound of oil". See Figure 5.4.

Let us examine some of the functions of the **ablative**. Its name (*ab-lātus* is the passive participle of *ā-ferrō* "take away") suggests that one of its semantic functions is local (or spatial)

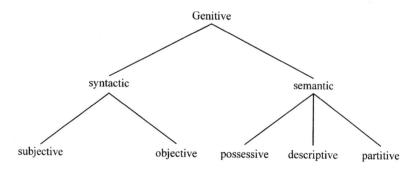

Fig. 5.4 Types of the genitive

since this case could express the 'point of departure' (i.e., place from which): *Rōmā exeō* "I go from Rome" and *domō abeō* "I am leaving the house". It should be mentioned that prepositionless constructions of this type were common only with proper names of cities and smaller islands; elsewhere it was necessary to use the preposition *ex Itāliā eō* "I go from Italy". However, in the following examples we can talk of the point of departure only metaphorically:

(34) Venus Iove nāta et Diōnā
"Venus born from Jupiter and Dione"
Nātus locō nōbilī
"Born from the noble family"

This abstract nuance of meaning of the former concrete local meaning was strong enough to ancient grammarians to justify a label *ablātīvus originis* "ablative of origin". This subtype of ablative could only co-occur with passive participles denoting "born from" (such as *nātus, genitus, ortus, satus*). We have to introduce another label to describe examples such as *vīvō Athēnīs* "I live in Athens" or *nocte dormiō* "I sleep during the night". Obviously, here we are not dealing with the 'point of departure' but with the spatiotemporal framework of utterances; hence, the traditional label *ablātīvus locī et temporis* "ablative of place and time". However, what is morphologically the genitive case could function in the same way, e.g., *Rōmae* "in Rome", *Corinthī* "in Corinth" (historically, here we are dealing with the Old Latin locative in *-ī*); the ablative has to be used with proper names of cities and smaller islands if they belong to the 3rd Declension or if they are morphologically plural, e.g., *Athēnae* "Athens"). Totally different semantic values of the ablative can be observed in the following examples:

(35) Vir summō ingeniō
"A man of great talent"

Cornibus taurī sē tūtantur
"Bulls defend themselves with horns"
Lacrimat gaudiō
"He weeps from joy"

Traditionally, these are called *ablātīvus qualitātis* "ablative of quality", *ablātīvus instrumentī* "instrumental" and *ablātīvus causae* "ablative of cause." These (and) some others, e.g., *comitative* "with" (as in *Caesar omnibus copiīs proficiscitur*... "Caesar goes with all the army...") are supposed to be subcategories of the **instrumental**. We may summarize our findings regarding the meaning of the Latin ablative in Figure 5.5. In dealing with the functions expressed by the Latin ablative an interesting observation can be made. It appears that there is a dichotomy between the more 'abstract' (grammatical) functions (such as comparison, quality, cause, accompaniment instrumentality) and the more 'concrete' ('local') functions (direction, space, time). This distinction, 'grammatical' vs. 'local', is fairly common in many treatments of case-systems found in a variety of languages. Since Latin gravitates toward 'grammatical' functions (the loss of the Old Latin locative was mentioned above) we may profit from examining another language where the 'grammatical' and 'local' notions are more in balance. An ideal language for this purpose is Turkish, which has three 'grammatical' cases (Nominative, Accusative, Genitive) and three 'local' cases (Dative, Locative, Ablative).

(36)		Case	Function
	ev "house"	Nominative	i) subject of a sentence
			ii) indefinite direct object
	ev-i	Accusative	definite direct object
	ev-in	Genitive	possessive
	ev-e	Dative	i) indirect object
			ii) allative; place to (whither)
	ev-de	Locative	time at (when) place in (where)
	ev-den	Ablative	place from (whence)

The system of 'local' oppositions in Turkish is very simple: *eve* "to the house", *evde* "in the house" *evden* "from the house". As in Latin these three cases may be used in a more abstract 'grammatical' sense such as the **dative of purpose**: *Kız çiçek dermieğ-e çıkıyor* "the girl is going out to pick flowers"; **locative of property**: *kahve rengin-de bir şapka* "a hat of coffee-colour"; **ablative of cause**: *açlık-tan bitkin* "exhausted from hunger". It may be noted that in contradis-tinction with Latin, **nominative** is a misnomer for Turkish and the term **absolutive** would be more appropriate. The reason is the peculiar syntactic behavior of the absolute (suffixless) form which can appear as both a subject of a sentence and an indefinite direct object of a verb, as shown in (37).

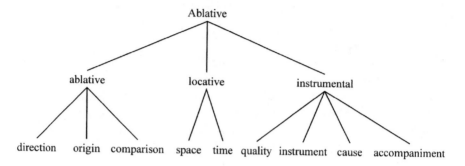

Fig. 5.5 Types of the ablative

(37) ev açıldı
"the house was opened"
ev aldım
"I bought a house"

The accusative case can only be used if the object is defined (i.e., the accusative marks the definite object of a verb):

(38) evi aldım
"I bought the house"

Case and **definiteness** intersect in similar ways in other languages such as Hebrew, Persian and Spanish. Observe, for instance, that in Spanish one has to say *Busco a mi professor* "I am looking for my professor" (definite) but *Busco un professor* "I am looking for a professor" (indefinite).

A more complex system of 'local' oppositions exists in Finnish. Here the three-way 'local' opposition of Turkish: "to" - "in" - "from" is combined with the features **exterior** vs. **interior**. As in Latin, there are also grammatical cases (Nominative, Genitive, Accusative and three specifically Finnish cases). The whole system consists of 15 cases (the record is probably held by Tabassaran from the North-East Caucasian family with 54 cases) which can be displayed as shown below for *talo* "house":

(39)   Grammatical Cases

	Case	Function
talo "house"	Nominative	subject of a sentence
talo-n	Genitive	possessive
talo-n	Accusative I	direct object
talo	Accusative II	direct object (in certain modal clauses)

talo-a	Partitive	mass or part of a whole from which a part is taken out
talo-na	Essive	state
talo-ksi	Translative	change of state
talo-n	Instrumental	instrument, means

Local cases

talo-ssa		Inessive	"in the house"
talo-sta	'Interior'	Elative	"from (inside) the house"
talo-on		Illative	"into the house"
talo-lla		Adessive	"at/near the house"
talo-lta	'Exterior'	Ablative	"from (outside) the house"
talo-lle		Allative	"to/towards the house"

There are two more cases which are not local cases (and which are better not classified as grammatical):

talo-tta	Abessive	"without the house"
talo-inensa	Comitative	"with the house/s"

Compared with Turkish the Finnish system of local cases is more precise in marking explicitly the contrast exterior vs. interior, shown in Figure 5.6. This, of course, is not to claim that distinctions such as "from inside the house" and "from outside the house" cannot be made in Turkish. What is meant is that Turkish ablative *ev-den* "from the house" does not show any overt marking for one of the above distinctions and only extra-linguistic context or additional lexical material (as in the English translation) may show it; on the other hand, Finnish *talo-sta* means unambiguously "from *inside* the house" (elative) and *talo-lta* "from *outside* the house" (ablative), i.e., the marking for local contrast exterior vs. interior is explicit.

A few comments on the Finnish grammatical cases. First of all, there is morphological **syncretism** (formal identity) of the nominative and accusative II (Ø-suffix), cf. Turkish in (36); and that of the genitive and accusative I (*-n* suffix). Thus the suffixless form is to be used to express both a subject (e.g., *Talo on korkea* "The house is high") and a direct object; to be more specific, only in certain modal contexts such as optative and imperative, exemplified in (40).

Fig. 5.6 The Finnish system of local cases

(40) Antakaa   minu-lle   pullo   viini-ä
     give   me-ALLAT   bottle   wine-PART
     "Give me a bottle of wine"

Accusative I is to be used elsewhere. This case is morphologically identical with the genitive (and actually also with the instrumental; this case, however, is used very rarely in the singular). It is of interest to observe that the Slavic languages display the same type of syncretism of accusative and genitive (with animate masculine nouns) and of accusative and nominative (with inanimate masculine and neuter nouns). Examine the following Russian data:

(41)   Masculine   Masculine
                        Animate   Inanimate
     Nominative   byk "bull"   stol "table"
     Genitive   byk-á   stol-á
     Accusative   byk-á   stol

The so-called **partitive** is used to denote totality from which a part is taken out (*pullo maito-a* "bottle of milk") or indefinite mass.

Both **essive** and **translative** are used to express a complement in sentences with **equational predication**, i.e. with verbs "be, become". Choice between these two is determined semantically in that the lexeme expressing someone's (permanent) state has to be realized as the essive, whereas the lexeme expressing someone's past or future state (i.e., changed state) has to be expressed as the translative. Contrast the following sentences:

(42) Velje-ni   on   opettaja-na   keskikoulu-ssa
     Brother-my   is   teacher-ESS   high-school-INESS
     "My brother is a teacher at high-school"

     Velje-ni   aikoo   lääkäri-ksi
     Brother-my   wants to become   physician-TRANS
     "My brother wants to become a physician"

Again, it may be of interest to observe a similar situation in Russian. Here, in equational predication speakers have the choice of expressing the state someone is in as permanent (by using the nominative, corresponding to the Finnish essive) or as acquired (by using instrumental, corresponding to the Finnish translative). Examine the following minimal pair of sentences:

(43) Lomonósov byl velíkyj učénnyj (= NOM)
     "Lomonosov was a great scholar"

Lomonósov byl velíkym učénnym (= INSTR)
"Lomonosov was (= became) a great scholar"

5.2.4 *Alignment*

The term 'alignment' (cf. Harris & Campbell 1995:240) is used to refer to the distribution of morphological markers; the 'alignment of case marking' refers in a neutral way to **nominative-accusative**, **ergative-absolutive** (and other patterns such as **double-oblique** and **active-inactive**). The languages we studied in 5.2.3 (Latin, Russian, Turkish, but not Finnish) are of familiar nominative-accusative typology which assigns the same suffix to both the **agent** (subject of the transitive verb) and the **subject** (of the intransitive verb). On the other hand, languages, such as Inuktitut (Eskimo), Georgian, and Hindi, are of less familiar ergative-absolutive typology which assigns the same suffix to the subject of the intransitive verb and the **patient** (object of the transitive verb) while the agent is marked by a special suffix (so-called **ergative case**). The situation in Latin vs. Hindi is as follows:

(43)

	Latin	Hindi
	Nominative-accusative	Ergative-absolutive
	Alignment	Alignment

Agent	}	-us		=nē
Subject			}	
Patient		-um		-ā

Consider Latin (44) and Hindi (45) equivalents of the two sentences: "The friend saw a horse" and "The horse came" (it may be observed that English displays **neutral alignment** with no morphological markers for any of the three semantic functions):

(44) Amīc-us   equ-um   vīdit   (Latin)
     friend+NOM   horse+ACC   see+PERF+3SG
        Agent   Patient

     Equ-us   vēnit
     horse+NOM   come+PERF+3SG
        Subject

(45) Dōst=nē   ghōṛ-ā   dēkh-ā   (Hindi)
     friend=ERG   horse+ABS   see+PP
        Agent   Patient

Ghōṛ-ā   āy-ā
<u>horse+ABS</u> come+PP
 Subject

In Hindi **ergative-absolutive alignment** is used only in the past tense and the perfect aspect (perfect, pluperfect and future perfect); hence the label **split ergative typology**. Contrast (45) with (46) where the noun "friend" appears in the absolutive form because the predicate is in the present tense:

(46) Dōst   ghōṛ-ā dēkhtā hai   (Hindi)
   friend+ABS horse+ABS see+PRT is
   "The friend sees a horse"

If the object is definite (marked by the DAT/ACC postposition *=kō*), in the ergative tenses the verb is always in the unmarked ('masculine') form in *-ā* irrespectively of the number of the object. This is shown in (47):

(47) i. Dōst=nē   ghōṛ-ē=kō   dēkh-ā
    friend=ERG horse+OBL=DAT/ACC see+PP
    "The friend saw the horse"

(47) ii. Dōst=nē   ghōṛ-õ=kō   dēkh-ā
     friend=ERG horse+OBL/PL=DAT/ACC see+PP
     "The friend saw the horses"

If, however, the object is indefinite, typical ergative agreement may be observed in the plural:

(48) Dōst=nē   ghōr-ē dēkh-ē
   friend=ERG horse+PL see+PP/PL
   "The friend saw horses"

RECOMMENDED READINGS

Anderson, John M. 1971. *The Grammar of Case*. Cambridge: Cambridge University Press.

Applegate, Joseph R. 1958. *An Outline of the Structure of Shilḥa*. New York: American Council of Learned Societies.

Bach, Emmon W. & Robert T. Harms, ed. 1968. *Universals in Linguistic Theory*. New York: Holt, Rinehart and Winston.

Campbell, A. 1959. *Old English Grammar*. Oxford: Clarendon Press.

Cowell, Mark W. 1964. *A Reference Grammar of Syrian Arabic*. Washington, D.C.: Georgetown University Press.

Curme, George O. 1960. *A Grammar of the German Language*. New York: Frederick Ungar.

Diakonoff, Igor M. 1988. *Afrasian Languages*. Moscow: Nauka.

Falkenstein, Adam. 1949. *Grammatik der Sprache Gudeas von Lagaš*. Roma: Pontificium Institutum Biblicum.

Fillmore, Charles J. 1968. "The case for case". Bach & Harms 1968.1–88.

Fodor, I. 1959. "The origin of grammatical gender". *Lingua* 7.1–41, 186–214.

Harris, Alice C. & Lyle Campbell. 1995. *Historical Syntax in Cross-Linguistic Perspective*. Cambridge: Cambridge University Press.

Havránek, Bohuslav & Alois Jedlička. 1963. *Česká mluvnice*. Praha: Státní pedagogické nakladatelstvi.

Hjelmslev, Louis. 1935. *La catégorie des cas. Etude de grammaire générale*. Acta Jutlandica VII.1.xij–184 and IX.2.viij–78.

Jakobson, Roman. 1936. "Beitrag zur allgemeinen Kasuslehre". *Selected Writings* II, 23–71. The Hague: Mouton.

Joly, André. 1975. "Toward a theory of gender in Modern English". *Studies in English Grammar* ed. by André Joly, 229–287. Lille: Presses de l'Université de Lille.

Katz, Jerrold J. 1966. *The Philosophy of Language*. New York: Harper and Row.

Kuryłowicz, Jerzy. 1964. *Inflectional Categories of Indo-European*. Heidelberg: Carl Winter.

Lewis, Geoffrey L. 1967. *Turkish Grammar*. Oxford: Clarendon Press.

Lewis, M. B. 1968. *Malay*. London: The English Universities Press.

Lyons, John. 1977. *Semantics*. Volume 2. Cambridge: Cambridge University Press. (Chapter 15).

Moreland, Floyd L. & Rita M. Fleischer. 1973. *Latin: An Intensive Course*. Berkeley: University of California Press.

Robins, Robert H. 1967. *A Short History of Linguistics*. London: Longmans.

Rosén, Haiim B. 1977. *Contemporary Hebrew*. The Hague: Mouton.

Schachter, Paul. 1985. "Parts-of-speech systems". *Language Typology and Syntactic Description*. Volume 1 ed. by T. Shopen, 3–61. Cambridge: Cambridge University Press.

EXERCISES

1. Analyze the system of possessive suffixes in Biblical Hebrew.

(a) How are the sex and the number of the possessor, and the grammatical gender and the number of the possessed object realized morphologically?

Hint: Before answering this question construct FOUR paradigmatic sets of Hebrew possessive suffixes for the following categories:

Possessed Sg - Possessor Sg	Possessed Pl - Possessor Sg
Possessed Sg - Possessor Pl	Possessed Pl - Possessor Pl

and specify their sex/gender distinctions in appropriate persons. Be careful with English "your" which is four-way ambiguous: Masc Sg, Masc Pl, Fem Sg, Fem Pl.

Use the following data:

(1)	malkī́	"my king"
(2)	sūsōθēhén	"their (F) mares"
(3)	šīrəxā́	"your (M) song"
(4)	məlāxōθēhém	"their (M) queens"
(5)	dəβārī́	"my word"
(6)	malkāθṓ	"his queen"
(7)	šīrēxém	"your (M) songs"
(8)	sūsāθā́h	"her mare"
(9)	məlāxḗnū	"our kings"
(10)	sūsōθǽhā	"her mares"
(11)	malkḗnū	"our king"
(12)	šīrəxém	"your (M) song"
(13)	dəβarxén	"your (F) word"
(14)	səfāráyix	"your (F) book"
(15)	šīrǽxā	"your (M) songs"
(16)	sūsāθā́n	"their (F) mare"
(17)	diβrēxén	"your (F) words"
(18)	malxēxém	"your (M) kings"
(19)	məlāxōθáyix	"your (F) queens"
(20)	sifrēxén	"your (F) books"
(21)	sifrḗx	"your (F) books"

(22) dəβāréx   "your (F) word"
(23) sūsōθǽxā   "your (M) mares"
(24) malkó́   'his king"
(25) malkǎn   "their (F) king"
(26) sifrǎm   "their (M) book"
(27) dəβārǎh   "her word"
(28) malkəxém   "your (M) king"
(29) məlāxōθǎw   "his queens"
(30) sifrəxén   "your (F) book"
(31) malkāθǎm   "their (M) queen"
(32) məlāxáy   "my kings"

The basic forms of the above nouns and their plural forms are as follows:

mélex	"king"	məlāxím
séfer	"book"	səfārím
malkǎ	"queen"	məlāxōθ
šír	"song"	šīrím
dāβǎr	"word"	dəβārím
sūsǎ	"mare"	sūsóθ

(b) Describe the distribution of morphophonemic variants of the root.

(c) Comment on the 'leak' in the system of the possessive suffixes.

(d) Translate into Hebrew:

(33) "our words"
(34) "our song"
(35) "their words"
(36) "your (M) word"
(37) "your (M) queens"
(38) "our songs"

2. Analyze the system of possessive affixes in Coptic.

(a) How are the sex, number and person of the possessor, and the gender and the number of the possessed realized morphologically? Note: Coptic distinguishes two genders: masculine, e.g., *kas* "bone" and feminine, e.g., *ovhe* "tooth".

(b) Construct the paradigmatic set of Coptic possessive affixes. Use the following data:

(1)	pajōt	"my father"
(2)	pefkot	"his basket"
(3)	pekkah	"thy (M) earth"
(4)	nefkot	"his baskets"
(5)	penjōt	"our father"
(6)	peukōhit	"their fire"
(7)	tenk'ič	"our hand"
(8)	nenjōt	"our fathers"
(9)	tekbō	"thy (M) tree"
(10)	netinovhe	"your teeth"
(11)	toubō	"thy (F) tree"
(12)	tesmāu	"her mother"
(13)	taape	"my head"
(14)	nekehe	"thy (M) cows"
(15)	nakot	"my baskets"
(16)	nesojk	"her breads"
(17)	teumāu	"their mother"
(18)	tesk'ič	"her hand"
(19)	tefehe	"his cow"
(20)	teubō	"their tree"
(21)	tesovhe	"her tooth"
(22)	nouovhe	"thy (F) teeth"
(23)	poujōt	"thy (F) father"
(24)	nenbō	"our trees"
(25)	petinlas	"your tongue"
(26)	netinehe	"your cows"
(27)	tetinbō	"your tree"
(28)	poukot	"thy (F) basket"
(29)	neukas	"their bones"
(30)	nekovhe	"thy (M) teeth"

3. Plural formation in German can be described in its interplay with grammatical gender (M, F, N). There are several plural suffixes (-e, -er, -en, -Ø) and the root can be umlauted (a → ä, u → ü, o → ö, au → äu).

(a) Elaborate as many plural patterns as possible in the following data.

(b) Reduce their number by disregarding 'exceptions' (single occurrences).

(c) Endeavor to make significant general statements regarding the distribution of four pluralizing suffixes and umlaut, and their interplay with gender.

(1)	Tag	"day"	Tage (M)
(2)	Bach	"brook"	Bäche (M)
(3)	Onkel	"uncle"	Onkel (M)
(4)	Sohn	"son"	Söhne (M)
(5)	Hand	"hand"	Hände (F)
(6)	Otter	"otter"	Otter (M)
(7)	Jahr	"year"	Jahre (N)
(8)	Rand	"margin"	Ränder (M)
(9)	Vogel	"bird"	Vögel (M)
(10)	Löwe	"lion"	Löwen (M)
(11)	Apparat	"utensil"	Apparate (M)
(12)	Biss	"bite"	Bisse (M)
(13)	Fluss	"river"	Flüsse (M)
(14)	Trübsal	"sorrow"	Trübsale (F)
(15)	Kunst	"art"	Künste (F)
(16)	Tafel	"tablet"	Tafeln (F)
(17)	Endung	"ending"	Endungen (F)
(18)	Ente	"duck"	Enten (F)
(19)	Schaf	"sheep"	Schafe (N)
(20)	Bild	"picture"	Bilder (N)
(21)	Haus	"house"	Häuser (N)
(22)	Schloss	"castle; lock"	Schlösser (N)
(23)	Fenster	"window"	Fenster (N)
(24)	Kloster	"monastery"	Klöster (N)
(25)	Auge	"eye"	Augen (N)
(26)	Ohr	"ear"	Ohren (N)
(27)	Geist	"ghost"	Geister (M)
(28)	Kessel	"kettle"	Kessel (M)
(29)	Balken	"beam"	Balken (M)
(30)	Graben	"ditch"	Gräben (M)
(31)	Lehrer	"teacher"	Lehrer (M)
(32)	Vater	"father"	Väter (M)
(33)	Bruder	"brother"	Brüder (M)
(34)	Bruch	"fraction"	Brüche (M)
(35)	Mensch	"man"	Menschen (M)
(36)	Buckel	"hump"	Buckel (M)

(37)	Büchse	"box"	Büchsen (F)
(38)	Eber	"boar"	Eber (M)
(39)	Einfahrt	"entrance"	Einfahrten (F)
(40)	Einfall	"intrusion"	Einfälle (M)
(41)	Glas	"glass"	Gläser (N)
(42)	Graf	"count"	Grafen (M)
(43)	Gunst	"favor"	Günste (F)
(44)	Gut	"merchandise"	Güter (N)
(45)	Haar	"hair"	Haare (N)
(46)	Hacken	"heel"	Hacken (M)
(47)	Haifisch	"shark"	Haifische (M)
(48)	Hahn	"rooster"	Hähne (M)
(49)	Halle	"hall"	Hallen (F)
(50)	Herr	"lord"	Herren (M)
(51)	Hirn	"brain"	Hirne (N)
(52)	Holz	"wood"	Hölzer (N)
(53)	Floss	"raft"	Flösse (N)
(54)	Floh	"flea"	Flöhc (M)
(55)	Fohlen	"foal"	Fohlen (N)
(56)	Flut	"flood"	Fluten (F)
(57)	Jude	"Jew"	Juden (M)
(58)	Jagd	"hunt"	Jagden (F)
(59)	Joch	"yoke"	Joche (N)
(60)	Order	"command"	Ordern (F)

4. There are various phenomena in adjectival and verbal agreement found in the Semitic languages which are unknown in the Indo-European languages. Describe at least four of them using the following data of Classical Arabic:

(1)	al-rajulu	wasixun	"the man is dirty"
(2)	al-kalbu	wasixun	"the dog is dirty"
(3)	al-marʔatu	wasixatun	"the woman is dirty"
(4)	al-rijālu	wasixūna	"the men are dirty"
(5)	al-kilābu	wasixatun	"the dogs are dirty"
(6)	al-marʔātu	wasixatun	"the women are dirty"
(7)	al-rajulu	daxala	"the man came in"
(8)	al-kalbu	daxala	"the dog came in"
(9)	al-marʔatu	daxalat	"the woman came in"
(10)	al-rijālu	daxalū	"the men came in"

(11) al-kilābu   daxalat   "the dogs came in"
(12) al-marʔātu daxalna   "the women came in"

5. (a) Using the following data elaborate the rules of verbal agreement in Biblical Hebrew;
do it separately for the future and the past:

(1) tišmōr hā-ʔiššā   "the woman will protect"
(2) yiqtəlū hā-ʔāβōθ   "the fathers will kill"
(3) baθ, tiftəhī   "daughter, you will open"
(4) bēn, tiqtōl   "son, you will kill"
(5) tilkōdnā han-nāšīm   "the women will catch"
(6) yiftah hā-ʔāβ   "the father will open"
(7) nāšīm, tišmōrnā   "women, you will protect"
(8) ʔənāšīm, tiftəhū   "men, you will open"
(9) pāθəhā hab-baθ   "the daughter opened"
(10) šāmərū han-nāšīm   "the women protected"
(11) lāxad hab-ben   "the son caught"
(12) qātəlū hā-ʔənāšīm   "the men killed"

(b) There are three phenomena in Hebrew verbal agreement which are unknown in the
Indo-European languages. Identify them clearly using appropriate terminology.

(c) Translate into Hebrew:

(13) "sons (= bānīm), you will kill"
(14) "the father protected"
(15) "daughter, you will protect"
(16) "the women opened"

6. Berber (Tašelḥit) spoken in southwest Morocco (according to Applegate 1958):

(1) asif (M)   "river"   isafn
(2) tagžif (F)   "palm tree"   tigžaf
(3) tahanut (F)   "stove"   tihuna
(4) amdakul (M)   "friend"   imdukal
(5) tamdakult (F)   "friend"   timdukal
(6) agudid (M)   "bird"   igudad
(7) agadir (M)   "fortress"   igudar
(8) adrar (M)   "mountain"   idrarn

(a) Describe the formation of the plural in Berber.
(b) What type of affix is used to mark the feminine gender?
(c) How does marking for the gender relate to marking for the plural?

7. Elaborate the rules of adjectival agreement (in gender and number) governing the morphology of numerals and counted objects in Biblical Hebrew:

(1)	ʔiššā	ʔahaθ	"one woman"
(2)	ʔīš	ʔæhāð	"one man"
(3)	šənayim	kəlāβīm	"two dogs"
(4)	šətayim	nāšīm	"two women"
(5)	šālōš	ʕārīm	"three cities"
(6)	šəlōšā	kəlāβīm	"three dogs"
(7)	ʔarbaʕ	bānōθ	"four daughters"
(8)	ʔarbāʕā	məlāxīm	"four kings"
(9)	ʔarbaʕ	bēṣīm	"four eggs"
(10)	ʔarbāʕā	ʕefrōnōθ	"four pencils"
(11)	həmiššā	ʔāβōθ	"five fathers"
(12)	ḥāmēš	məlāxōθ	"five queens"

Translate into Hebrew:

(a) "three women"
(b) "one father"
(c) "two queens"
(d) "three books"
(e) "four bitches"
(f) "one egg"
(g) "two kings"
(h) "two pencils"
(i) "five women"
(j) "one pencil"

Vocabulary:

keleβ	"dog"	ʔāβ	"father"
ʕīr	"city" (Fem)	malkā	"queen"
baθ	"daughter"	sēfer	"book" (Masc)
melek	"king"	kalbā	"bitch"

bēṣā   "egg"   ʕippārōn   "pencil"

8. Describe the semantic values of Turkish 'local' cases. Use the following data (from Lewis 1967):

Locative
(1) su-da   "in the water"
(2) Ramazan-da   "in Ramadan" (the month of fasting)
(3) ihtiyarlık-ta   "in old age"
(4) yirmi yaşın-da   "twenty years old"
(5) bu fikir-de değilim   "I am not of this opinion"

Ablative
(6) şehir-den ayrıldı   "he departed from the city"
(7) pencere-den girdi   "he entered by the window"
(8) on-dan   "for that reason"
(9) Türkiye Lübnan-dan büyük-tür   "Turkey is bigger than Lebanon"
(10) naylon-dan   "of nylon"
(11) komşular-dan biri   "one of the neighbors"
(12) bu elmaları kaç-tan aldın?   "at what price did you buy these apples?"

Dative
(13) mektubu Ali-ye gösterdim   "I showed the letter to Ali"
(14) Türkiye-ye döndüler   "they returned to Turkey"
(15) talebe imtihan-a hazırlanıyor "the student is preparing for the examination"
(16) bu elmaları kaç-a aldın?   "what was the total amount you paid for these apples?"

Vocabulary:
yirmi	"twenty"	alma	"apple"
bu	"this"	al-dın	"you bought"
değilim	"I am not"	mektub	"letter"
ayrıl-dı	"he departed"	göster-dim	"I showed"
dön-dü-ler	"they returned"	talebe	"student"
hazırlan-ıyor	"he/she is preparing"		

CHAPTER SIX
INFLECTIONAL CATEGORIES ASSOCIATED WITH VERBAL ELEMENTS

6.1 *Verb as a Primary Grammatical Category*

As established under 5.1.1, the verb could be defined as a primary grammatical category the domain of which includes secondary categories of **person, number, tense, aspect, mood**, and **voice**. It was also mentioned that Plato grouped verbs and adjectives together since he considered the most typical function of both being that of **predication**; as we put it, verbs express dynamic features on substances (nouns) and adjectives express static features on substances. Whereas both verbs and adjectives predicate, the most typical function of the noun is that of naming the subject of predication. In other words, the definition of these two primary grammatical categories cannot be made independently of syntactic and logical considerations — subject and noun and predicate and verb are simply indissolubly associated in traditional grammatical and logical theory. A full discussion of **functional categories** of subject and predicate would of course bring us far beyond the domain of morphology proper. Suffice it to say that there is a far reaching agreement between the categories of logic and grammar in simple declarative sentences such as *John ran away* where the individual person (substance) is an instigator of the action.

Apparently, in all languages of the world, the individual person in such a sentence would be grammaticalized as a noun and its action as a verb. Thus the correspondence between grammatical and logical categories are shown in Figure 6.1.

At this point, it is important to establish the distinction between morphological and syntactic predication. The latter concerns the predication of one word on another, in this case of verb on subject, such as in English and Latin:

(1)   John ran away.
       Ioannēs effūgit

However, in the context which is suitable to pronominal substitution, such as in answering the question *Quid fēcit Ioannēs* "What did John do?", the strategies of English and Latin will differ. Compare the answers to this question:

(2)   He ran away.
       Effūgit.

In this case, Latin displays **morphological predication**, which may be defined as a predication which takes place within the system of the Latin verb. The Latin verb, in contrast to

Grammar	Morphology	Noun	Verb
	Syntax	Subject	Predicate
Logic		Agent	Action

Fig. 6.1 Correspondence between grammatical and logical categories

that of English, allows for morphological predication using the secondary grammatical categories of person and number. With this particular verb it is possible to predicate a different grammatical category of number in the same person (3rd): *fūgērunt* "they ran away" or different grammatical categories of person in the same number (singular): *fūgī* "I ran away", *fūgistī* "you ran away" etc. See further discussion under 6.3.1.

6.2 Quasi-Nominal Categories of the Verb: Infinitive and Participle

Quasi-nominal categories, namely, **infinitive** and **participle** (called also **infinite** or **non-finite forms**) share properties of both nouns and verbs. Participles in heavily flective languages behave like adjectives, i.e., they can be inflected for the nominal categories of number, case and gender (to a limited degree) and similarly to adjectives, they can form the positive and superlative (to a limited degree). With verbs they share the categories of aspect (to a limited degree), and also of voice and mood. Infinitives are more abstract in that they can be inflected only for the nominal category of case (but not for gender and number), and with verbs they share the categories of aspect and voice. In both infinitives and participles the essential verbal categories of person and tense are missing: hence the label non-finite forms (opposed to finite verbal forms). Participation in nominal and verbal categories may be schematized as shown in Figure 6.2.

Since many of these nominal and verbal categories are not realized by synthetic morphology in English, we may use Latin and Greek as examples in these cases. Compare the contrasts of **aspect** and **voice** with the **infinitive** in these languages.

(3)	English	Latin	Greek
	(to) praise	laudāre	epaineîn
	(to) have praised	laudāvisse (Perfect)	epainésai (Aorist), epēynekénai (Perfect)
	(to) be praised	laudārī	epaineîsthai (Passive)

The perfect infinitive is realized **synthetically**, i.e., by means of inflections in Latin and Greek (in Greek there are two other infinitives in the passive: *epēynethénai* (Aorist) and *epēynêsthai* (Perfect), cf. (6)) but by means of the grammatical auxiliary *have* in English. The passive infinitive is realized **analytically** by means of the grammatical auxiliary *be* in English.

All these languages allow for the aspectual contrast even in the **passive infinitive**. The English system may be portrayed as a double binary opposition:

(4)		non-Perfect	Perfect
	Active	(to) praise	(to) have praised
	Passive	(to) be praised	(to) have been praised

The Latin system may be diagrammed similarly and it is of interest to observe an analytic formation in the **perfect passive infinitive** (where English has two grammatical auxiliaries *have* and *be*):

(5)		Infectum	Perfectum
	Active	laudāre	laudāvisse
	Passive	laudārī	laudātum esse

Greek distinguishes the **perfective** (Aorist) and **retrospective** (Perfect) **infinitives** (see more under 6.3.3) and realizes all these distinctions synthetically:

(6)		Imperfective	Perfective	Retrospective
	Active	epaineîn	epainésai	epēynekénai
	Passive	epaineîsthai	epainethênai	epēynêsthai

A parallel situation exists in the **participle** in English and Greek. English possesses four forms (*praising, being praised, having praised* and *having been praised*) and Greek six forms:

(7)		Imperfective	Perfective	Retrospective
	Active	epainôn	epainésās	epēynekôs
	Passive	epainoúmenos	epainetheís	epēynēménos

Latin does not possess the aspectual contrast of perfectivity in its participial system: *laudāns* "praising" is an active participle and *laudātus* "praised" its passive counterpart. But Latin (and also Greek) has participles which have modal meaning. The so-called **future participle** (formed curiously from the passive base by the suffix *-ūr-us*: *laudā-t-ūr-us*) is used only with the auxiliary *esse* "to be" in phrases which imply 'volition' on the part of the speaker. They correspond to English phrases "going to", "be about to": *scrīptūrus sum* means "I intend to write" or "I am going to write". *Hostēs bellum illātūrī erant* may be translated "The enemy were likely to make war". The so-called **gerundive** (formed by the suffix *-nd-us* from the stem) is a passive participle whose contextual meanings are classifiable as follows:

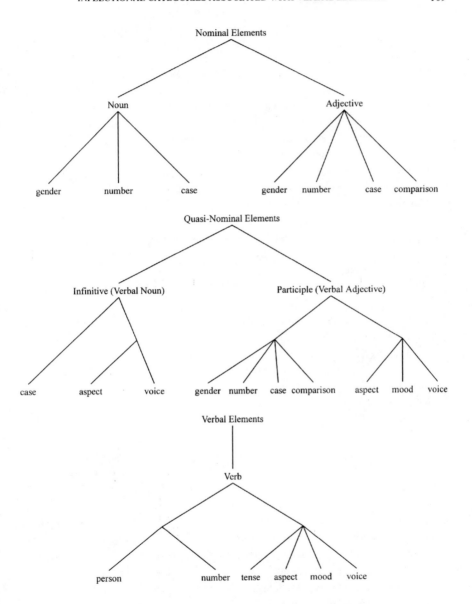

Fig. 6.2 Primary and secondary grammatical categories

(i)   the action which will be done in the future (i.e., the temporal category of futurity);

(ii) the action which should be done (i.e., the modal category of necessity);

(iii) the action which is under way (i.e., the aspectual category of progessivity).

The modal meaning is the most common; for instance *nōbīs eundum est* "we have to (ought to) go", *memoria nōbīs exercenda est* "we have to train our memory", etc. In *hīs librīs legendīs* "by reading these books" the third meaning can be exemplified.

Let us now examine the nominal categories of participles and infinitives. As mentioned above, inflection for gender may be limited in participles. Thus in Latin, the **active participle** is not inflected for three genders, whereas the **passive participle**, the **future participle** and the **gerundive** are:

(8)

	Present Participle	Passive Participle	Future Participle	Gerundive
Masc		laudāt-us	laudātūr-us	laudand-us
Fem	laudāns	-a	-a	-a
Neuter		-um	-um	-um

Greek, on the other hand, inflects unfailingly all its six participles, even the **present participle**, for three genders:

(9)

	Latin	Greek
Masc		epainôn
Fem	laudāns	epainoûsa
Neuter		epainoûn

As far as case and number are concerned, Latin and Greek participles show the same number of forms as adjectives. It is astonishing to realize that all the six participles of Greek can be inflected for three genders, three numbers (Sg, Dual, Pl) and four cases.

It remains to demonstrate that the infinitive can be inflected for **case**. In Latin the syntactic cases (nominative and accusative, called also direct cases) are formally identical with the usual form in *-āre*. English may use either the infinitive or the verbal noun in *-ing* in the function of the subject: *Errāre hūmanūm est* "To err is human" or "Erring is human". Similarly, English may use both forms in the function of the object: *Incipiō scrībere* "I start to write" or "I start writing". On the other hand, neither Latin nor English can use the infinitive in instances such *ars scrībendī* "art of writing". The genitive of the infinitive (and other semantic cases, dative and ablative, called also **oblique cases**) are formed from the verb base in *-nd* plus the endings of the *o*-stem masculine nouns:

(10) Nom   laudāre
     Gen   laudandī
     Dat   laudandō
     Acc   laudāre ~ ad laudandum
     Abl   laudandō

These oblique cases are called **gerunds** (verbal nouns). The dative of the infinitive is quite rare; it occurs in constructions such as *nōn sum solvendō* "I cannot pay" (lit. I am not [up] to paying). On the other hand, the ablative is quite common in adverbial phrases such as *iniuriās ferendō* "by (from) sustaining the injustice" and *dēfessus dīcendō* "tired by (from) talking". As is well-known, English has the option of constructing the gerundial phrase verbally (as above) or nominally "by sustaining of the injustice". Latin has an active option (as above) or a passive option *iniuriīs ferendīs*, where the gerundive has to be used. It is of interest to note that Greek has nothing comparable with Latin infinitival inflection by means of the gerund in oblique cases. Greek inflects its infinitive simply by inflecting the preposed neuter article *tò* (gentive *toû*, dative *tôy*, accusative = nominative *tò*). Greek *aéthēs toû hupakoúein* "not used to obey" would be translated by the gerund in Latin: *īnsuētus oboediendī*. An example of the dative: *Nikēson orgền tôy logídzesthai kalôs* "Win over wrath by correct reasoning."

6.3 *Secondary Grammatical Categories Associated with Verbal Elements*

6.3.1 *Person and Deixis*

The category of person is definable with reference to the notion of **participation in the discourse**: the **first person** is used by the speaker to refer to her/himself as a **subject of discourse**; the **second person** represents the **listener** when spoken to about her/himself; the **third person** is used to refer to the persons (or things) other than the speaker and addressee. Tesnière (1959) introduced the following terms for these distinctions into French structural linguistics:

(11) 'ontif'   =   subject of discourse
     'antiontif' =   its antipode, i.e. addressee
     'anontif'   =   neither subject nor addressee, i.e. spoken about

The first and the second person are the positive members of the category of person (in that they refer to participants in discourse), whereas the third person is a negative notion. It is of interest to note that in many languages there is no overt marking for the third person and its meaning is given by the absence of the markers for the first and second person. Consider the personal endings in Turkish:

(12) Sg 1   gel-iyor-um   "I am coming"   (-*iyor* = progressive aspect)
         2   -sun   "you are coming"
         3   -Ø   "he/she/it is coming"

Paradoxically, in English it is the negative member of the category of person which is marked overtly by -*s*, whereas the first and second persons are left unmarked. Typologically, other constellations of markers are possible: (i) markers in all persons, e.g., Latin; (ii) no markers, e.g., Chinese, Japanese; (iii) first person unmarked, second and third marked. This is a very unusual pattern which may be found in Old Norse: *ek kalla* "I call" vs. *θu kallar* and *hann kallar*. However, in Modern Norwegian the personal suffix -*r* appears in all persons.

The third person is distinguished from the first and second persons in many respects. First of all, the speaker and the addressee are necessarily present in any discourse; they coincide if someone talks to himself. While the speaker and the addressee are always given, other persons and things to which reference is made may be absent in both time and space from the situation of discourse. In grammatical terms, the category of the third person may combine with categories such as **definiteness** (definite vs. indefinite) and **proximity** (proximate vs. remote). On the other hand, personal pronouns of the first and second person are necessarily only definite and typically only proximate (unless we consider situations such as speaking on the telephone; here, of course, the remoteness is of non-linguistic referential character). Normally, pronouns of first and second person refer to human beings (unless we consider anthropomorphized or personified animals and things in the world of fairy-tales) whereas pronouns of the third person may refer to both inanimate things and animate beings (human and non-human). See Figure 6.3.

Let us exemplify these notions. We may be inclined to think that the contrast such as English *he/she* and *it* (third person **definite**) versus *somebody* and *something* (third person **indefinite**) is universal. Turkish (and other Altaic languages) cannot grammaticalize the distinction of sex in the third person definite (*o* refers to both a male or female being) but it has the distinction of definiteness: *o* "he/she" versus *biri* "someone". The same situation obtains in other languages, e.g. in Plains Cree (Algonkian family): *wīya* "he/she" versus *awiyak* "someone". Furthermore, in Turkish the category of definiteness has to be marked obligatorily with personal pronouns by the suffix -*i* (personal pronouns are definite), whereas the marking with nouns depends on whether the noun is definite or indefinite:

(13) sen-i   gör-dü-m
      you-ACC   see-PAST-1SG
      "I saw you"

      ev   al-dı-m
      house   buy-PAST-1SG
      "I bought a house"

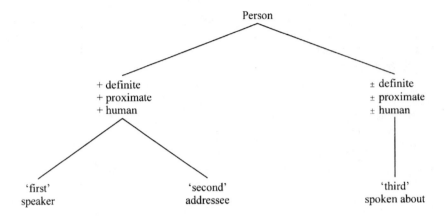

Fig. 6.3 The category of person

```
ev-i          al-dı-m
house-ACC     buy-PAST-1SG
"I bought the house"
```

The category of proximity plays an important role with **demonstrative pronouns** (*this* vs. *that*). This category is obviously determined in relation to the speaker (subject of discourse). *This* and *here* are proximate and *that* and *there* are remote with respect to the speaker. It may be observed that other languages have a more complex three-way system of proximity. Let us juxtapose Latin, Turkish, and English systems of demonstrative pronouns:

(14) Latin   Turkish   English   (dialectical)
      hīc   bu   this   this
      iste   şu   ⎫   that
                           ⎬   that
      ille   o   ⎭   yon

Latin *hīc* and Turkish *bu* (= "this") indicate proximity to the speaker, *iste* and *şu* (= "that") remoteness from the speaker, and *ille* and *o* (= "that", dialectical "yon", cf. German *jener*) indicate remoteness from both the speaker and the addressee. A more subtle distinction connected with three-way systems has to do with the notion of **old** vs. **new information** (in functional sentence perspective). In Turkish the pronoun *bu* is used when referring to old information, whereas the pronoun *şu* will be used when referring to new information introduced into consciousness of listeners by the speaker. Hence, *bu* has to be used in the phrase *bu teklif* "this proposal" when referring to the aforesaid proposal, the proposal which has just been mentioned (old information), whereas if the speaker wants to introduce a new proposal he has to say *şu teklif* "the following proposal", this proposal which he is about to mention (new information). Similarly, in Ancient Greek *hóde ho lógos* means "the following word" whereas *hoûtos ho lógos* means "the aforesaid word". The three members of the system are: *hoûtos* "this", *hóde* "this, that" *ekeînos* "that".

Traditionally, person has been regarded as a category of the verb since in flective languages it is marked by the personal suffixes. Since English and spoken French are poor in this respect we may profit from examining richer morphological systems such as those of Latin and Turkish.

(15)		Latin	Turkish	
Sg	1	am-ō	sever-im	"I love"
	2	-ās	-sin	"you love"
	3	-at	-Ø	"he/she loves"

Latin and Turkish (and many other flective languages) in contrast with English and French do not need analytic specification of the subject since they rely on morphological predication. To say "I love you" in Latin it is enough to say *tē amō*, or in Turkish *seni severim*. If we specify the subject by using the independent pronoun *egō* (or *ben* in Turkish) the meaning of *egō tē amō* would be different. The speaker in this case emphasizes that HE (or SHE) loves the addressee in contrast with someone who does not love (or hates, etc.) the addressee. This contrast, of course, may only be implied and not realized linguistically. Thus we may translate *egō tē amō* either by using **sentential stress** "*I* love you" or by a so-called **clefted sentence** "I am the one who loves you". The latter version might be preferable when the contrast is realized linguistically as in *egō tē amō nōn frāter tuus* "It is I who loves you not your brother!". Given these differences in discourse strategies of analytic (English-type) and synthetic (Latin-type) languages, we may wonder whether there are similar differences in what is called **underlying** or **deep structure**. It seems that these differences are here non-existent since in both cases we have to postulate an abstract pronominal element PRO (determined with respect to person and number) which is the subject of the verb, as shown in Figure 6.4. It might be tempting to talk about a pronominal element 'replacing' the subject (or NP) to obtain more universal diagrams than the usual S → NP+VP, as shown in Figure 6.5.

However, this would be a controversial procedure. First of all, pronouns as deictic elements depend on other elements in discourse. The first person is used by the speaker to refer to her/himself as a subject of discourse, the second person to refer to the hearer when spoken to about her/himself; on the other hand, the third person is used to refer to persons or things other than the speaker and hearer. The replacement of the subject by pronouns (linguistic **pronominalization**), in the realm of what is spoken about is qualitatively different from assuming the role of the subject in discourse. To exemplify this statement, it is a normal procedure to pronominalize in cases such as *John came* → *he came* but in *I came* the first person (subject of discourse) cannot be replaced by the noun *John*. Of course, we may say *I, John Smith,*

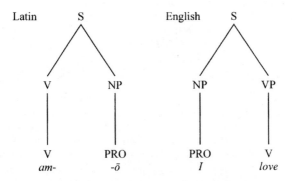

Fig. 6.4 1ˢᵗ Sg derived by pronominalization

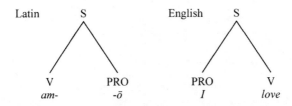

Fig. 6.5 Deep PRO

testify... in testimonies, oaths, etc. but this represents another type of discourse. Thus, it is preferable to consider personal pronouns and other deictic elements as basic, not derived from a deep NP. Let us remind ourselves that pronouns are universal and that we cannot imagine a language without pronouns, whereas there are languages without adjectives or articles.

6.3.2 *Tense*

The term **tense** goes back to the Latin word *tempus* meaning "time" (Latin *tempus* is calqued on Greek *khrónos*). Since antiquity, this term has been used for labelling time-relations which are expressed by systematic grammatical contrasts such as Latin *laudābat* "he/she praised" vs. *laudat* "he/she praises", or English *(I) loved* vs. *love*. Jakobson (1957) characterized tense as a **deictic category**, (a **shifter**) which puts the **narrated event** in reference to the **speech event**. Since the time of the utterance is always 'now', the tense of the narrated action (or event or state) can be either 'before-now' (past time) or 'after-now' (future time), or 'simultaneous-with-now' (present time). Hence, the typical three-way analysis of tense which prevails in many traditional grammars of various languages: Present, Past, Future. Even some linguists (e.g. Jespersen in his *Philosophy of Grammar*, 1929) believed this trichotomy to be representative of the 'natural' division of time into 'present', 'past' and 'future'. It is also noteworthy that this trichotomy, shown in (16) is reflected nicely in the system of adverbs of time: 'now', 'before' and 'after'.

(16)

before   now   after

PAST   PRESENT   FUTURE

Thus Jespersen talks about the past as before-now and the future as after-now. The primary distinctions of the past and future are then subdivided by means of a secondary application of the notions 'before' (past) and 'after' (future):

(17)

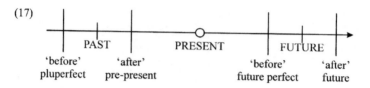

      PAST   PRESENT   FUTURE

'before'   'after'   'before'   'after'

pluperfect   pre-present   future perfect   future

The result is a seven term notional tense-system, which is suitable for the analysis of the **relative aspect** (or **anteriority**) in terms of its Pluperfect, Pre-Present and Future Perfect.

6.3.3 *Aspect*

It is fundamental to distinguish between **tense** and **aspect**. Both are concerned with time (both are **designators** in Jakobson's terms) but in different ways. Whereas, as pointed out above, tense is a deictic category which relates the time of the action (or event or state) to the time of utterance which is 'now', aspect is concerned with representing different positions of the subject within **Event Time**. Put differently, aspect is concerned with the internal temporal constituency of the event (situation-internal time), whereas tense, as we saw above, allocates event within the cover of **Universal Time**.

Using vertical lines to represent the initial and final limits of an event, we may discern five positions within Event Time:

(18)   A|B··C····························· D|E

    Prospective   Inceptive   Progressive   Perfective   Retrospective

Position A represents **prospective aspect** (*I will write*, Turkish *yaz-acağ-ım*); B represents **inceptive** (Russian *ja vý-p'ju* "I will drink (= empty the glass)"); C represents **progressive** or **imperfective** (*I am writing,* Turkish *yaz-ıyor-um*); D represents **perfective** (Russian *ja vý-pil* "I drank (= emptied the glass)" or Greek 'aorist' *é-lū-s-a* "I solved"); and E represents **retrospective** (traditional perfect: *I have written* or Greek *gé-graph-a*). B, C, D positions represent **immanent aspects** (interior to the event), while A and E represent **transcendent aspects** (exterior to the event).

It is of interest to observe that the term aspect is a translation of the Russian word *vid* (from *videt'* "see, view") and it was used for the first time in the analysis of Russian and other Slavic languages: *soveršennyj* = **perfective** and *nesoveršennyj vid* = **imperfective aspect**. The terms perfective and imperfective should not be confused with *perfectum* and *infectum*, terms used by Ancient grammarians for similar notions referring to completion of action or process. Thus the Latin verbal system may be analyzed along the following lines:

(19)   Aspect

Tense	Infectum	Perfectum
Present	amō	amāvī
Past	amābam	amāveram
Future	amābō	amāverō

There are three binary contrasts in this paradigm:

(i)   aspectual contrast: **perfect** vs. **nonperfect**. Marking for the perfect is *-v* (there are other types of marking for the same category, most notably *-s*, and reduplication);

(ii)   temporal contrast: **present time** vs. **non-present time**. Marking for non-present is *-b* in the non-perfect forms and *-er* in the perfect forms;

(iii) temporal contrast: **experienced** (past) **time** vs. **non-experienced** (future) **time**. This contrast operates only for non-present time.

The morphological marking is less consistent and may be best demonstrated for the 1st and 2nd Conjugation. Consider the paradigm of the 1st Conjugation:

(20)		Past	Future
Sg	1	am-ā-b-a-m	am-ā-b-ō
	2	-ā-s	-i-s
	3	-a-t	-i-t
Pl	1	-ā-mus	-i-mus
	2	-ā-tis	-i-tis
	3	-a-nt	-u-nt

In the majority of forms (2nd and 3rd Sg, 1st and 2nd Pl) the contrast Past vs. Future is identifiable by the contrast *-a* vs. *-i*. These contrastive vowels occur immediately after the marker for non-present time in the system of the non-perfect aspect. Traditional grammars talk rather about Imperfect and Future endings *-ās* vs. *-is*; however, it is obvious that these are analyzable. Thus the whole Latin system of aspect and tense in terms of its morphological markers may be represented as shown in Figure 6.6 (the final *-t* marks the 3rd Sg).

Let us examine some simple examples for the values enumerated above.

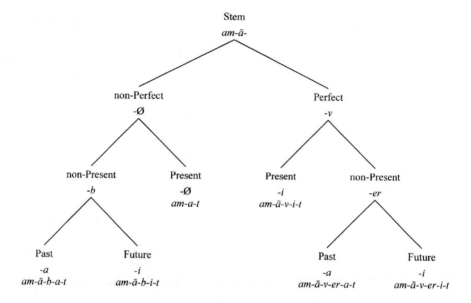

Fig. 6.6 Latin system of aspect and tense

(21) i. Domum aedificat "he builds/is building (his) house"
    ii. Domum aedificāvit "he built/has built (his) house"

The first sentence with the imperfective verb *aedificat* suggests an incomplete event (somebody's building activity takes place in the very moment of the narrator's utterance). It may be best translated into English by the progressive form "is building". The event is simply in progress and it will last for some time after someone's utterance has come to an end. On the other hand, the second sentence with the perfect *aedificāvit* suggests a completed event at the time of the utterance (somebody's building activity went to its end before the narrator's utterance). It is usually said that this form (called traditionally **perfect**) covers simultaneously the perfective aspect and the present time reference; in semantic terms, that it relates the present state to the past event. To demonstrate this point, we may consider the following pair of English sentences:

(22) i. I have lost (Perfect) my wallet
    ii. I lost (Preterit) my wallet

The first sentence suggests that my wallet is still lost, whereas the second one with the simple past (preterit) may or may not (depending on the context). This stipulation makes the perfect a marked form, as was argued in 3.3.

It is well-known that in English the **present perfect** may not be used with specification of past time. Thus it is impossible to say *I have seen that film yesterday*; on the other hand, the perfect in *I have recently learned that Bill is leaving* is acceptable, although *recently* refers to some point of time in the past. However, the English type of incompatibility of the perfect with adverbials of past time is far from being universal. For instance, in Spanish the perfect may co-occur with adverbs of past time: *Gustavo Ferrán ha muerto* (Perfect) *ayer... se ha estrellado anoche en los montes de nieve* "Gustavo Ferran died yesterday ... he crashed last night on the snow-covered mountains" (Stevenson, 1970:62).

Similarly, it is possible to say in German *Gestern habe ich viel gearbeitet* (Perfect), but it is impossible to say in English *I have worked* (Perfect) *much yesterday*. This restriction on the co-occurrence of temporal adverbs and the perfect should be further investigated in a variety of languages. The contrast present time vs. non-present time may be exemplified with the following Latin sentences:

(23) Domum suam aedificat
      "He/she builds/is building (his/her) house"
      Domum suam aedificābat
      "He/she built/was building (his/her) house"
      Domum suam aedificābit
      "He/she will build (his/her) house"

There is no space in an introductory book on morphology to discuss the wide variety of tense-aspect systems found in different languages. Nevertheless, we may be interested in examining briefly a more complicated system than that of Latin. Contrasted with Latin, the system of Ancient Greek exhibits an additional form, called **aorist**, which may be analyzed as a perfective aspect. Let us use the verb *lúō* "solve" as an example:

(24)		Imperfective	Perfective	Retrospective
	Non-past	lú-ō (Present)	lú-s-ō (Future)	lé-lu-k-a (Perfect)
	Past	é-lū-on (Imperfect)	é-lū-s-a (Aorist)	e-le-lú-k-ēn (Pluperfect)

Compared with the Latin system of two aspects and three tenses, the Greek paradigm has to be analyzed as consisting of three aspects: the imperfective, perfective and retrospective; and two tenses: non-past and past. The perfect is formed by partial reduplication; the aorist by the suffix *-s*. Temporal contrast non-past vs. past is marked morphologically by the opposition Ø- vs. augment *e-* (plus different personal endings). It is surprising to see the future listed under the perfective aspect but this may be justified morphologically, since both the aorist and future use the suffix *-s* (of course, with different personal endings). On semantic grounds one may observe that the perfective non-past event must necessarily refer to the future. Greek *-s* performs very much the same task as the Russian prefixes used to perfectivize the non-past tense and thus refer to the future; compare Greek *gráp-s-ō* "I will write" with Russian *ja na-piš-ú*. The traditional term aorist is taken from Greek *aóristos* (meaning "unbounded, unlimited, unqualified"). We may best understand the meaning of the aorist vis-à-vis that of the perfect and the imperfect. In Ancient Greek the aorist denoted a simple past occurrence of the event where the subject of Event Time is in position D (perfective aspect). The perfect, on the other hand, denoted past events resulting in the present state where the subject is in position E (retrospective aspect). For instance, the perfect *pepoíēke toûto* could be translated "he has (already) done this" (the past event with present relevance), whereas the aorist *epoíēse toûto* means simply "he did this". If we want to express aspectual qualifications such as progressivity or habituality we have to use the imperfect *epoíei toûto* "he was doing this" or "he used to do this". Traditional grammars maintain that the aorist **narrates** the event whereas the imperfect **describes** it; more importantly, both are **Immanent** aspects, whereas the perfect in viewing the event externally is classified as a **Transcendent aspect**. This is shown in Figure 6.7.

It is of interest to observe that the tense-aspect system of Modern Greek is essentially the same (in terms of oppositions) even if perfect and future forms were replaced by analytical formations (the perfect is nowadays formed by means of the auxiliary *éxo* "have" and the future by *θa* "will"). We may use the verb *pédzo* "play" as an example:

(25)		Imperfective	Perfective	Retrospective
	Present	pédz-o	pék-s-o (modal form)	éx-o pék-si
	Past	épedz-a	épek-s-a	íx-a pék-si
	Future	θa pédz-o	θa pék-s-o	θa éx-o pék-si

6.3.4 *Mood*

Traditional grammar distinguishes three main classes of sentences: **statements, questions** and **commands**. In terms of their grammatical structure, these are referred to as **declarative, interrogative** and **jussive** sentences. The term command covers requests, entreaties, demands, as well as commands in the narrower sense. To avoid confusing these various senses of **command** some linguists employ the term **mand** (e.g. Lyons, 1977:745). In many languages the difference between mands and statements is realized in terms of the grammatical category of **mood**. For example, the 2nd Pers Sg imperative form of the Latin verb *laudāre* "praise" is *laudā* and the 2nd Pers Sg of the present indicative is *laudās*. It may be observed that the form of the 2nd Pers imperative is a bare stem (= root *laud* + thematic vowel *-ā*) with no overt indication of person or tense. In contradistinction with English, Latin marks the person in the plural: *laudāte* "praise!" (2nd Pers Pl Imp) vs. *laudātis* "you praise" (2nd Pers Pl Ind). Other languages, e.g. Ancient Greek, indicate the person in the plural but show no difference between the indicative and the imperative; (26) displays the pertinent forms of the verb *leípein* "to leave":

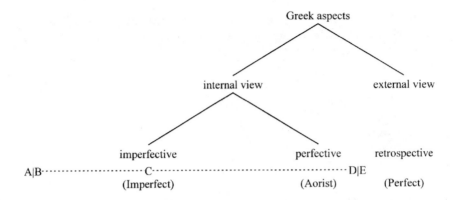

Fig. 6.7 Greek aspects

(26) Ancient Greek Indicative and Imperative

	2nd Sg	2nd Pl
Indicative	leípeis	leípete
Imperative	leîpe	

It is no coincidence that the imperative forms carry no overt indication of tense; the past is ruled out by the fact that is impossible to command someone to carry out some course of action in the past. The only tense distinctions that may be expressed in the imperative are those of more immediate and more remote futurity. The formal contrast of the **present** vs. **future imperative** is found, for instance in Latin (-Ø vs. *-tō*) and Hindi (-Ø vs. *-gā*):

(27) Crās petitō, dabitur. Nunc abi. (Plautus)
       "Tomorrow ask, it will be given. Now go away."

The present imperative of *petere* "ask" would be *pete*; its future form *petitō* indicates that the compliance with the command is not expected immediately but in the future (tomorrow). Similarly, in Hindi the future imperative will be used for those actions that are to be done after some lapse of time. Contrast the following two sentences:

(28) Bil dījiē. "Give [me] the bill (right away)!"   (Hindi)
       Bil dījiegā "Give [me] the bill (after a while)!"

The present imperative would be uttered by an impatient customer who wants to leave the restaurant, whereas the future imperative implies that the waiter may bring the bill at his leisure.

As far as the aspectual contrasts are concerned, these are possible in the imperative but are not particularly common. As in the indicative, Ancient Greek allows for a three-way aspectual contrast: Present (= imperfective) - Aorist (= perfective) - Perfect (= retrospective); cf. the forms of the verb *leípein* 'leave' in the 2ⁿᵈ Sg:

(29) Aspectual Contrasts in the Ancient Greek Imperative

		Indicative	Imperative
Present		leípeis	leîpe
(imperfective)		"you leave/are leaving"	"leave/be leaving!"
Aorist		élipes	lipé
(perfective)		"you left"	"leave!"
Perfect		léloipas	léloipe
(retrospective)		"you have left"	lit. have left!

In Russian we also find the usual aspectual contrast imperfective - perfective in the imperative:

(30) Imperfective   píj vódku   "drink vodka"
      Perfective   výpij vódku "empty (this glass of) vodka" (lit. have drunk)

As far as the category of person is concerned, it is implicit in the notion of commanding that the command is addressed to the person who is expected to carry it out. In other words, the subject of an imperative sentence normally refers to the addressee. However, many languages possess a **third-person imperative** which is typically used in a more polite style, since the third-person imperative typically requires an intermediary to transmit a command. Examples of the third-person imperative are available from Ancient Greek and Sanskrit; their forms of the verb "to carry" are contrasted in (31):

(31) 3ʳᵈ Person Imperatives in Ancient Greek and Sanskrit

	Ancient Greek	Sanskrit	
2ⁿᵈ Pers Sg	phér-e	bhár-a	"carry"
3ʳᵈ Pers Sg	pher-étō	bhár-atu	"may he carry"

Another piece of evidence that the subject of a **jussive sentence** containing an imperative does not have to coincide with the addressee is supplied by the passive imperative. Thus in Sanskrit we have a choice of constructing the command in the active or in the passive voice, the latter typically in a more polite style. Contrast:

(32) Mahyam imāṃ (Acc) dehi   "Give me her!"
      Mahyam iyaṃ (Nom) dīyatām   "May she be given to me!"

Subjunctive sentences are another subset of jussive sentences. The subjunctive in the main clause is most typically used to express **wish** and the subjunctive in this function is called **optative**. In English we use the *s*-less form in the 3rd Pers Sg and in French the subjunctive (without *que*):

(33) Long live the Queen!
      Vive la république!

Used with *que* in the 3rd Pers, the subjunctive expresses a **demand**:

(34) Qu'il écrive.
      "May he write!"

Used with the negative particle in the 3rd Pers, the subjunctive expresses a **polite prohibition**:

(35) Qu'ils ne le fassent pas.
      "May they not do it!"

In the 1st Pers the subjunctive may express **indignation**:

(36) Que je vienne à cette heure?
      "That I would come at this hour?"

Used with the negative particle in the 1st Pers, the subjunctive expresses a weak **negative assertion**. Contrast the following minimal pair of sentences:

(37) Je ne sais rien (strong negative assertion)
      "I know nothing."
      Je ne sache rien (weak negative assertion)
      "I know nothing."

The subjunctive is used in a variety of **subordinate clauses**, whose full treatment belongs to syntax. Thus in French we have to use the subjunctive if the main clause contains the verb "to wish":

(38) Je veux que vous le fassiez.
"I want you to do it."

The subjunctive has to be used in a variety of subordinate clauses (**final, consecutive, conditional, causal**) after their specific conjunction:

(39) Il est content que je le lui aie dit.
"He is satisfied that I have told him."

In terms of morphology, Romance languages present full-fledged sub-systems of the subjunctive that are typically organized as their indicative counterparts. Thus in Latin we find the contrasts past - non-past and perfectum - infectum in the subjunctive. Contrast the non-modal (indicative) and the modal (subjunctive) forms of the verb *laudāre* 'praise' in the 3rd Pers Sg:

(40) Latin Modal Forms

Indicative	Infectum	Perfectum
Present	laud-at	-āvit
Past	-ābat	-āverat
Future	-ābit	-āverit

Subjunctive		
Present	laud-et	-āverit
Past	-āret	-āvisset

The Spanish system is similar; here the parallelism is even more complete in that Spanish possesses the future subjunctive. In contradistinction with Latin the retrospective forms are analytic (formed by the auxiliary *haber* "have" + passive participle in *-ado*). The following are the forms of the verb *trabajar* "work" in the 3rd Sg:

(41) Spanish Modal Forms

Indicative	Imperfective	Retrospective	
Present	trabaj-a	ha	trabajado
Past	-aba	había	"
Future	-ará	habrá	"

Subjunctive			
Present	trabaj-e	haya	"
Past	-ára/ase	hubiera/ese	"
Future	-are		

The past forms of the subjunctive are used most typically in **hypothetical judgements** (i.e., those judgements which are qualified in terms of possibility). In Latin, for example, one may contrast the **real wish** *laudet* "may he praise" (the present subjunctive) or *laudāverit* "may he have praised" (the perfect subjunctive) with the wish which is not realizable (**irrealis**):

(42) Sī mē laudāret, amīcus meus esset (Imperfect)
"If he praised me, he would be my friend"
Sī mē laudāvisset, amīcus meus fuisset (Pluperfect)
"If only he had praised me, he would have been my friend"

The second sentence strongly implies that "he did not praise me".

6.3.5 *Voice*

The term **voice** (*vōx*) was originally used by Roman grammarians in two senses: (i) in the sense of 'sound' (translating the Greek *phōnḗ* "sound"), hence the terms 'vowel' (from Latin *sonus vocālis*) and 'voice' (the effect of the vibration of the vocal cords); (ii) and in the sense of the 'form' of a word as opposed to its 'meaning' (in this sense, the term has disappeared from modern usage). The term has developed a third sense, deriving ultimately from (ii), in which it refers to the active and passive forms of the verb. The Greek term for voice as a category of the verb was **diathesis** 'state', 'disposition', 'condition'. The two extreme positions in the state of affairs expressed by the predicate are 'acting upon someone' (the active voice) and 'being acted upon by someone' (the passive voice). The **middle voice** can be thought of as being intermediate between the primary opposition of **active** and **passive**. It is found most typically in **reflexive sentences** where the use of the middle voice indicates that the results of the action affect the agent. We may contrast the active voice in *I am washing the baby* with the middle voice in the **reflexive sentence** *I am washing myself* (called also 'pronominal' voice). In some languages the middle voice may also be used in a transitive sentence with an object that is distinct from the agent but which typically belongs to the agent. Thus in Ancient Greek we would use the middle voice in *loúomai* "I am washing myself" (vs. the active voice in *loúō tò téknon* "I am washing the baby") but also in *loúomai tòn khitȏna* "I am washing (my) shirt". Here the implication of the middle voice is that the action is being carried out by the agent for his/her own interest: in our case, it affects an object possessed by the agent. Some modern languages have a similar construction, e.g., in French we would use the **pronominal voice** in both *je me lave* "I am washing myself" and *je me lave une chemise* "I am washing (myself) a shirt"; similarly in Czech we would say *umývám se* "I am washing myself" and *umývám si košili* "I am washing myself a shirt" (*se* is the accusative form and *si* is the dative form of the reflexive pronoun which can be used in any person). It is of interest to observe that in many languages the **verbs of saying and perception** (*verba dīcendī et sentiendī*) occur in middle voice (formally identical with the passive). These verbs are different from typical transitive verbs, such as *kill*, *hit*, etc., in that the agent is affected by the action (the speaker normally hears himself through total feedback; the agent of perceiving is rather an undergoer of perception). Thus in Latin we find the middle voice in *loquor* "I speak", *hortor* "I admonish" (called **verba deponentia**); in Ancient Greek in *akroômai* "I listen", *theômai* "I watch", *aisthánomai* "I perceive", etc. Verbs indicating **change of state** occur also typically in middle voice, e.g. Latin *morior* "I die", Sanskrit *mriye* "I die"; Latin *nascitur* "he is born", Sanskrit *jāyate* "he is born"; Greek *gígnetai* "it becomes".

In terms of morphology, voice differences in the verb may be expressed analytically by the auxiliary and the passive participle of the verb) or synthetically (special endings different from the active ones). English realizes the passive voice analytically with the auxiliary "be"; in German the auxiliary is *werden* "become" and in Hindi *jānā* "go".

(43) Das Buch wird geschrieben   (German)
      "The book is (being) written"

Yah	kitāb	likhī	gaī	(Hindi)
this	book	written+FEM	gone+FEM	

      "This book is written"

Latin and other archaic Indo-European languages may be used to exemplify synthetic passive morphology. (44) lists the forms of the 3rd Pers Sg in all tenses and moods for the verb *laudāre* "praise". The forms of **infectum** are synthetic, the forms of **perfectum** analytic (formed by the auxiliary *esse* "be" + passive participle).

(44) Latin Passive Forms: Indicative

Present	laudātur	"he is praised"
Imperfect	laudābātur	"he was praised"
Future	laudābitur	"he will be praised"
Perfect	laudātus est	"he has been praised"
Pluperfect	laudātus erat	"he had been praised"
Future Perfect	laudātus erit	"he will have been praised"

Latin Passive Forms: Subjunctive

Present	laudētur	"may he be praised"
Imperfect	laudārētur	"might he be praised"
Perfect	laudātus sit	"may he have been praised"
Pluperfect	laudātus esset	"might he have been praised"

It may be said that Latin neutralizes the contrast of voice in its participial system in that the active participle is imperfective and the passive participle is retrospective. However, the contrast of voice can be realized with the verbs which occur in the middle voice called **verba deponentia** 'deponent verbs' (lit. verbs which 'lay aside' certain forms). Here the passive participle has also the meaning of the active retrospective participle. Contrast the participial forms of the transitive verb *laudāre* "praise" and those of the deponent verb *loquor* "speak":

(45)

	Infectum	Perfectum	Infectum	Perfectum
Active	laudāns	---	loquēns	locūtus
	"praising"		"speaking"	"having spoken"
Passive	—	laudātus	—	locūtus
		"praised"		"spoken"

This anomaly in the participial system was solved during a later development of Romance languages when the auxiliary "have" + passive participle in the meaning of the active retrospective participle was introduced. Hence French developed the analytical participial expression *ayant loué* "having praised" while in Latin we cannot say **habēns laudātum*.

In functional perspective (cf. under 10.3), the use of the passive has to do with different presentations of the state of affairs designated by the predication. In the case of the active voice the subject coincides with the agent (Ag); in the passive voice the subject coincides with the patient or goal (Go). In either case the subject function is interpreted as marking the entity which is taken as the primary vantage point for presenting the state of affairs:

(46)   Mary (Ag Subj) kissed John (Go Obj)
       John (Go Subj) was kissed by Mary (Ag)

In the passive sentence our attention is drawn to the goal which becomes the topical element of the sentence (for details see 10.3). It is important to realize that not all languages have the passive voice (e.g. Chadic languages, many languages in New Guinea, Zapotec, Yidiɲ); those which have the passive voice do not have to realize the **agentive phrase**, e.g., in Classical Arabic the above passive sentence would be literally translated as *John was kissed, kissed-him Mary*; furthermore, the passive is avoided, especially in colloquial speech, even in languages which have a fully productive basic passive (cf. Keenan 1985:248). Thus the most natural way of saying "He was killed yesterday" in Russian would be "They killed him yesterday":

(47)   Včerá   egó   ubíli
       Yesterday him   killed
       "They killed him yesterday"

Finally, it is worth mentioning that in many languages even intransitive verbs are passivizable (e.g., in Turkish, Latin, Sanskrit). For instance, in Sanskrit the verb "to go" may be found in both **impersonal** and **personal passive constructions**:

(48) Mayā   grāmaṃ   gamyate
      I+INSTR   village + ACC   go+PASS+3SG

      Mayā   grāmo   gamyate
      I+INSTR   village + NOM   go+PASS+3SG

Both versions mean "I am going to the village". Similarly, in Latin we may use the impersonal passive of "to go" as in (49).

(49) Sīc   itur   ad   astra
      Thus   go+3SG+PASS   to   stars
      "This is the way (to go) to the stars."

RECOMMENDED READINGS

Comrie, Bernard. 1976. *Aspect: An Introduction to the Study of Verbal Aspect*. Cambridge: Cambridge University Press.

____. 1985. *Tense*. Cambridge: Cambridge University Press.

Goodwin, William W. 1894/1965. *A Greek Grammar*. London: Macmillan.

Hewson, John & Vit Bubenik. 1997. *Tense and Aspect in Indo-European Languages: Theory, Typology, Diachrony*. Amsterdam: Benjamins.

Hirtle, Walter H. 1975. *Time, Aspect and the Verb*. Québec: Presses de l'Université Laval.

Jakobson, Roman. 1957. *Shifters, Verbal Categories and the Russian Verb*. Cambridge, Mass.: Harvard University Press.

Jespersen, Otto. 1929. *The Philosophy of Grammar*. London: Allen and Unwin.

Keenan, Edrward L. 1985. "Passive in the world's languages". *Language Typology and Syntactic Description* ed. by T. Shopen, 243–281. Cambridge: Cambridge University Press.

Kuryłowicz, Jerzy. 1964. *Inflectional Categories of Indo-European*. Heidelberg: Carl Winter.

Lewis, Geoffrey L. 1967. *Turkish Grammar*. Oxford: Clarendon Press.

Lyons, John. 1977. *Semantics*. Volumes 1 and 2. Cambridge: Cambridge University Press.

Matthews, Peter H. 1972. *Inflectional Morphology: A Theoretical Study Based on Aspects of Latin Verb Conjugation*. Cambridge: Cambridge University Press.

____. 1974. *Morphology: An Introduction to the Theory of Word-Structure*. Cambridge: Cambridge University Press.

Meillet, Antoine & Joseph Vendryes. 1948. *Traité de grammaire comparée des langues classiques*. Paris: Champion.

Mitchell, Terence F. 1962. *Colloquial Arabic*. London: The English Universities Press.

Moreland, Floyd L. & Rita M. Fleischer. 1973. *Latin: An Intensive Course*. Berkeley: University of California Press.

Palmer, Frank R. 1965. *A Linguistic Study of the English Verb*. London: Longmans.

Schwyzer, Eduard. 1959. *Griechische Grammatik*. München: Beck.

Stevenson, C. H. 1970. *The Spanish Language Today*. London: Hutchinson.

Tesnière, Lucien. 1959. *Éléments de syntaxe structurale*. Paris: Klincksieck.

Tzermias, Paul. 1969. *Neugriechische Grammatik*. Bern/München: Francke.

EXERCISES

1. Analyze the whole Ancient Greek system of aspect and tense in terms of its morphological markers. Use the following data:

   (1) Present   leípō   "I leave"
   (2) Imperfect   éleipon   "I left" ~ "was leaving"
   (3) Aorist   élipon   "I left"
   (4) Future   leípsō   "I will leave"
   (5) Perfect   léloipa   "I have left"
   (6) Pluperfect   eleloípēn   "I had left"

2. Using the following data, analyze and describe the morphological make-up of the system of tense and aspect in Hindi. Note: The progressive forms are built on the past participle *rah-ā* of the verb *rahnā* "remain".

   I. Verb *honā* "to be"
       mɛ̃ hū̃   "I am"
       mɛ̃ thā   "I was"
       mɛ̃ hū̃gā   "I will be"

   II. Verb *calnā* "to go"
       mɛ̃ čaltā hū̃   "I go"
       mɛ̃ čaltā thā   "I went" ~ "I used to go"
       mɛ̃ čal rahā hū̃   "I am going"
       mɛ̃ čal rahā thā   "I was going"
       mɛ̃ čalā   "I went"
       mɛ̃ čalā hū̃   "I have gone"
       mɛ̃ čalā thā   "I had gone"
       mɛ̃ čalū̃   "I may go"
       mɛ̃ čalū̃gā   "I will go"

3. Analyze the whole Sanskrit system of aspect and tense in terms of its morphological markers. Use the following data:

   (1) Present   karomi   "I make"
   (2) Imperfect   akaravam   "I made" ~ "I was making"
   (3) Aorist   akārṣam   "I made" ~ "I have made"
   (4) Future   kariṣyāmi   "I will make"

(5)	Perfect	čakara	"I have made"
(6)	Pluperfect	ačakram	"I had made"
(7)	Conditional	akariṣyam	"I would make"

4. Analyze the aspectual system of Modern Hebrew. Consider the following forms:

(1)	dibbēr	"he/she has spoken, had spoken, spoke"
(2)	mədabbēr	"is speaking, was speaking, speaks habitually"
(3)	yədabbēr	"will speak, would speak, would be speaking"

(a)   Establish three basic aspectual categories.

(b)   Describe their morphology.

5. Identify the morphemes marking tense, aspect and mood in Spanish in the following data. Be as formal as possible.

(1)	trabaja	"he/she works"
(2)	trabajaba	"worked"
(3)	trabajó	"worked" ~ "has worked"
(4)	ha trabajado	"has worked"
(5)	había trabajado	"had worked"
(6)	trabajará	"will work"
(7)	habrá trabajado	"will have worked"
(8)	trabajaría	"would work"
(9)	habría trabajado	"would have worked"
(10)	trabaje	"may he/she work"
(11)	trabaja	"work!"

6. Identify the morphemes marking tense, aspect and mood in Italian, and attempt to hierarchize them in a tree diagram. Note: The auxiliary *avere* "have" has *h-* in some persons.

(1)	ama	"he/she loves"
(2)	ami	"may he/she love"
(3)	ama	"love!"
(4)	amera	"will love"
(5)	amerebbe	"would love"
(6)	amava	"loved"
(7)	ha amato	"has loved"
(8)	aveva amato	"had loved"

(9)   avra amato   "will have loved"
(10)   avrebbe amato   "would have loved"

7. Analyze the whole Russian system of aspect, tense and mood in terms of its morphological markers. Use the following data:

(1)   nesú   "I carry"
(2)   nés   "carried"
(3)   nés by   "would carry"
(4)   prinesú   "will have brought"
(5)   prinés   "have brought"
(6)   prinés by   "would have brought"
(7)   nošú   "am carrying"
(8)   nosíl   "was carrying"
(9)   búdu nosít'   "will be carrying"
(10)   nosíl by   "would be carrying"
(11)   prinošú   "am bringing"
(12)   prinosíl   "was bringing"
(13)   búdu prinosít'   "will be bringing"
(14)   prinosíl by   "would be bringing"

8. Analyze the whole Lithuanian system of aspect, tense and mood in terms of its morphological markers. Use the following data:

(1)   dìrbu   "I work" ~ "am working"
(2)   dìrbau   "worked"
(3)   dìrbdavau   "used to work"
(4)   dìrbsiu   "will work"
(5)   dìrbčiau   "would work"
(6)   esù dìrbęs   "have worked"
(7)   buvaũ dìrbęs   "had worked"
(8)   būdavau dìrbęs   "had worked (at intervals)"
(9)   būsiu dìrbęs   "will have worked"
(10)   būčiau dìrbęs   "would have worked"
(11)   buvaũ bedirbą̃s   "was working"
(12)   būdavau bedirbą̃s   "used to be working"
(13)   būsiu bedirbą̃s   "will be working"

9. Analyze the Farsi (Modern Persian) system of aspect, tense, and mood in terms of its morphological markers:

(1)	porsad	"he/she asks"
(2)	mīporsad	"is asking"
(3)	beporsad	"may he/she ask"
(4)	porsīd	"asked"
(5)	mīporsīd	"was asking"
(6)	porsīde ast	"was asked"
(7)	mīporsīde ast	"has been asking"
(8)	mīporsīde būd	"had been asking"
(9)	porsīde bāšad	"may he/she have asked" ~ "if only he/she (had) asked"
(10)	porsīde būd	"had asked"
(11)	xvāhad porsīd	"will ask"
(12)	xvāhad porsīde būd	"will have asked"

(a) Provide traditional labels for all the forms, e.g. (6) Perfect

(b) Attempt to hierarchize the markers identified in the forms above in a tree diagram organized binarily.

(c) There are two forms which are difficult to accommodate in the tree. Identify them and explain why. (Hint: Use the theory of markedness outlined in 3.3).

10. Using the Word and Paradigm model, analyze the Kurdish (dialect of Suleimaniye) system of tense, aspect, and mood in terms of its morphological markers. Use the following data:

(1)	akáwim	"I fall"
(2)	bíkawim	"if I fall" ~ "let me fall"
(3)	káwtim	"fell"
(4)	akáwtim	"kept on falling"
(5)	bíkawtimāya	"would fall"
(6)	kawtúwim	"have fallen"
(7)	kawtíbim	"if I should have fallen"
(8)	kawtíbūm	"had fallen"
(9)	(bí)kawtibām	"would have fallen" ~ "if I should have fallen"
(10)	(bí)kawtibāmāya ~ (bí)kawtābāmāya	*"I would have had fallen"

Consider the following data which will help you to analyze the above forms:

akáwī(t)	"you fall"	(bí)bim	"let me be"	
kawtū̃	"fallen"	būm	"I was"	
abím	"I am"	būwim	"I have been"	

Answer the following questions:

(a) Attempt to hierarchize the identified markers for tense, aspect, and mood in a tree diagram organized binarily.

(b) Provide 'traditional' labels for (1) – (9), e.g. (6) = Perfect.

(c) Comment on the absence of *bí* in (7) and its optionality in (9) and (10). Hint: Use the theory of markedness outlined in 3.3.

(d) What is 'unexpected' (non-prototypical) on the sequence of markers in (5) and (10)?

11. Analyze the Ancient Greek system of aspect, tense and voice in terms of its morphological markers. Attempt to hierarchize these markers in a tree diagram. Use the following data:

(1) ágei   "he/she leads"
(2) êgen   "led"
(3) áksei   "will lead"
(4) égagen   "has led" ~ "led"
(5) êkhe(n)   "has led"
(6) ékhein   "had led"
(7) ágetai   "leads for himself" ~ "is (being) led"
(8) égeto   "led for himself" ~ "was (being) led"
(9) áksetai   "will lead for himself"
(10) ēgágeto   "has led for himself" ~ "led for himself"
(11) êkhtai   "has led for himself" ~ "has been led"
(12) êkhto   "had led for himself" ~ "had been led"
(13) ékhthē   "has been led" ~ "was led"
(14) akhthēsetai "will be led"

12. Using the Word and Paradigm model analyze the following Modern Greek system of tense, aspect, and voice in terms of its morphological markers. Note: Read carefully B. Comrie (1976), *Aspect* (Chapter 4) before you start working on this assignment.

(1) féri   "he/she carries"
(2) vlépi   "sees"
(3) θa pléni   "will be washing"
(4) θa vlépsi "will see"

(5)	ékleve	"stole"
(6)	égrapse (Aorist)	"has written" ~ "wrote"
(7)	éxi dísi	"has dressed"
(8)	íxe grápsi	"had written"
(9)	íxe klépsi	"had stolen"
(10)	θa éxi grápsi	"will have written"
(11)	θa íxe dísi	"would have dressed"
(12)	plénete	"is washed"
(13)	θa skotónete	"will be being killed"
(14)	θa diθí	"will be dressed"
(15)	(e)vlepótane	"was seen"
(16)	skotóθike (Aor)	"has been killed" ~ "was killed"
(17)	éxi pliθí	"has been washed"
(18)	íxe skotoθí	"has been killed"
(19)	θa íxe diθí	"would have been dressed"

Answer the following questions:

(a) Hierarchize the identified markers for tense, aspect and voice in a tree diagram organized binarily.

(b) Provide 'traditional' labels for all the identified verb forms.

(c) Comment on the 'leak' in the system of tense and aspect.

(d) Translate (20) – (29) into Modern Greek:

(20) "he/she will be carrying"
(21) "has stolen"
(22) "was dressed"
(23) "has seen" ~ "saw"
(24) "was washed"
(25) "will be seen"
(26) "would have stolen"
(27) "would have been killed"
(28) "would have seen"
(29) "has been washed" ~ "was washed"

13. Analyze the whole Latin system of aspect, tense and mood in terms of its morphological markers as systematically as you can. Use the following data:

(1)   dūcit   "he/she leads"

(2)	dūxerit	"he/she will have led"
(3)	dūcēbat	"led"
(4)	dūcat	"may lead"
(5)	dūcet	"will lead"
(6)	dūceret	"would/might lead"
(7)	dūxit	"has led"
(8)	dūxerit	"may have led"
(9)	dūxerat	"had led"
(10)	dūxisset	"would/might have led"

14. Analyze the whole Turkish system of aspect, tense and mood in terms of its morphological markers as systematically as you can. Use the following data:

(1)	geliyorum	"I am coming"
(2)	gelecektim	"would come"
(3)	geliyordum	"was coming"
(4)	gelmeliyim	"ought to come"
(5)	gelirim	"come"
(6)	gelmeliydim	"ought to have come"
(7)	gelirdim	"used to come"
(8)	geldim	"came"
(9)	geleceğim	"will come"
(10)	geldiydim	"had come"

15. Analyze the Turkish system of participial forms in terms of its morphological markers. Use the following data:

(1)	yazan adam	"the man who writes"
(2)	yazıyor olan adamlar	"the men who are writing now"
(3)	yazırlar	"those who usually write"
(4)	yazmış olan adamlar	"the men who wrote/have written"
(5)	yazacak olan adam	"the man who is about to write"
(6)	yazılıyor olan mektuplar	"the letters that are being written"
(7)	yazılır olan mektup	"the letter that is usually written"
(8)	yazılmış olan mektup	"the letter that was/has been written"
(9)	yazılacak olan mektuplar	"the letters that will be written"
(10)	yazılmalı olan mektup	"the letter that ought to be written"

Translate the following relative clauses into Turkish. Use the participles and observe the rules of vowel harmony:

(11) "the man who ought to die"
(12) "the woman who is coming now"
(13) "those who will come"
(14) "the men who came/have come"
(15) "the women who ought to be loved"

Vocabulary:

öl-	"die"	sev-	"love"
ol-	"be"	adam	"man"
gel-	"come"	kadın	"woman"
yaz-	"write"	-lar	(plural suffix)

16. Comrie (1976:52) notes that the perfect is an aspect in a sense different from the representation of the internal temporal constitution of a situation "since it tells us nothing directly about the situation in itself, but rather relates some state to a preceding situation". His reason for writing a chapter on the perfect is that "given the traditional terminology in which the perfect is listed as an aspect, it seems most convenient to deal with the perfect in a book on aspect".

Comment on this dilemma. Hint: Distinguish carefully between perfect (as defined traditionally) and perfective (as used in modern linguistics).

17. Matthews (1974:139) illustrates the concept of formative ambiguity by means of the present indicative and present subjunctive in Spanish:

	Indicative	Subjunctive
Conjugation 1	compro 'I buy'	compre
	compras 'you buy'	compres
	compra 'he/she buys'	compre
Conjugation 2	como 'I eat'	coma
	comes 'you eat'	comas
	come 'he/she acts'	coma

Then he wonders: "What is the point . . . in saying that 'SUBJUNCTIVE' is an element in sequence which is located in its allomorphs *e* or *a* specifically? Obviously we CAN say so if we must. But the traditional view seems more revealing. Mood is a category of words as wholes, which is identified by the oppositions of whole stems or word-forms in the individual paradigm."

Explain, as best you can, these two viewpoints. Hint: Think of the two basic approaches to the study of morphology: the Item and Arrangement model vs. the Word and Paradigm model.

CHAPTER SEVEN
MORPHOSYNTACTIC PROPERTIES AND THEIR EXPONENTS

Secondary grammatical categories, such as gender and number (see Chapter Five), and person, number, tense and aspect (see Chapter Six) are frequently referred to as 'morphosyntactic' categories. Their individual terms (such as Masculine, Singular, Third Person, Past, Imperfective) are called **morphosyntactic properties** since they are properties of the word which play roles in both morphology and syntax.

In the framework of the Word and Paradigm model the elements which identify morphosyntactic properties are called **exponents**. For instance, in Moroccan Arabic *t-šuf-u* "you see" the prefix *t-* is an exponent of the 2nd Pers and the suffix *-u* is an exponent of the Plural. In Latin, on the other hand, exponents of Person and Number are fused in a suffix which is not analyzable for these two properties:

(1)   Moroccan Arabic   Latin
    "you see"   t-šuf   vid-ēs
    "ye see"   t-šuf-u   vid-ētis

Examination of a sufficient number of typologically divergent languages enabled linguists to establish five types of exponence:

(i)   cumulative
(ii)   fused (originally separate)
(iii)   extended
(iv)   agglutinative (non-cumulative)
(v)   overlapping

7.1 *Cumulative versus Agglutinative Exponenence*

The best examples of **cumulative exponence** can be found in Ancient or conservative Indo-European languages (Latin, Russian). If we examine the nominal paradigm of Latin *o*-stems it will become obvious that there is no exponent which could be said to identify consistently Plural versus Singular.

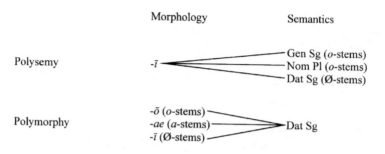

Fig. 7.1 Polysemy and polymorphy in Latin

(2)   Case and Number in Latin (*o*-stems)

	Singular	Plural
Nominative	serv-us "slave"	serv-ī
Accusative	serv-um	serv-ōs
Genitive	serv-ī	serv-ōrum
Dative	serv-ō	serv-īs
Ablative	serv-ō	serv-īs

In other words, in Latin, Number is 'fused' with Case in the sense that the inflectional suffixes mark the lexical item for a particular case and a particular number simultaneously. A result of this situation is **polysemy** of individual suffixes (when the same suffix marks different combinations of case and number) and **polymorphy** of syntactic functions (when the combination of a particular case and a particular number is marked by different suffixes in different declensions). See Figure 7.1.

The situation in Turkish is diametrically opposed in that Number is not fused with Case. Both number and case are marked by their own exponents and in all instances it is possible to establish the boundary between them. Unlike in Latin, Turkish nominal suffixes are always segmentable and constant for all nouns; while Latin has five patterns of declension, Turkish has only one. This type of exponence is called **agglutinative** (or **non-cumulative**).

(3)   Case and Number in Turkish

	Singular	Plural
Nominative	ev "house"	ev-ler
Accusative	ev-i	ev-ler-i
Genitive	ev-in	ev-ler-in
Dative	ev-e	ev-ler-e
Locative	ev-de	ev-ler-de
Ablative	ev-den	ev-ler-den

Similarly, in Turkish verbal paradigms, Number is not fused with Person whereas in Latin it is. Let us contrast the following verbal forms from Turkish and Latin:

(4)		Turkish	Latin	
Sg	1	gör-üyor-um "I see"	vid-e-ō	"I see"
	2	-sun	-ē-s	
	3	-Ø	-e-t	
Pl	1	-uz	-ē-mus	
	2	-sunuz	-ē-tis	
	3	-lar	-e-nt	

In Turkish we may identify the plural morpheme *-uz* (in the 1ˢᵗ and 2ⁿᵈ person) and *-lar* in the 3ʳᵈ Person. Surprisingly, the 1ˢᵗ Pers Pl is not the expected *gör-üyor-um-uz; rigidly agglutinative forms, however, obtain in possessive pronouns as shown in (5).

(5)	ev-im	"my house"	ev-im-iz	"our house"
	ev-in	"thy house"	ev-in-iz	"your house"

A similar morphological analysis is simply impossible for Latin (cf. 5.1.2).

As with all typological distinctions, of course, we are speaking of a continuum. The following data from Moroccan and Syrian Arabic may demonstrate that Arabic occupies an intermediate position between Latin and Turkish on the scale of cumulative ↔ agglutinative exponence:

(6)			Moroccan Arabic	Syrian Arabic
Sg	1		n-šuf "I see"	šūf "I see"
	2m		t-šuf	t-šūf
		f	t-šuf-i	t-šūf-i
	3m		i-šuf	y-šūf
		f	t-šuf	t-šūf
Pl	1		n-šuf-u	n-šūf
	2		t-šuf-u	t-šūf-u
	3		i-šuf-u	y-šūf-u

In Moroccan Arabic it is possible to identify separately Person (*n-* = 1ˢᵗ, *t-* = 2ⁿᵈ, *i-* = 3ʳᵈ) and Number (-Ø = Sg, *-u* = Pl), and we may conclude that we are dealing with agglutinative exponence. On the other hand, in Syrian Arabic in the 1ˢᵗ Pers we are dealing with cumulative exponence (Ø- = 1ˢᵗ + Sg, *n-* = 1ˢᵗ + Pl).

(7)   Moroccan Arabic (Agglutinative Exponence)

(8)   Syrian Arabic (Cumulative Exponence)

However, in both Moroccan and Syrian Arabic, Gender is expressed identically by two different strategies: suffixation in the 2nd Pers Sg (-Ø vs. -i = Masc vs. Fem) and prefixation in the 3rd Pers Sg (y- or i- vs. t- = Masc vs. Fem). Thus in both Moroccan and Syrian Arabic marking for morphosyntactic properties of Person and Gender is of an agglutinative character. One observes, however, polysemy of the form tšuf = 2nd + Masc or 3rd + Fem; this is a consequence of the fact that prefixation is used primarily for marking Person.

7.2 Fused, Extended and Overlapping Exponence

It is more difficult to distinguish cumulative from **fused exponence**. We saw in (4) that in Latin Person and Number are identified cumulatively; in Latin, it is impossible to analyze further the suffixes appearing after the thematic vowel. Now, let us examine the marking for these two properties in Spanish. Consider the following data:

(9)   Spanish
   Pl   1   vivímos "we live"
        2   vivís
        3   víven
   Pl   1   llamámos "we call"
        2   llamáis
        3   lláman

In Spanish viv-is "ye live" the ending -is identifies the form as Present Indicative + 2nd Pers Pl. However, examining the rest of the same paradigm and the paradigm of the 1st Conjugation (llamá-is "you/ye call") we would predict a form *viví-is. The same form can be established on the basis of an Indicative - Subjunctive contrast (*viviis - viváis) but this form simply does not 'surface' since its occurrence would violate phonotactic rules of Spanish. (Spanish allows for vocalic clusters such as uo and ao but not for homorganic *ii). Consequently, we may treat the form vivís as a form resulting from underlying viví + is by a regular phonological process in

Spanish. Thus it may be said that in this case the resulting **fused exponence** is **underlyingly agglutinative**. The corresponding subjunctive form *viváis* "may ye live" displays agglutinative exponence at both levels (underlying and surface). These matters are surveyed in Figure 7.2.

Another type of exponence-relationship is that of **extended exponence**. It is customarily referred to as **double marking**. Classical examples are supplied by German plural forms involving simultaneous use of the process of **umlaut** and the **suffixation**. Consider the following German plural formations:

(10) Tag "day"   Tag-e "days"
      Vater "father"   Väter "fathers"
      Mann "man"   Männ-er "men"
      Fuss "foot"   Füss-e "feet"

Their plural is indicated either by the suffix (*Tag-e*) or by the process of umlaut (*Väter*) or by both (*Männ-er, Füss-e*). The latter strategy (combining morphological process and suffixation) is in a sense 'redundant' as the later state of affairs present in Dutch and English may indicate. Thus English relies only on umlaut in distinguishing plural counterparts of *man* and *foot* (*men* and *feet*, respectively); their plural suffixes which caused umlaut in the root were lost during the pre-Old English period.

Another example of extended exponence is available from Ancient Greek which double-marks its past verbal categories by the **augment** and **secondary endings** (cf. 6.3.3); see some representative examples in (11):

(11) leíp-ō "I leave"   é-leip-o-n "I was leaving"
      lé-loip-a "I have left" e-le-loíp-ē-n "I have left"

The secondary suffix carried more 'weight' and the augment could be left out (especially in Homeric Greek).

And finally, linguists recognize a fifth type of exponence, called **overlapping**. Strictly speaking, this is not a new type of exponence but rather an 'interplay' or 'interdigitation' of two

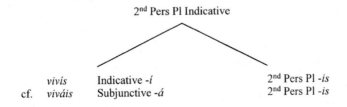

2ⁿᵈ Pers Pl Indicative

      vivís   Indicative -*i*   2ⁿᵈ Pers Pl -*is*
cf.   viváis   Subjunctive -*á*   2ⁿᵈ Pers Pl -*is*

Fig. 7.2 Fused exponence in Spanish

extended exponences. In Ancient Greek the categories of aspect, tense and voice pattern in this fashion. Let us examine the following verbal forms:

(12) Active Present   lŭ-ei "he solves"
     Imperfect   é-lū-e(n) "he was solving"
     Perfect   lé-lu-k-e(n) "he has solved"
     Pluperfect   e-le-lú-k-ei(n) "he had solved"
     Mediopassive Perfect   lé-lu-t-ai "it has been solved"
     Pluperfect   e-lé-lu-t-o "it had been solved"

The active pluperfect shows the overlap of markers for tense, aspect and voice in the following fashion:

(13) Active Pluperfect (Ancient Greek)

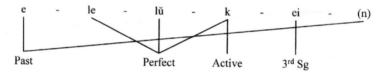

The mediopassive pluperfect shows the overlap of markers for tense, aspect and voice in the following fashion:

(14) Mediopassive Pluperfect (Ancient Greek)

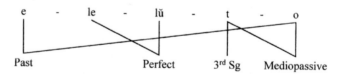

In (13), the perfect is marked by the suffix -k and two processes (reduplication of the root and the shortening of the root-vowel lū → lu). The suffix -k also marks the active voice vs. mediopassive -t in (14); here the perfect is only double-marked by the two processes of reduplication and vocalic shortening. As mentioned above the category of tense (past) is also double-marked at both extremities of the word resulting in the line crisscrossing the lines with aspectual markers. Consequently, this state of affairs may fittingly be described by the term overlapping exponence.

RECOMMENDED READINGS

Bazell, Charles E. 1966. "Linguistic typology". *Five Inaugural Lectures* ed. by P. D. Strevens, 29–49. London: Oxford University Press.

Cowell, Mark W. 1964. *A Reference Grammar of Syrian Arabic*. Washington, D.C.: Georgetown University Press.

Harrell, Richard S. 1965. *A Short Reference Grammar of Moroccan Arabic*. Washington, D.C.: Georgetown University Press.

Lewis, Geoffrey L. 1967. *Turkish Grammar*. Oxford: Clarendon Press.

Matthews, Peter H. 1974. *Morphology: An Introduction to the Theory of Word-Structure*. Cambridge: Cambridge University Press. (Chapter 8).

EXERCISES

1. Identify and exemplify the following types of exponence:

   (a) cumulative
   (b) fused
   (c) extended
   (d) agglutinative
   (e) overlapping

2. It is claimed that Sanskrit inflectional endings show a considerable degree of fusion of grammatical meanings whereas those of agglutinating languages are typically composed of a sequence of morphemes, with each morpheme corresponding to one meaning. Discuss this statement using the following data:

		Sanskrit	Finnish
Sg	Nom	gṛham "house"	talo "house"
	Gen	gṛhasya	talon
	Loc	gṛhe	talossa (Inessive)
	Abl	gṛhāt	talolta
Pl	Nom	gṛhāṇi	talot
	Gen	gṛhāṇām	talojen
	Loc	gṛheṣu	taloissa (Inessive)
	Abl	gṛhebhyas	taloilta

3. Marking for the verbal categories of person and number in Syrian Arabic differs from that of Moroccan Arabic. Describe and explain the following data in terms of cumulative and agglutinative exponence:

			Syrian Arabic	Moroccan Arabic
Present Sg	1		šūf "I see"	nšuf "I see"
	2	(M)	tšūf	tšuf
		(F)	tšūfi	tšufi
	3	(M)	yšūf	išuf
		(F)	tšūf	tšuf
Pl	1		nšūf	nšufu
	2		tšūfu	tšufu
	3		yšūfu	išufu

Past   Sg 1   katabt "I wrote"   ktebt "I wrote"
            2 (M)   katabt   ktebi
              (F)   katabti   ktebti
            3 (M)   katab   kteb
              (F)   katbet   ketbet

4. Analyze several grammatical forms of the five aspectual categories of Ancient Greek (cf. 6.3.3) in terms of their extended and overlapping exponence. You should consult Matthews (1974:148–149) before working on this question.

	1st Sg	1st Pl	3rd Pl
Present	lú-ō	lû-omen	lû-ousi
Imperfect	é-lū-on	e-lû-omen	é-lū-on
Aorist	é-lū-sa	e-lû-sa-men	é-lū-sa-n
Perfect	lé-lu-ka	le-lú-ka-men	le-lú-kā-si
Pluperfect	e-le-lú-k-ēn	e-le-lú-ke-men	e-le-lú-ke-san

5. Languages are frequently classified into structural types of isolating, agglutinative, flective/inflectional (the latter subdivided into inflected externally and internally).

(a) Define these three types.

(b) Demonstrate that this classification is ultimately based on the distinction between morpheme and sememe.

CHAPTER EIGHT
MORPHEME AND ALLOMORPH

8.1 The Alternation of Allomorphs

It was mentioned in Chapter Two that a particular morpheme is quite often represented not by the same morph but by different morphs in different contexts. These alternate representations of a particular morpheme are called **allomorphs**. One of the important tasks of morphology is to account for these allomorphic alternations. For instance, the plural morpheme in English, which is homophonous with the possessive noun suffix or the verb suffix for the 3rd Pers Sg Indicative is regularly represented by the allomorphs /s/, /z/ and /əz/:

(1)	Plural	Possessive	3rd Pers Sg
/əz/	glasses	glass's	(he) sneezes
/s/	cats	cat's	(he) meets
/z/	dogs	dog's	(he) feeds

These three allomorphs occur in three **mutually exclusive environments**. If the morph representing the noun morpheme with which the plural morpheme is combined ends with

(i)   a (strident) alveolar or alveo-palatal sibilant fricative /s/, /z/, /š/, /ž/ or a (strident) affricate /č/, /ǰ/, the plural morpheme is represented by /əz/;

(ii) a voiceless consonant other than the strident /s/, /š/, /č/, the plural morpheme is represented by /s/;

(iii) elsewhere the plural morpheme is represented by /z/.

It may be observed that the orthographical conventions of English distinguish only two of these three allomorphs, with -s or -'s representing both /s/ and /z/, and -es or -'s representing /əz/. The question arises how to represent the morpheme underlying these three allomorphs, or, in other words, what is the phonic substance of the underlying morpheme? Obviously, we have a choice between /s/ and /z/. Those linguists who favor the latter alternant rely on the distributional account; if the contexts (ii) and (iii) as listed above are brought within the scope of a more systematic statement it will appear that /z/ occurs in more environments than /s/. Since all vowels of English are voiced, the environment of /s/ includes only three voiceless stops /p, t, k/ and two voiceless fricatives /f/, /θ/; on the other hand, the environment of /z/ includes three voiced stops /b/, /d/, /g/, two voiced fricatives /v/, /ð/, three nasals /m/, /n/, /ŋ/ two liquids /l/, /r/, five tense vowels /i/, /e/, /u/, /o/, /ɑ/ and three diphthongs, /aj/, /aw/, /oj/. The allomorph /z/ is distributionally the **major variant** (to use the Prague School term) of the plural (and the possessive and the 3rd Pers Sg) morpheme and may thus be favored as most convenient for the phonetic representation of the underlying morpheme.

The process description (in terms of Generative Phonology) of this allomorphic variation would run along these lines. We have to postulate an epenthesis rule which inserts schwa /ə/ between a stem final sibilant and the suffixed /z/. Sibilants (alveolar and alveo-palatal fricatives and affricates in English) comprise the set of sounds which are [+strident +coronal]. The occurrence of /s/ after voiceless consonants would be attributed to assimilation of /z/ to the normal voicelessness of the preceding consonant, and of course no conditioning would occur after voiced non-strident consonants. Schematically:

(2)	/glæs + z/	/kæt + z/	/dɑg + z/
Epenthesis	ə	-	-
Devoicing	-	s	-
	[glæsəz]	[kæts]	[dɑgz]

It may be noted that if we had chosen the **minor variant** /s/ of the plural morpheme as the underlying form we would have to posit a voicing rule. This rule would voice /s/ after a voiced consonant or vowel:

(3)	/glæs + s/	/kæt + s/	/dɑg + s/
Epenthesis	ə	-	-
Voicing	z	-	z
	[glæsəz]	[kæts]	[dɑgz]

It may be argued that z is a less common sound than s (notice that it is possible for a language not to include any voiced obstruents in its phonemic inventory) but, on the other hand, to postulate the final devoicing rule for English seems to be very natural given the universal constraint that no voiced consonant follows a voiceless one in the same syllable coda. Another reason why {z} is preferable to {s} has to do with words ending in sonorants (n and l) such has *hens, sins,* and *falls, ells.* If we chose {s} for the representation of the plural morpheme, the voicing rule would have to be made sensitive to other words which do not voice their final s after n or l; *hens* /hɛnz/ but *hence* /hɛns/; *sins* /sɪnz/ but *since* /sɪns/; *falls* /fɑlz/ but *false* /fɑls/; *ells* /ɛlz/ but *else* /ɛls/.

There is another familiar case of allomorphic alternation in English which is similar to the above. The allomorphs of the regular past tense and past participle are /əd/, /t/ and /d/:

/əd/ in petted, padded
/t/ kicked, ...

/d/   begged, ...

The environments for these three allomorphs can be stated as follows:

(i)   /əd/ after /t/, /d/;
(ii)   /t/ after voiceless consonants other than /t/;
(iii)   /d/ elsewhere.

The allomorph represented by a voiced consonant only (in this case the voiced alveolar stop /d/) proves again to be a major variant. The process description of this allomorphic alternation has to work with two phonological rules similar to those of the plural morpheme, namely, the rule inserting schwa (epenthesis rule) and the rule of devoicing:

(4)	/pɛt + d/	/kɪk + d/	/bɛg + d/
Epenthesis	ə	-	-
Devoicing	-	t	-
	[pɛtəd]	[kɪkt]	[bɛgd]

We may conclude that {z} and {d} should represent plural and past tense morphemes in English.

8.2 Morphological vs. Phonological Conditioning of Allomorphs

The alternation found in the suffixes of the plural and the past tense in English has thus far been attributed to the phonological shape of the preceding nominal or verbal stem. Such alternations, which are explicable on purely phonetic grounds without reference to the notions of morphology, are said to be **phonologically conditioned**. However, the distribution of some morphemes cannot be accounted for phonologically. In such a case, it is inevitable to list the specific set of lexemes with which each irregular alternate occurs. When some morphemes are distributed in this manner, we have to say that they are **conditioned lexically**.

Familiar examples may be found in English. The plural morpheme beside showing three phonologically conditioned allomorphs /z/, /s/ and /əz/ displays also several other pluralizing morphemes which may be classified into ten groups:

(i)   oxen, children, brethren
(ii)   deer, sheep . . .; bass, pike . . .; quail, grouse . . .
(iii)   geese, teeth, feet, lice, mice, men, women
(iv)   data, media, memoranda/memorandums, curricula/curriculums
(v)   radii, fungi
(vi)   cherubim/cherubs, seraphim/seraphs
(vii)   criteria, phenomena

(viii) formulae, larvae
(ix)   crises, theses
(x)   indices/indexes

It is obviously true that the plural of *ox* or *goose* has the same kind of meaning as the plural of *cat*; in all these instances we are dealing with more than one individual. However, on the phonological side, we are dealing with different morphemes expressing the same meaning, namely plurality. Consequently, the equation in (5) holds semantically but not morphologically in that different morphemes represent the same semantic unit.

(5)   Polymorphy:

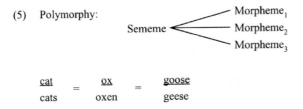

$$\text{Sememe} < \begin{array}{l} \text{Morpheme}_1 \\ \text{Morpheme}_2 \\ \text{Morpheme}_3 \end{array}$$

$$\frac{\text{cat}}{\text{cats}} = \frac{\text{ox}}{\text{oxen}} = \frac{\text{goose}}{\text{geese}}$$

The nouns in (i) do not add /əz/ and /z/ but /ən/; in addition, the last two change their root vowel and *child* also adds -*r* before -*ən*. The nouns in (ii) have a Ø-suffix. It is notable that the words in this group are the names of edible domesticated and game animals (fish and birds). Of course, there are similar words with a regular plural: *pigs, goats, pheasants, ducks*. But it is of interest to note that some have both forms, the forms with the Ø-suffix appearing in the dialect of hunters: a farmer who has *ducks* on his pond may go out hunting *duck*. In such cases we are not dealing with plural forms but rather with **collectives** (see 5.2.2). The nouns in (iii) exhibit a vowel change (umlaut) of various types: /u/ → /i/, /aw/ → /aj/, /æ/ → /ɛ/. The nouns in (iv) replace the (Latin) singular suffix -*um* by the plural suffix -*a* /ə/. The nouns in (v) replace the (Latin) singular suffix -*us* by the plural suffix -*i* /aj/ and the nouns in (vi) keep the (Hebrew) plural suffix /ɪm/, beside the regular plural in /z/. There are various terminological problems connected with this state of affairs. If we use the term allomorph indiscriminately for all the pluralizing suffixes /s/, /z/, /əz/, /ən/, /Ø/, /ə/, /aj/, /ɪm/, it will become impossible to state what the phonic substance of the plural morpheme is, since only the first three are phonologically related. Consequently, we should prefer to talk about six different pluralizing morphemes and to keep the term allomorph for the phonologically conditioned variants. This admittedly is a somewhat pedantic insistence on terminology since the whole problem is a marginal area of English grammar. What is essential after all is the fact that we may identify phonologically the regular pluralizing morpheme of English as {z} and the residuum has to be considered as exceptional (regardless of whether we decide to label /ən/ etc. morphemes or allomorphs).

However, the situation is more complicated when we deal with languages where it is impossible to identify the regular pluralizing morpheme. This state of affairs is found in languages which subcategorize their nouns into various inflectional classes. For instance, it is impossible to talk about regular pluralizing morpheme in Latin without specifying the declension (and gender and case) of the noun, such as in the nominative case *o*-stems take -*ī* if the noun is masculine and -*a* if the noun is neuter. Similarly, Arabic uses three plural suffixes: -*īn*, -*e* and -*āt* and their distribution can be stated only with reference to rather complicated morphological phenomena. The situation in Syrian Arabic can be outlined along the following lines:

(i)   -*īn* is used with nouns denoting male human beings: *mʕallem* "teacher" → *mʕallmīn* and most occupational nouns of the pattern $C_1aC_2C_2\bar{a}C_3$: *nažžār* "carpenter" → *nažžārīn*;

(ii)   -*e* is used with nouns ending in the suffix -*ži* or -*i*: *xədarži* "green-grocer" → *xədaržiyye*; *ḥarāmi* "thief" → *ḥaramiyye*; also with many occupational nouns of the pattern $C_1aC_2C_2\bar{a}C_3$: *ṣarrāf* "moneychanger" → *ṣarrāfe*;

(iii) -*āt* is used with feminine derivatives: *xāl* "(maternal) uncle" → *xāle* "aunt" *xālāt* and with singulatives (see 5.2.2): *žāž* "chicken(s)" → *žāže* "a chicken" → *žāžāt* "some chickens".

There are other subgroups which we may omit at this point but what is of interest is the fact that the suffix -*āt* is used with most loanwords. This might indicate that this suffix is the most productive of the three pluralizing morphemes:

(6)   bābōr "steamship" → bābōrāt
       ʔamirāl "admiral" → ʔamirālāt
       bēbē "baby" → bēbiyāt
       trēn "train" → trēnāt

Returning to our theoretical discussion, we cannot call these three pluralizing suffixes of Syrian Arabic allomorphs since they are not phonologically related. For similar reasons as in English we may keep the term allomorph for a phonologically conditioned variant of the morpheme -*e* which obtains after pharyngeals or *r* (e.g., *baḥḥār* "sailor" → *baḥḥāra* "sailors"). Thus in both English and Arabic we are dealing with polymorphy of the plural meaning (one-to-many relationships between semantics and morphology), cf. Figures 8.1 and 8.2.

8.3 *Turkish Vowel Harmony*

We may be interested in examining less familiar examples of phonological conditioning of allomorphs than those of the English plural and past tense morphemes. We saw above that this particular alternation was ultimately reducible to phonological **assimilatory processes**. In Turkish, the alternations found in allomorphs of case, plural, and possessive suffixes are also

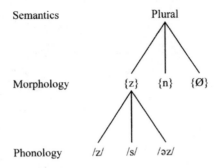

Fig. 8.1 Polymorphy and allomorphy in English

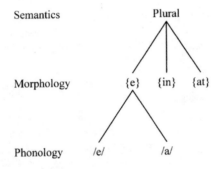

Fig. 8.2 Polymorphy and allomorphy in Arabic

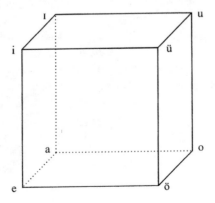

Fig. 8.3 Turkish Vowels

reducible to assimilatory processes. Here the alternations affect vowels and they are frequently referred to as **vowel harmony**.

For the purposes of the following discussion, we have to classify Turkish vowels by three pairs of familiar features: front vs. back (*i, e, ü, ö* vs. *ı, a, u, o*) high vs. low (*i, ü, ı, u* vs. *e, ö, a, o*) and unrounded vs. rounded (*i, e, ı, a* vs. *ü, ö, u, o*). We may portray this three-dimensional system as a cube in Figure 8.3. The first set of data in (7) contains all the case forms of Turkish nouns.

(7)			"house"	"room"	"eye"	"friend"
Sg	Nom		ev	oda	göz	dost
	Acc		evi	odayı	gözü	dostu
	Gen		evin	odanı	gözün	dostun
	Dat		eve	odaya	göze	dosta
	Loc		evde	odada	gözde	dostta
	Abl		evden	odadan	gözden	dosttan
Pl	Nom		evler	odalar	gözler	dostlar
	Acc		evleri	odaları	gözleri	dostları
	Gen		evlerin	odaların	gözlerin	dostların
	Dat		evlere	odalara	gözlere	dostlara
	Loc		evlerde	odalarda	gözlerde	dostlarda
	Abl		evlerden	odalardan	gözlerden	dostlardan

The order of morphemes in this data is as follows: ROOT $\left\{ \begin{array}{c} \text{Case} \\ \text{Pl} \end{array} \right\}$ Case. These morphemes are realized by various morphs: the plural suffix is realized by two morphs /ler/ ~ /lar/; the accusative (and genitive) suffix is realized by four morphs showing the alternation /i/ ~ /ı/ ~ /ü/ ~ /u/; the dative (locative and ablative) suffix is realized by two morphs showing the alternation /e/ ~ /a/; furthermore, if the plural morpheme intervenes between the lexical root and the case even the accusative (and genitive) is realized by only two morphs /i/ ~ /ı/. So far, the conditioning for this distribution can be expressed along these lines:

(i)   the plural suffix or the case (Dat, Loc, Abl) contains the vowel /e/ if the preceding vowel is front (/e/, /ö/); elsewhere, it is /a/;

(ii) the case (Acc, Gen) contains: the vowel /i/ if the preceding vowel is low front /e/; the vowel /ı/ if the preceding vowel is low back (/a/); the vowel /ü/ if the preceding vowel is low front rounded /ö/; the vowel /u/ if the preceding vowel is low back rounded /o/.

We need additional data to complete our analysis. Below are listed words which contain high vowels (only three cases will be necessary, the rest of the paradigm is predictable):

(8)   "name"   "forehead"   "measure"   "fear"
   Sg Nom   isim   alın   ölçü   korku
          Acc   ismi   alnı   ölçüyü   korkuyu
          Dat   isme   alına   ölçüye   korkuya

These forms show that our previous tentative conclusions were correct, in that

(i)   the plural suffix or the case (Dat, Loc, Abl) contain the vowel /e/ if the preceding vowel
       is front (/i/, /e/, /ü/, /ö/); furthermore, we may simplify our statement under (ii);
(ii) the case (Acc, Gen) contains: the vowel /i/ if the preceding vowel is front unrounded
       (/i/, /e/); the vowel /ı/ if the preceding vowel is back unrounded (/ı/, /a/) — notice *alın
       → alnı; the vowel /ü/ if the preceding vowel is front rounded /ü/, /ö/); the vowel /u/ if
       the preceding vowel is back rounded /u/, /o/.

Let us use additional data for elaborating on the sequence of morphemes and this allomorphic
alternation. The possessive suffixes meaning "my" and "our" can be added to these forms as
shown below:

(9)   evim   "my house"
        evimin   "of my house"
        evimiz   "our house"
        evimizin   "of our house"

        evlerim   "my houses"
        evlerimin   "of my houses"
        evlerimiz   "our houses"
        evlerimizin   "of our houses"

        odam   "my room"
        odamın   "of my room"
        odamız   "our room"
        odamızın   "of our room"

        odalarım   "my rooms"
        odalarımın   "of my rooms"
        odalarımız   "our rooms"
        odalarımızın   "of our rooms"

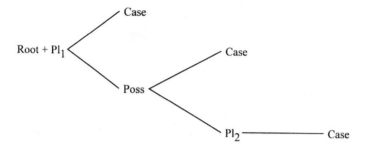

Fig. 8.4 The sequence of morphemes in Turkish nouns

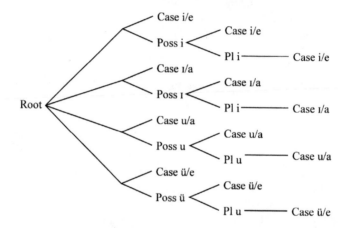

Fig. 8.5 Turkish four-way vowel harmony

(Other forms are predictable — thus *gözüm* "my eye", *gözlerim* "my eyes" etc.; *dostumuz* "our friend", etc.). The sequence of morphemes seen in (9) can be visualized in Figure 8.4. The forms which do not have a plural suffix intervening between the lexical root and the case/possessive suffix exhibit the type of allomorphy shown in Figure 8.5. This type of allomorphy is frequently referred to as **four-way vowel harmony**. If the plural suffix intervenes only **two-way vowel harmony** results as shown in Figure 8.6. We may wish to formalize these conclusions. First, we have to express the eight vocalic phonemes of Turkish as 'bundles' of three distinctive features; this is shown in Figure 8.7.

As we saw above, the suffixes undergoing the four-way vowel (Poss Pl_2) $\begin{Bmatrix} \text{Gen} \\ \text{Acc} \end{Bmatrix}$ harmony have to agree with the preceding vowel in two features, namely backness and roundness (the feature of height is irrelevant, i.e., it does not matter if the preceding vowel is *i* or *e*, the vowel of the suffix has to be *i* etc.). Thus in (10) we write the four rules of agreement in two features.

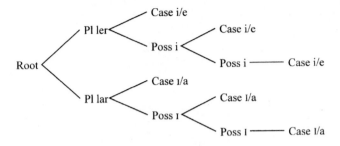

Fig. 8.6 Turkish two-way vowel harmony

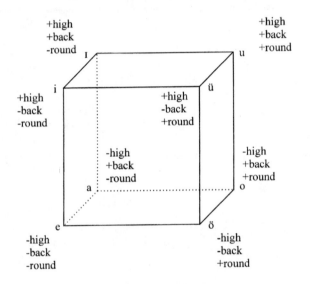

Fig. 8.7 Turkish vowels

(10)   (i, ü, ı, u) →   (i)   (i, e)
              V   V

         [+high] → $\begin{bmatrix} -back \\ -round \end{bmatrix}$ / $\begin{bmatrix} -back \\ -round \end{bmatrix}$ $C_o + C_o$ —

                       (ü)   (ü, ö)
                                     V

                  → $\begin{bmatrix} -back \\ +round \end{bmatrix}$ / $\begin{bmatrix} -back \\ +round \end{bmatrix}$ $C_o + C_o$ —

$$(\textsc{i}) \qquad\qquad (\textsc{i, a})$$

$$\rightarrow \begin{bmatrix} +\text{back} \\ -\text{round} \end{bmatrix} \Big/ \overset{V}{\begin{bmatrix} +\text{back} \\ -\text{round} \end{bmatrix}} C_0 + C_0 \text{ ——}$$

$$(\text{u}) \qquad\qquad (\text{u, o})$$

$$\rightarrow \begin{bmatrix} +\text{back} \\ +\text{round} \end{bmatrix} \Big/ \overset{V}{\begin{bmatrix} +\text{back} \\ +\text{round} \end{bmatrix}} C_0 + C_0 \text{ ——}$$

Using the usual conventions of Generative Phonology we may collapse these four rules into a single rule:

$$\overset{V}{[+\text{high}]} \rightarrow \begin{bmatrix} \alpha \text{ back} \\ \beta \text{ round} \end{bmatrix} \Big/ \begin{bmatrix} \alpha \text{ back} \\ \beta \text{ round} \end{bmatrix} C_0 + C_0 \text{ ——}$$

The suffixes undergoing the two-way vowel harmony $(P1_1 \left\{ \begin{matrix} \text{Dat} \\ \text{Loc} \\ \text{Abl} \end{matrix} \right\})$ have to agree with the preceding vowel in a single feature, namely backness. We may write the following two rules of agreement:

$$(11) \qquad (\text{e,a}) \qquad \rightarrow \qquad (\text{e}) \qquad\quad (\text{i, e, ü, ö})$$

$$\overset{V}{\begin{bmatrix} +\text{high} \\ -\text{round} \end{bmatrix}} \rightarrow [-\text{back}] \Big/ \overset{V}{[-\text{back}]} \ C_0 + C_0 \text{ ——}$$

$$(\text{a}) \qquad\quad (\textsc{i, a, u, o})$$

$$\rightarrow [+\text{back}] \Big/ \overset{V}{[+\text{back}]} \ C_0 + C_0 \text{ ——}$$

These two rules may be collapsed into a single rule given below:

$$(12) \qquad \overset{V}{\begin{bmatrix} +\text{high} \\ -\text{round} \end{bmatrix}} \rightarrow [\alpha \text{ back}] \Big/ \overset{V}{[\alpha \text{ back}]} \ C_0 + C_0 \text{ ——}$$

Our story would be incomplete without discussing exceptions to the rules of vowel harmony. This means preparing a list of morphemes after which suffixes do not undergo the changes predicted by the rules above. Some examples follow.

(i)   Arabic or French words ending in clear *l* [l]: e.g. *mahsul* "produce" forms its accusative
        mahsulü, not according to the rules of vowel harmony which would give: **mahsulu*;
(ii)   Arabic words ending in *k*: *idrak* "perception" forms its accusative *idraki*, instead of the
        predicted **idrakı*;
(iii)   Arabic monosyllabic words with an *a* followed by two consonants (the second of which
        is a front consonant): *harp* "war" forms its accusative *harbi*, not **harbı*.

There are exceptions to the rules of vowel harmony even among native Turkish words. For
instance, the following simple words contain both back and front vowels: *elma* "apple", *kardeş*
"brother". Examples can also be found among compound words: *bu* "this" + *gün* "day" → *bugün*
"today" (*bügün* can be heard sometimes), *baş* "head" + *müfettiş* "inspector" → *başmüfettiş* "chief
inspector". Many loanwords do not show any effects of vowel harmony: *mikrop* (< French)
"microbe", *feribot* (< English) "ferry boat" *piskopos* (< Greek) "bishop". On the other hand, many
loanwords have been turkicized by undergoing vowel harmony: Arabic *mumkin* "possible" >
Turkish *mümkin* > *mümkün*; French *épaulette* > Turkish *apolet* (see Lewis 1967 for more
examples).

8.4 *Morphonology*

The term **morphonology** was proposed 70 years ago by Trubetzkoy (1929). For Trubetzkoy
morphonology was a particular section of linguistic descriptions (distinct from phonology dealing
with the system of phonemes and distinct from morphology dealing with the system of
morphemes) which studies the morphological utilization of phonological differences (1929:85).
To use Trubetzkoy's example, in the Russian words *ruká* "hand" and *ručnój* "manual" the
allomorphs /ruk/ and /ruč/ represent one morpheme. These two allomorphs are held together on
the phonological side by the regular alternation *k ~ č* (regular means that there are more instances
such as *óko* "eye" *óčnyj* "ocular", *kulák* "fist" *kuláčnyj* "having to do with the fist") and they are
linked to the same semantic unit (the perusal of similar numerous examples would reveal that we
are dealing with a productive process of the forming of derived adjectives from nouns).
According to Trubetzkoy /ruk/ and /ruč/ represent one morpheme "which exists in linguistic
consciousness ... in the form *ruk/č*, where *k/č*, is a complex unit". Thus morphophonemes, in
contrast to phonemes which are of strictly unitary nature, are complex units of two (or more)
phonemes capable of alternating in one and the same morpheme. That /k/ and /č/ are two distinct
phonemes of Russian can be shown easily by minimal pairs such as *kumá* "godmother" vs. *čumá*
"plague". Furthermore, it is not the phonetic context of the derivational suffix *-no/ny* that
'changes' the /k/ of *ruká* into the /č/ of *ručnój*, since /k/ is retained in *oknó* "window". This of
course is not to say that all of the alternations *k ~ č* are of a morphophonemic nature; for example,
we are dealing with true phonological conditioning in the verbal set of *skakát'* "to spring": *skakál*
"he used to spring" vs. *skáčeš* "you spring," *skáčet* "he springs" (here *k* →*č* before front vowel
e). A problem, however, arises if we examine other inflectional forms of *ruká*; for instance, the

Dat Sg is [ruk'é] which has to be phonemicized as /ruké/ — here the [k] of [ruká] alternates with [k'] of [ruk'é] in the same phonetic environment of the front vowel e (k → k' / -e). This is why some linguists would prefer to consider even the above alternation of ruká ~ ručnój as phonologically conditioned. This assumption, however, necessitates the introduction of very abstract underlying representations such as /ruk + in + oj/ from which the correct phonetic form [ručnój] has to be derived by means of **morphophonemic rules**, bypassing the phonemic level of representation. Thus more recently the classical phonemics /k/ = [k] ~ [k'] ~ [č] and morphophonemics (morphonology) {k} = /k/ ~ /č/ have been collapsed in **Generative Phonology**, which named Trubetzkoy's morphophoneme **systematic phoneme**. The latter is a building unit of **underlying representations**. The underlying representation contains only part of the information about the pronunciation of the morpheme stored in the lexicon, and the other aspects of pronunciation are determined by phonological rules which apply to morphemes of the language. Thus the pronunciation of /ruk + in + oj/ is determined by at least two phonological rules: the rule which palatalizes and affricates k before the front vowel i and the rule which subsequently deletes i after it has triggered the palatalization and affrication:

(13)   ruk - in - ój
        palatalization/affrication   č
        deletion   Ø
        phonetic output   [ručnój]

Needless to say, this type of analysis cannot be considered as truly synchronic analysis in terms of 'here and now'. The alternation of k ~ č in ruká ~ ručnój is only a legacy of diachrony which cannot be explained phonetically except by reference to conditions which have become obsolete for many centuries; the derivational suffix -in was a productive suffix in prehistoric times (cf. Greek phēgós "beech" and its adjectival derivative phēginos) but its high front vowel was reduced to schwa and subsequently lost in Modern Russian.

To use an example from a Romance language. Are we dealing with purely phonogical conditioning in the case of Italian amico "friend" [amiko] whose root is pronounced [amič] before the plural suffix -i? There are hundreds of words undergoing the same change: medico "doctor", medici; civico "urban", civici, etc. However, Italians have no difficulty in pronouncing k before the same plural form i: stomaco "stomach", stomachi [stomaki], antico "ancient", antichi [antiki]. Since /k/ and /č/ are two distinct phonemes of Italian, how do we explain this alternation? The usual explanation has to do with the accent pattern — the words which are accented on their penultimate syllable keep their velar consonants (k, g) unchanged before the plural suffix, whereas those accented on the antepenult show the effects of palatalization (č, ǰ). Consider the following data:

(14) Penultimate Stress　　　　　　　　Antepenultimate Stress

fuóco	"fire"	fuóchi	médico	"doctor"	médici
antíco	"ancient"	antíchi	mónaco	"monk"	mónaci
lágo	"lake"	lághi	magnífico	"magnificent"	magnífici
albérgo	"hotel"	albérghi			

There are, however, several exceptions to these accentual rules. The words *amíco, nemíco* "enemy", *pórco* "pig" and *Gréco* "Greek" although accented on the penult palatalize the velar consonant; on the other hand, *stómaco* "stomach" and *cárico* "load", although accented on the antepenult, do not palatalize their velar consonant before *-i*.

Another typical morphophonemic alternation exists between a voiceless consonant and its voiced counterpart. The familiar examples come from English which has the alternation between /f/ and /v/ in the forms *knife/knives, wife/wives, leaf/leaves* etc. Here the morphophoneme {f} is realized as /f/ in the allomorph /najf/ occurring in the singular, and as /v/ in the allomorph /najv/ occurring in the plural. In German *Rat* "advice" and *Rad* "wheel" are both represented phonemically as /ra:t/ (as is well-known, in German voiced obstruents are devoiced syllable-finally). However, this analysis fails to account for the fact that /ra:t/ "advice" alternates in the plural with /re:tə/, while /ra:t/ "wheel" alternates with /re:dər/. In the second word *t* is a morphophoneme {t} which is realized as /t/ in the singular but as /d/ in the plural. This analysis is open to objections if we want to pay due attention to the facts of morphology. If we consider the whole paradigm of *Rad* "wheel" we have to conclude that the form with a final /t/ is a minor variant in that it occurs only in the Nom/Acc Sg whereas in the remaining six forms exhibiting suffixes *-es, -e, -er, -ern* the vowel of the suffix does not allow for the devoicing. Even better examples would come from Slavic languages which have longer nominal paradigms. For instance, to insist that the morphophonemic representation of Russian *dub* "oak" is {dup} (Russian has the same rule of devoicing voiced obstruents syllable-finally as German) is strange given the fact that the remaining ten members of the inflectional paradigm contain *b* before a vowel (*dubá* Gen Sg, *dubú* Dat Sg, *dubóm* Instr Sg, *dubé* Loc Sg, *dubý* Nom Pl, etc). Thus we may favor process-analysis which would derive a phonetic representation [dup] from the morphological representation {dub} by means of the rule of devoicing *b* → *p* before word or morpheme boundary. The fruitfulness of this approach may be demonstrated by working out a solution of more complicated data such as the following from Latin. Latin verbs belonging to the 3rd conjugation show two allomorphs of the verbal root: one with the voiced obstruent /g/ in the infinitive and another one with the voiceless /k/ in the passive participle:

(15)
agere	"act"	āctus
legere	"read"	lēctus
frangere	"break"	frāctus
pangere	"fix"	pāctus

fingere	"create"	fictus
pingere	"paint"	pictus
pungere	"hit"	pūnctus
cingere	"gird"	cīnctus

Given the fact that the form with /g/ is a major variant we may attempt to account for the form with /k/ by deriving it from underlying {agtus}. We will need the rule devoicing the root-final consonant g in the cluster -gt- and the rule of **compensatory lengthening** (compensating for the loss of voice). Furthermore some forms simplify the cluster nkt by losing the nasal: nkt → kt. Thus the process description of these forms can be elaborated along these lines:

(16)		ag-tus	frang-tus	fing-tus	cing-tus
	Cluster Simplification	-	Ø	Ø	-
	Devoicing	k	k	k	k
	Compensatory lengthening	ā	ā	-	ī
		āktus	frāktus	fiktus	cīnktus

RECOMMENDED READINGS

Anderson, Stephen R. 1985. *Phonology in the Twentieth Century*. Chicago: University of Chicago Press.

Bloomfield, Leonard. 1935. *Language*. London: Allen and Unwin. (Revised edition.) (Chapter 13).

Dressler, Wolfgang U. 1985. *Morphonology: The Dynamics of Derivation*. Ann Arbor: Karoma Publishers.

Gleason, H. A. 1961. *An Introduction to Descriptive Linguistic*. New York: Holt, Rinehart and Winston. (Revised edition.)

Hockett, Charles F. 1958. *A Course in Modern Linguistics*. New York: The Macmillan Company (Chapters 32–35).

Hyman, Larry M. 1975. *Phonology: Theory and Analysis*. New York: Holt, Rinehart and Winston. (Chapter 3).

Lewis, Geoffrey L. 1967. *Turkish Grammar*. Oxford: Clarendon Press.

Martinet, André. 1965. "De la morphonologie". *La linguistique* 1.16–31.

Trubetzkoy, Nikolai S. 1929. "Sur la morphonologie". *Travaux du cercle linguistique de Prague*. 1.85–88.

_____. 1934. "Das morphonologische System der russichen Sprache". *Travaux du cercle linguistique de Prague*. Volume 5, Part 2.

EXERCISES

1. Describe the allomorphy in Sanskrit verbal forms whose stem contains a nasal infix (in the present and the imperfect): *yṇj̊-* "to join". The root is seen in the passive participle: *yuk+tá* "joined".

Present Sg	1	yunájmi "I join"	Imperfect	áyunajam
	2	yunákṣi		áyunak
	3	yunákti		áyunak
Pl	1	yuṇjmás		áyuṇjma
	2	yuŋkthá		áyuŋkta
	3	yuṇjánti		áyuṇjan

2. Describe the allomorphy seen in the nouns whose stem is formed by *-an(t)* in Vedic Sanskrit. Monosyllabic nouns are to be taken as a basis for your predictions regarding the location of accent.

	"king"	"soul"	"eating"	"voice"
Sg Nom	rájā	ātmā́	adán	vā́k
Acc	rájānam	ātmā́nam	adántam	vā́cam
Instr	rájñā	ātmánā	adatā́	vācā́
Dat	rájñe	ātmáne	adaté	vācé
Gen	rájñas	ātmánas	adatás	vācás
Loc	rájñi	ātmáni	adatí	vācí
Pl Nom	rájānas	ātmā́nas	adántas	vā́cas
Acc	rájñas	ātmā́nas	adatás	vācás
Instr	rájabhis	ātmábhis	adábhis	vāgbhís
Dat	rájabhyas	ātmábhyas	adádbhyas	vāgbhyás
Gen	rájñām	ātmánām	adatā́m	vācā́m
Loc	rájasu	ātmásu	adátsu	vākṣú

(a) Start by identifying the roots, the stem-forming elements and the suffixes.

(b) Specify the distribution of allomorphs of individual stems.

(c) Apply the IP model, i.e., specify the phonological and morphological conditioning which account for the shape of the allomorphs of the stems.

3. Describe and try to explain as best as you can morphophonemic variants of the root in the following sets of Hebrew nominal forms:

I.

(1) nāβī́   "prophet"
(2) nəβī́ʔí   "my prophet"
(3) nəβīʔəxém   "your (Pl) prophet"
(4) nəβīʔím   "prophets"
(5) nəβīʔēxém   "your (Pl) prophets"

II.

(1) dāβ́ar   "word"
(2) dəβārí   "my word"
(3) dəβarxém   "your (Pl) word"
(4) dəβārím   "words"
(5) diβrēxém   "your (Pl) words"

III.

(1) mélex   "king"
(2) malkí   "my king"
(3) malkəxém   "your (Pl) king"
(4) məlāxím   "kings"
(5) malxēxém   "your kings"

4. Describe and try to explain as best as you can morphophonemic variation in the following set of Latin verbal forms:

1st Sg Present		1st Sg Perfect
(1) vertō	"turn"	vertī
(2) fodiō	"dig"	fōdī
(3) fundō	"pour"	fūdī
(4) rumpō	"break"	rūpī
(5) findō	"split"	fidī
(6) scindō	"split"	scidī
(7) dēfendō	"protect"	dēfendī
(8) prehendō	"grasp"	prehendī

CHAPTER NINE
DERIVATIONAL MORPHOLOGY

9.1 *Theory of Word Formation*

Word formation may be defined as that branch of linguistics which "studies the patterns on which a language forms new lexical units, i.e. words" (Marchand, 1969:2). According to Marchand, word formation is concerned only with **composites** or **complex lexemes** (**derivatives and compounds**) and not with simple one-morpheme words which are the subject matter of lexology and morphology. For instance, simple nouns and verbs such as *brain*, *bird* and *make* can be studied morphologically (as shown in Chapters Five and Six), but not derivationally since these words are not composites. On the other hand, their derivatives such as *brain-y* (formed by suffixation) or *re-make* (formed by prefixation) or compounds such as *bird-brain* may be studied derivationally for their motivation, semantic restriction, etc. For reasons given under 4.1 we cannot consider word formation either as a part of inflectional morphology or as a part of the lexicon as suggested by generative-lexicalists such as Chomsky (1970) and Aronoff (1976). The most obvious counter-argument to the latter hypothesis comes from polysynthetic languages (such as Inuktitut or Ainu) where lexicalists have to store whole sentences in the lexicon in order to account for 'sentence-words'.

An interesting article was devoted to this problem by M. Halle (1973) who entertains the following model of the coexistence of morphology and lexology; see Figure 9.1. However, a closer scrutiny of Halle's article will reveal that Halle did not distinguish clearly between inflectional and derivational morphology (p. 7, "the rules of word formation generate the inflected forms"). This confusion is, of course, a result of handling both inflectional and derivational morphology by means of an oversized transformational component (or, in other words, of handling morphology syntactically). Hence, Halle's attempt to accommodate both inflectional and derivational morphology in the dictionary: (i) the dictionary contains only (and all) fully inflected forms of the language, (ii) the dictionary must be organized into derivational paradigms. Thus, according to Halle, the lexical entries for WRITE and PLAY are organized along these lines:

		Inflected Forms
		- ->
	WRITE	write, writes, wrote, writing, written
derivatives	rewrite	write, writes, wrote, writing, written
"	writer	writers

(1)

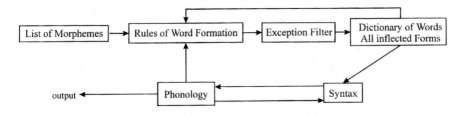

Fig. 9.1 Word formation according to Halle (1973)

	PLAY	play, plays, played, playing
derivatives	replay	play, plays, played, playing
"	player	players

Obviously, the first proposal, which de facto enshrines the grammar in the lexicon, would be highly impractical in the case of heavily flective languages where the number of inflections may run into the hundreds (versus 5 inflections of English, 11 inflections of French). Furthermore, the functioning of the 'exception filter' (corresponding essentially to the lists of exceptions in traditional grammars) is surrounded by uncertainty. The second assumption that the dictionary must be organized into **derivational paradigms** is nothing new. Dictionaries of Sanskrit and Arabic were organized in this fashion centuries ago. We may examine the lexical entry for *barad* "be or become cold" in any traditional dictionary of Arabic (i.e. any dictionary which has not been organized alphabetically in imitation of dictionaries of European languages):

(2) | barad | "be or become cold" | (Verb, Class I) |
     |----------|-------------------------------|-----------------------------------|
     | bard | "coldness" | (Verbal Noun, Class I) |
     | barad | "hail" | (Verbal Noun, Class I) |
     | burūd | "coldness, frigidity" | (Verbal Noun, Class I) |
     | barrād | "refrigerator" | (Occupational Noun, see 9.5) |
     | bārid | "cold" | (Adjective = Participle, Class I) |
     | barrad | "make cold, cool" | (Verb, Class II = Causative) |
     | tabrīd | "cooling" | (Verbal Noun, Class II) |
     | mubarrid | "cooling, refreshing" | (Participete, Class II) |
     | ?abrad | "enter upon the cold season" | (Verb, Class IV) |
     | tabarrad | "refresh oneself" | (Verb, Class V) |
     | ?ibtarad | "become cold" | (Verb, Class VIII) |

Actually the first information given will be a vowel in the stem of the imperfective:

(3) barada   (u)   bard

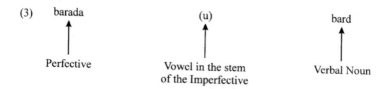

Perfective   Vowel in the stem   Verbal Noun
of the Imperfective

This, of course, is far from including 'only (and all) fully inflected forms' in the dictionary, since all these forms will have to appear in the grammar. Thus the grammar of Arabic — not its lexicon — contains the information on deictic categories of person (1, 2 and 3) and the category of number (Sg, Dual and Pl). All this seems to be rather too obvious, but let us recall the fact that the morphology of tense and aspect is a grammatical (not lexical) issue in a variety of languages. However, the latter (actually the **Aktionsart**, i.e., lexical aspect) has to be handled in the dictionary in the case of Slavic languages. Since Semitic languages collapse aspect and tense, both will appear in the dictionary:

(4) barada   (-brud-)

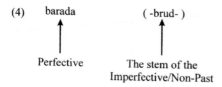

Perfective   The stem of the
Imperfective/Non-Past

Similarly, the dictionary of Russian will have to list the perfective counterpart of the verb *bit'* "to beat" since its lexical meaning has changed: *u-bit'* "to kill".

9.2 Derivation versus Compounding

A **derivative** (derived or complex lexeme) is a lexeme whose stem is formed from a simpler stem (derivational base) by some kind of morphological modification (most commonly **affixation**). For instance, the English suffix *-ic* derives denominal adjectives as in *democrat* → *democratic*. A **compound**, on the other hand, is a lexeme whose stem is formed by combining two or more stems (which may be separated by an **interfix** (cf. 2.3) as in *huntsman*). For instance, *blackbird* is a compound lexeme whose stem is formed by combining the adjective *black* and the noun *bird*.

According to Marchand (1969:11) the coining of new words proceeds by way of "combining linguistic elements on the basis of a determinant/determinatum relationship called syntagma". In terms of semantics, the **determinatum** represents that member of the composite lexeme which is modified or rather 'determined' by the **determinant**. For instance, in the composite lexeme *steamboat* the basic word *boat* underwent a semantic restriction or **determination** by the determinant *steam*. Marchand uses the same categories for the analysis of derivatives where the determinatum is the derivational suffix; in his words, derivation is "the transposition of a word to the role of determinant in a syntagma where the determinatum is a dependent morpheme" (p. 13). Whereas in the compound *steamboat* the determinatum was a noun *boat*, in the derivative *steamer* the determinatum is a derivational suffix *-er*. On the other hand, derivational prefixes have to be classified as determinants; *anti-* in *antifascist* determines the determinatum *fascist*.

Traditionally, the area of word formation was treated as consisting of **derivation** and **compounding**. The former was subclassified according to whether the derivational affix was prefixed or suffixed in **prefixation** and **suffixation**, shown in Figure 9.2.

However, as was shown by Marchand (1969:11), it is possible to regroup this traditional schema by subsuming prefixation and compounding under one heading of **expansion**. Marchand defines the expansion as "a combination AB in which B is a free morpheme (word) and which is analysable on the basis of the formula AB = B". This means that AB (*black-bird*, *counter-attack*) belongs to the same lexical class to which B (*bird*, *attack*) belongs. Put differently, compounds and prefixed words share the 'expanding' of the free determinatum:

(5)		Determinant	Determinatum
	Compound	free morpheme	free morpheme
		black	*bird*
	Derivative	bound morpheme	free morpheme
	prefixed word	*fore*	*see*
	suffixed word	free morpheme	bound morpheme
		king	*dom*

Consequently, we may wish to keep the term derivative only to derivatives formed by suffixation (deriving by bound morphemes), as shown in Figure 9.3. This reasoning may be supported on semantic grounds. As recognized by traditional grammarians, an important difference between prefixes and suffixes lies in the fact that the former have a distinct meaning of their own (even if they are not used as independent words), whereas the latter do not. Of course, there are exceptions on both sides. The prefixes *a-* [ə] and *be-* appear to have no distinct meaning of their own and to serve only as means of transferring a word from one lexical category to another. The former derives predicative adjectives from intransitive verbs (*He is asleep*) and the latter derives transitive verbs from nouns, adjectives and verbs (*bespectacled*, *belittle*, *bemoan*). On the other hand, the meaning of suffixes is usually best described grammatically; many suffixes convert one part of speech into another, e.g. *kind* → *kindness*. It is rather exceptional to find a suffix which modifies the lexical meaning of its determinant; for instance, the suffix *-ish* added to adjectives denoting color changes their lexical meaning from "X" into "rather X": *blue* → *bluish*.

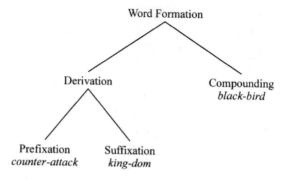

Fig. 9.2 Word formation

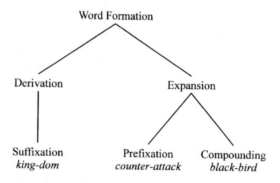

Fig. 9.3 Word formation according to Marchand (1969)

9.3.1 *Prefixation*

Prefixes may be defined as bound morphemes which are preposed to free (or bound) morphemes. As mentioned under 9.2, they function as determinants of the words (or bound stems) to which they are prefixed. For instance, the adjective *natural* may serve as a determinatum in various derivatives such as *un-natural, super-natural* and *counter-natural*. The bound stem *-fer* may serve as a determinatum in *re-fer, de-fer,* and *pre-fer*. Prefixes *un-, super-, counter-* are taken from the list of English prefixes which may be studied for their origin and **productivity** in various grammars in English. The list of productive English prefixes, taken from Zandvoort (1966:291–298), is reproduced in (6).

As is well known, almost all productive ('living') English prefixes are of non-Germanic origin, with the exception of *a-* (in *asleep*), *be-, fore-, mis-* and *un-; for-* as in *forget* and *with-* as in *withhold* are usually not included since these words are synchronically unanalyzable. It can be observed that negative *a-, auto-, hyper-,* and *mal-* combine only with non-Germanic words,

(6)   English prefixes:

a- [ə]	adrift, asleep, awash, a-flicker
a- [ɛɪ]	amoral, asexual
ante-	anteroom, antediluvian
anti-	antichrist, anti-aircraft
arch-	archbishop, arch-enemy
auto-	automobile, autobiography
be-	bespectacled, besmear
bi-	bilingual, bisexual
co-	co-operate, co-education
counter-	counter-attack, counteract
de-	decode, defrost, dehumanize
dis-	dishonour, disagree
en-, em-	embed, endanger, enslave
ex-	ex-premier, ex-service man
extra-	extraordinary, extra-mural
fore-	foreground, foreword, foresee
hyper-	hyper-critical, hyper-sensitive
in-, im-, il-, ir-	inaudible, impolite, illegible, irreligious
inter-	international, interschool
mal-	maladjustment, malodorous
mis-	mislead, misconduct
non-	non-payment, non-existent
post-	post-war, post-reformation
pre-	predate, pre-war (cf. premature)
pro-	pro-German (cf. propel)
re-	rebuild, refuel, rebirth (cf. remain, remote, recover)
semi-	semivowel, semicircle
sub-	submarine, subway
super-	supermarket, superstructure
trans-	transalpine, transplant
ultra-	ultra-violet, ultra-conservative
un-	unhappy, unkind, unrest, undress, unearth

whereas the rest combines with both Germanic and non-Germanic words. However, this type of study of derivational morphology belongs rather to diachrony. Synchronically, linguists are interested in semantic restrictions on combinability of various prefixes with various lexical classes (nouns, verbs, adjectives, adverbs). Why is it, for instance, that we may combine the prefix re- with both free stems and bound stems (such as -fer and -mit) but the prefix fore- only with free stems? Furthermore, we may combine sub- with -mit but not with -fer. To facilitate the study of these restrictions linguists construct various **derivational paradigms**. The following paradigm of the latinate verbs is taken from Aronoff (1976:12) and it includes only verbs which are stressed on the stem such as: refér, excluding verbs stressed on the prefix such as: súffer. (In the system of Sound Pattern of English by N. Chomsky and M. Halle this class is marked phonologically by the presence of a special boundary symbolized as =):

(7) Derivational Paradigm of Latinate Verbs

X=fer	X=mit	X=sume	X=ceive	X=duce
refer	remit	resume	receive	reduce
defer	demit		deceive	deduce
prefer		presume		
infer				induce
confer	commit	consume	conceive	conduce
transfer	transmit			transduce
	submit	subsume		
	admit	assume		adduce
	permit		perceive	

Aronoff uses this data to demonstrate that neither the prefix nor the stem has any 'fixed meaning'. Obviously, this statement is only half-true since we may establish a 'basic' meaning of some of these prefixes and bound stems. It seems reasonable to assume that the basic meaning of trans- is "across, beyond, through" (transfer "move from X to Y, transmit" (make) pass on/along", transduce "draw across"). Similarly, we may assume that the basic meaning of -fer is "give, bring, send" (confer "give, grant", transfer "send across", defer "delay, postpone"). We could proceed along these lines with certain other words from the chart. However, this analysis would be impossible in other cases when the meaning is too abstract; prefer "like better" is obviously difficult to analyze in this vein. Thus we have to assume that in some cases the meaning of the verb is associated with the whole lexeme. There is nothing particularly disturbing on this solution and English offers a host of similar examples of morphological opacity. To exemplify this phenomenon with native words we may try to analyze compounds with a determinatum -berry such as cranberry, strawberry, raspberry, blackberry, blueberry, gooseberry. It is no problem to identify determinants in these compounds but their semantic analysis is another problem. Cran- does not occur independently in Standard English or in other compounds and blackberries can be green or red. Does anybody connect geese and gooseberries or straw and strawberries? We have to simply acknowledge that cran- and similar bound morphemes are **semi-morphemic** elements since the usual definition of morpheme as a meaningful element (or more precisely the element connected with a particular sememe) does not hold. However, they are morphemes as distributional elements.

9.3.2 *Suffixation*

Suffixes may be defined as bound morphemes which are postposed to free morphemes. As mentioned under 9.2, they function as determinata of simple or composite (i.e. compound or derivative) free morphemes: *king-dom, color-blind-ness, dis-agree-ment*. Their origin and productivity may be studied in various grammars of English or in the study by Marchand (1969). For practical purposes, it is important to distinguish between two types of derivation by means of suffixation: (1) suffixation on a **native base** and (ii) suffixation on a **foreign base** (also called Neo-Latin base). The former method can be subdivided as follows (Marchand, 1969:215):

(a) Derivation by native suffixes (*good* → *goodness*) with no allomorphy.

(b) Derivation by imported suffixes (*love* → *lovable*) with no allomorphy.

(c) Derivation by imported suffixes involving allomorphy: *históric* → *historícity, áble* → *abílity*.

The latter method can be subdivided as follows:

(d) The suffix is added to a Latin stem which closely resembles a word that exists is English: *scient-* → *scientist* (cf. *science*).

(e) The suffix is added to a Latin (or Greek) stem which has no adopted English equivalent: *lingu-* → *lingual, chron-* → *chronic* (but see *crony* "an old chum").

A more traditional distinction would be simply (i) derivation by means of native suffixes and (ii) derivation by means of foreign suffixes — the latter being divided into suffixation on either native or foreign bases. (It may be noted that both approaches combine synchrony and diachrony).

Another subdivision of suffixation is based on the resulting grammatical category; thus we may distinguish suffixes deriving nouns, adjectives, verbs and adverbs. The list of the productive English suffixes shown in (8) was adopted from Zandvoort (1966:299–322).

(8) (i) Suffixes deriving nouns:

(a) **Personal** and **concrete non-personal nouns**

-ee	addressee, employee
-eer	mountaineer, profiteer
-er	hunter, writer, rooster, boiler
-ess	hostess, murderess, actress, lioness

-ist	violinist, copyist, loyalist
-ite	Sybarite, Wagnerite
-ster	gangster, trickster, songster

(b) **Diminutives**

-et(te)	kitchenette, owlet, islet
-ie/y	Annie, Johnny, piggie, doggie
-kin	catkin, lambkin
-let	booklet, leaflet, ringlet, piglet
-ling	duckling, fledgeling, weakling, gosling

(c) **Abstract** and **collective nouns**

-age	mil(e)age, orphanage, drainage, percentage
-al	approval, arrival
-(i)ana	Shakesperiana, Newfoundlandiana
-ance	furtherance, utterance
-ation	starvation, sedimentation
-cy	accuracy, diplomacy
-dom	dukedom, freedom, kingdom
-hood	childhood, neighbourhood
-head	godhead, maidenhead
-ing	bedding, matting
-ism	despotism, Calvinism, Americanism
-itis	appendicitis
-ity	identity, visibility
-ment	shipment, deferment
-ness	drunkenness, foolishness
-(e)ry	rivalry, chemistry, nursery
-ship	friendship, scholarship

(ii) Suffixes deriving **adjectives**:

-able	breakable, eatable
(ible)	convertible, discernible
-al	cultural, musical
-an	Indian, Lutheran
-ed	landed, wooded, blue-eyed

-en	wooden, earthen
-ese	Chinese, Viennese
-esque	Dantesque, picturesque
-fold	twofold, manifold
-ful	beautiful, cheerful
-ian	Dickensian, Shavian, Canadian
-ic	emphatic, phonetic, classic, historic
-ical	classical, historical
-ing	amusing, charming
-ish	Danish, Jewish, girlish
-ive	attractive, instructive
-less	endless, countless
-like	childlike, heartlike
-ly	lovely, manly, deadly
-ous	dangerous, mountainous
-some	troublesome, toothsome
-th	fourth, sixth
-ward	backward, forward, inward, outward
-y	noisy, catchy, empty

(iii) Suffixes deriving **verbs**

-en	blacken, darken, worsen
-fy	certify, satisfy
-ize	civilize, organize

(iv) Suffixes deriving **adverbs**

-ly	greatly, namely
-ways	lengthways, sideways
-wise	lengthwise, sidewise

9.4 *Compounding*

In discussing the status of compounds, linguists usually rely on three criteria: the **underlying concept**, **stress** and **spelling**. However, all these three criteria are notoriously unreliable as the perusal of various treatments of compounding may demonstrate. For instance, H. Koziol, the author of the first monograph on English word formation, published in 1937 in German, claims that the criterion of a compound is the psychological unity of a combination. Obviously, even syntactic groups such as *the Holy Roman Catholic Church* may function as psychological units and thus it is extremely difficult, if not impossible, to establish a clear cut distinction between a **compound** and a **syntactic group**. Stress has been used as a criterion by Bloomfield (1935:228): "Accordingly, wherever we hear lesser or least stress upon a word which would always show high stress in a phrase, we describe it as a compound member: *ice-cream* /ˈajs-ˌkrijm/ is a compound, but *ice cream* /ˈajs ˈkrijm/ is a phrase, although there is no denotative difference of meaning". The criterion of stress was rejected by Jespersen (1942:8.12): "If we stuck to the criterion of stress, we should have to refuse the name of compound to a large group of two-linked phrases that are generally called so, such as *headmaster* or *stone wall*". The spelling is, of course, the worst criterion, since some compounds are hyphenated, others are not, and others are spelled with no separation between the constituents, e.g. *gold-tail, stone wall, blackbird*. Perhaps the two-stressed syntactic groups (*stone wall, paper bag*, etc.) should be excluded from word formation. However, it is of interest to note that many such combinations have developed forestress (e.g. *bóy friend, mánservant*). Furthermore, they may be classified as compounds in languages which indulge in compounding more than English does. Thus *Steinmauer* "stone wall" is classified as a compound in German but *stone wall* is rather a syntactic group in English.

Compounds are usually studied according to their membership in the parts of speech (as given by their determinatum): (i) compound nouns (*steamboat, blackbird*) (ii) compound adjectives (*color-blind, heart-breaking*) and (iii) compounds verbs (*outbid, overflow, undertake*). There are also compound pronouns (*myself*) adverbs (*somewhere*), prepositions (*into*), conjunctions (*whenever*) and interjections (*heigh-ho*). However, in this book a different type of classification will be adopted — that which was elaborated centuries ago by Hindu grammarians:

(i)   **Coordinate compounds**
(ii)   **Determinative compounds** (these can be of two types — subordinate or descriptive)
(iii)   **Possessive compounds**
(iv)   **Syntactic compounds**

9.4.1 *Coordinate Compounds*

Some **coordinate compounds** are **additive**. In modern languages this relationship obtains most typically in numerals; for instance, *fourteen* is "four" + "ten" (we may note that on the phonological side these numerals may be realized with double stress /fɔ́rtín/ or single final stress /fɔrtín/). Hindu grammarians applied the term *dvandva* to this type of compound. This term translates literally "two" + "two" but it means "pair" or "couple". This 'illogicality' is explained by the fact that in Rigvedic compounds of this type (nearly always names of deities) each member of the compound is formally dual. For instance, *mitrá-váruṇā* means "Mitra and Varuna" (= twin deities) and not, as morphology suggests, *"two Mitras and two Varunas" (singular *Mitrás*, Rigvedic dual *Mitrā́*). Similarly *mātarā-pitarā* means "mother and father" even if morphologically we are dealing with two duals. More 'logical' compounds of this type appear in later post-Vedic documents, for instance, *indra-vāyū́* "Indra and Vaya" where the first member of the compound assumes the form of the stem and the second member takes the dual from (singular *Vāyús*, plural *Vāyū́*). It is also notable that at this stage the first member of the compound loses its stress (compare English /fɔ́rtín/ or /fɔrtín/). More complicated examples to analyze are pluralized coordinate compounds. They are formed when the pair of groups is to be denoted; for instance, *ajā́váyas* means "(the flock of) goats and (the flock of) sheep". 'Illogically', they show the stem-form in the first-member and the plural form in the second-member (the accent is on the final syllable of the second member *avís* "sleep"). There are other types of relationships which may be found in coordinate compounds. For instance, English *bitter-sweet* means roughly "sweet with an admixture or aftertaste of bitterness" (OED). Here we are not dealing with a pair but with a mixture of two properties (one being predominant). Similarly, in religious terminology *God-man* (German *Gottmensch*, French *Homme-Dieu*, all of them calqued on Greek *theánthrōpos*) denotes someone who is both God and man, i.e., a mixture of two properties one being predominant). Religious terminology of Hinduism abounds in terms such as *Hari-Hara* (Vishnu-Shiva), *Ardhanārīśvara* (Hermaphrodite Lord) and *Sūrya-Candra* (sun-moon). The deity known as Hari-Hara was represented with Shiva characteristics for the right side of the body (trident in his hand, snakes on his arms, etc.) and with Vishnu characteristics for the left side of the body (conch shell in his hands, necklace of flowers, crown on head, and half of the traditional V mark of Vishnu on the forehead). Ardhanārīshvara shows the male characteristics of Shiva on the right side and the female ones of Parvati on the left (according to an ancient legend Shiva and Parvati once engaged in such a violent sexual intercourse that they merged into one androgynous being). As is well known, the Greek Hermaphrodite combines male and female sexual features in a different way (here the myth tells us that the son of Hermes and Aphrodite grew together with the nymph Salmacis while bathing in her fountain). Obviously, the 'notional compounding' differs from culture to culture. To take an example from a totally different area, scientific terminology abounds in terms such as *russula cyanoxantha*, which is a "milk-mushroom" whose cap is both "dark-blue" (Greek *kuáneos*) and "yellow" (Greek *xanthós*). The mixture of these two colors in this case does not yield *green*; the cap of this mushroom is basically dark blue with yellow spots. Similar examples could be multiplied from any scientific terminology.

More interesting examples come from languages which do not have derivational morphology and have to rely totally on compounding. For instance, Chinese forms its abstract nouns by compounding two adjectives of exactly opposite meaning (antonyms):

(9)	ta-hsiao	literally	"big" + "little"	"size"
	ch'ang-tuan		"long" + "short"	"length"
	yuan-chin		"far" + "near"	"distance"
	kuei-chien		"dear" + "cheap"	"price"

The mental process illustrated by these Chinese examples is quite different from Indo-European coordinate compounds quoted above. English *bitter-sweet* does not mean "taste" but "sweet with bitter aftertaste". On the other hand, these Chinese examples must be analyzed figuratively, more specifically as examples of **metonymy** (usually defined as a semantic transfer based on temporal or spatial contiguity). This derivational type is extremely rare in Indo-European languages; nevertheless, some examples may be found in Hindi or Persian. For instance, in the latter language *āmad-o-raft* means literally "(he) came-and-(he) left" and figuratively "traffic". Similarly, *āb-o-havā* "water-and-air" means simply "weather".

9.4.2 *Determinative Compounds*

There are basically two types of **determinative compounds**. A noun may be determined by an adjective as in *blackbird*. Similarly, adjectives may be determined by the stem of a noun as in *color-blind* or they may be determined by another adjective as in *icy-cold*. In traditional grammars the first type is called **subordinate (dependent)** compound, the second type **descriptive** compound. It is possible to classify subordinate compounds according to the grammatical meaning which the determinant has at the level of the underlying sentence. For instance, the following three compound adjectives are quite different at the level of the underlying sentence: *heart-break-ing*, *easy-going* and *man-made*. The first one refers to the object of the sentence: *grief broke his heart* → *heart-breaking grief*; the second one is based on an adverbial phrase, and the third one refers to the subject of the underlying sentence: *man made the hut* → *man-made hut*. There are different relationships in combinations such as *color-blind* or *grass-green*. The first one is paraphrasable as "blind with regard to color", or possibly "he does not see colors" whereas the other one is based on the comparison "as green as grass is green". This type of analysis was elaborated centuries ago in Ancient India for Sanskrit by Pāṇini and his followers. Since Sanskrit is heavily flective they described subordinate compounds (called *tat-puruṣa*, lit. his man) by identifying the case function the determinant would have at the level of the underlying sentence. Thus in the subordinate compound *go-ghna* "cow-slaying" the determinant "cow" is a direct object (accusative in Sanskrit) underlyingly (compare English *heart-breaking*). In the compound adjective *agni-dagdhá* "burnt with fire", the determinant "fire" is an instrumental in Sanskrit. The underlying sentence has to be constructed in the mediopassive voice: *agnínā dahyáte*: "he is burnt with fire" or "he burns himself with fire" (where *agnínā* is morphologically an instrumental). In the compound adjective *go-jā* "produced from cows" the determinant "cow" is an ablative at the level of the underlying sentence: *góbhyas jāyate* "it is produced from cows" (where *góbhyas* is morphologically an ablative). The most common type of subordinate compounds in Sanskrit are the nouns determined by the genitive (in the broadest sense). The compound noun such as *rāja-putrá* "king's son" is analyzable as a nominal phrase *rā́jñas putrás* where *rā́jñas* is morphologically the genitive of origin. In historical perspective, in all these cases we are dealing with syntactic groups (phrases) becoming compounds. In Vedic Sanskrit it is still possible to find compounds whose determinants retain the case ending: *abhayaṃ-kará* "producing security" (with accusative, not *abhaya-kará*), *śúneṣita* "driven by dogs" (with instrumental *śúnā*, Nom *śvā*), *divo-jā* "produced from heaven" (with ablative *divás*,

Nom *dyú*), *jās-pati* "lord of a family" (with genitive *jas*, Nom *jā́*) and *divi-yáj* "worshipping in heaven" (with locative *divi*).

Descriptive compounds with the adjective as a determinant (the type *blackbird*) are rare in Sanskrit: *kṛṣṇa-śakuni* "raven" (lit. "black" + "bird"). This type of determinative compounds is very common in Germanic languages. In English, here belong combinations with adjectives denoting color: *bluebird, redfish, blackboard*; dimension: *longboat, broadside, shortcake*; taste: *sweetbread, sourdough*; genealogical compounds with the determinant meaning "standing in the second degree of ancestry or descent": *grandfather*; ethnic names: *Englishman, Irishman*.

Specific morphological problems in compounding appear in all flective languages. They have to do with the fact that many flective languages became analytic during their history and consequently it is hard to use the terminology of the case grammar in the analysis of compounds. This problem is rather marginal in English which has few compounds of the type *craftsmen* where *-s-* represents the old genitive ending. However, in modern English this type is not productive, i.e. all formations such as *huntsman, kingsman* etc. were formed in previous centuries. But in German this problem is more serious. On the one hand, we find parts of subordinate compounds such as *Volkskunde* "folklore" vs. *Völkerkunde* "ethnography" (*Gottesdienst* "divine service" vs. *Götterdienst* "idolatry"; *Landeskunde* "areal studies" vs. *Länderkunde* "regional geography (of different countries)" with the opposition —*(e)s* vs. —*er*. This might imply that speakers of German still identify these suffixes on the determinant of the compound with the case endings of the genitive singular vs. the genitive plural. However, these examples are isolated and it is more common to find *-s-* in environments where we would postulate a genitive plural: for instance, we find *Bischofsmütze* "mitre" but also *Bischofskonferenz* "bishops' conference" (not *Bischöfekonferenz*). On the other hand, (—)*r-* occurs in environments where we would postulate a genitive singular: *Kindermörder* "murderer of a child", *Hühnerkeule* "chicken leg" etc. Furthermore, *-s-* can appear with feminine determinants while it never appears in the declension of the feminine nouns: *Wohnungsinhaber* "tenant" but the form in the genitival group has a Ø-suffix: *ein Inhaber der Wohnung*. For these reasons various grammars of German handle this particular morpheme as a 'boundary marker' (*Fugenzeichen*) and they have to go into lengthy descriptions of its phonological shape: *e, (e)n, er, (e)s, ens*. In Section 2.3 we called this morpheme an **interfix**.

9.4.3 *Possessive Compounds*

Possessive compounds are analyzed as combinations with a compound determinant and a zero determinatum. These are cases where the relationship between the two members of the compound does not provide the essential meaning and an external element must be added. For instance, a *birdbrain* is not a "bird's brain" but rather a "stupid person", i.e. "someone having a birdbrain", On the other hand, *humpback* can denote both "a back with a hump" or (by metonymy) "a person with a humped back". Hence, adjectival derivatives from possessive compounds such as *humpbacked, palefaced*, etc. For this reason, these compounds are called

exocentric, as opposed to **endocentric** compounds including coordinate and determinative compounds. Another common term coming from Pāninian grammar is *bahuvrīhi* meaning literally "someone whose rice is plentiful" (*yasya vrīhir bahur asti*). In Sanskrit adjectival possessive compounds were formed from both descriptive and subordinate compounds and this process was accompanied by a shift of accent from the final member of the compound to the first. For instance, a descriptive compound *bṛhad-aśvá* "great horse" could be transformed into an adjectival possessive compound by the shift of accent *bṛhád-aśva* "possessing great horses". Similarly, a subordinate compound *rāja-putrá* "king's son (= prince)" could be transformed into an adjectival possessive compound *rājá-putra* "having kings as sons". The most common possessive compounds are those with numerals as a determinant found in all Indo-European languages: Sanskrit *aṣṭấ-pad* "eight-footed", Greek *oktṓpous* "octopus", Latin *bipes* "two-footed". The accentual shift can be found elsewhere, most notably in Ancient Greek, where the pairs such as the following can be found: *patro-któnos* "patricide" vs. *patró-ktonos* "killed by the father"; *thēro-tróphos* "feeding the beasts" vs. *thēró-trophos* "nourished by the beasts". However, the relationship between them is rather active vs. passive at the level of the underlying sentence (*kteínei tòn patéra* "he kills the father" → *patro-któnos* vs. *hupò toû patròs kteínetai* "he is killed by the father" → *patró-ktonos*). Possessive compounds are fairly common in Sanskrit poetic discourse which abounds in opaque formations such as *vṛkṣá-keśa* "whose trees are like hair" or "tree-haired" = "mountain" or *tapó-dhana* "whose wealth is penance" = "ascetic".

9.4.4 Syntactic Compounds

Any **syntactic group** or phrase may have a meaning that is not the same as the sum of the meanings of its constituents. Lexicalized prepositional groups are extremely common; here belong examples such as *lady in waiting, maid of honor, man in the street, good-for-nothing, cat-o'-nine-tails*, etc. In many cases the process of their lexicalization, as analyzed by Jespersen (1942:8.83), was a lengthy one. This is shown especially by the uncertainty as to the place of the plural morpheme in Early Modern English and it may often be attached to the whole combination instead of the determinatum. The following forms for *sons-in-law* from King Lear may exemplify this point: *sonne in lawes, sonnes in law, sons in laws* (also hyphenated *Sons-in-Laws*).

Another common type is represented by derivations from a verbal phrase such as *looker-on, hanger-on, listener-in, passer-by*. Their pluralization by 'infixed' *-s* shows that we are not dealing with a compound.

Another common type is represented by additive phrases such as *bread and butter, soap-and-water, deaf-and-dumb* and, of course, by (archaic and dialectal) numerals: *five and twenty*. It is of interest to note that German uses exclusively the latter type in forming its numerals (*fünfundzwanzig*) whereas Standard English uses exclusively coordinate *twenty-five*. As mentioned in 4.2, Czech has both additive *pětadvacet* and coordinate *dvacetpět*.

9.5 *Noun Derivation in Arabic*

It is often said that the absence of compounding is one of the typical features of word formation in Semitic languages. This statement will not stand the scrutiny and it is really possible to find rare examples of compounding. Some of them are based on foreign models. Thus Arabic *bāš-mufattiš* "chief inspector" or *bāš-kātib* "chief clerk" etc. are calqued on Turkish compounds *baş* "head" + *bakan* "minister" = "prime minister" (synchronically, *bāš* may be taken as a prefix in Arabic). Modern Hebrew has formations which have to be analyzed as determinative compounds; for instance, *ram* "high" + *kol* "voice" = "microphone"; *rəʔi* "appearance" + *dak* "thin" = "microscope"; *karn* (<*keren*) "horn" + *af* "nose" = "rhinoceros". The latter type "someone whose nose is horn" corresponds fairly closely to the possessive (exocentric compounds) of Indo-European languages. Examples of this type could be multiplied but it will soon become obvious that we are dealing with syntactic groups rather than with compounds: *tob leb* "kindhearted", *rak leb* "mild-hearted". As mentioned under 9.4, the two stressed syntactic groups such as *stone wall* have to be excluded from word formation; here the use of *stone* as a preadjunct is a purely syntactic phenomenon. On the same grounds we may exclude Hebrew constructions such as *kəli zahab* "golden dish(es)" from word formation, since the use of *zahab* "gold" as a postadjunct is a syntactic phenomenon (so-called **status constructus**). Similarly has to be evaluated *roš hammemšala* lit. the head of the government "premier minister". On the other hand, *jošeb roš* lit. sitting-head "chairman" may be considered as a compound. Nevertheless, we may somewhat misleadingly state that the only viable strategy of forming new words in the Semitic group of languages is derivation. Where English or German compound Semitic languages have to use syntactic groups. Thus versus German compound *Flugzeugträger* "aircraft carrier" we find Arabic syntactic group *nāqila al-ṭāʔirāt* (lit. the carrier of aircrafts). Otherwise they have to draw on their derivational potential; for instance, German *Panzerschiff* "armored ship" would be translated as *darrāʕa* or *dāriʕa* in Arabic (both these words are derived from the base *dirʕ* "armor").

In what follows nominal derivatives in Syrian Arabic will be examined. The discussion of verbal derivation would actually be more interesting (given the fact that Arabic does not use the verbal prefixes), but it is of considerable complexity which does not make it a suitable topic for an introductory course in morphology.

Nominal derivatives of Syrian Arabic (the same holds true of Classical Arabic) are traditionally classified as belonging to one of the following morphological or semantic categories:

(i)   Abstract
(ii)   Verbal (or gerundial)
(iii) Singulative
(iv)   Feminine
(v)   Occupational
(vi)   Instrumental

(vii) Locative
(viii) Hypostatic
(ix)   Diminutive
(x)   Elative

Abstract nouns are denominal and deadjectival derivatives formed on the patterns $C_1aC_2\bar{a}C_3e$, $C_1C_2\bar{u}C$ ȩ, and C əC Ģ (e); it will be observed that -e is lowered to -a after pharyngeals, ʔ and r.

(10) Adjective   Abstract Noun
      šəžāʕ   "brave"   šažāʕa   "bravery"
      saʕb   "difficult"   sʕūbe   "difficult"
      kbīr   "large"   kəbr   "large size"

      Noun
      sadīʔ   "friend"   sadāʔa   "friendship"
      saheb   "friend"   səhbe   "friendship"
      ʔabb   "father"   ʔubuwwe   "fatherhood" (< earlier ʔubūw-)

Verbal nouns (or gerundial nouns) are deverbal derivatives formed on a variety of patterns. In the case of simple triradical verbs there is no sure way of predicting which pattern is to be used. Some of the patterns are: $C_1aC_2C_3$, $C_1\partial C_2C_3$, $C_1aC_2aC_3$, $C_1aC_2\bar{a}C_3$, $C_1(i)C_2\bar{a}C_3(e)$, $C_1(u)C_2\bar{u}C_3$, $C_1aC_2aC_3\bar{a}n$, and $C_1\partial C_2C_3\bar{a}n$.

(11) Verb   Verbal Noun
      žarah   "cut, wound"   žarh   "cutting, wounding"
      hakam   "judge"   həkm   "judging"
      talab   "request"   talab   "requesting"
      nažāh   "succeed"   nažāh   "succeeding"
      ʕabad   "worship"   ʕbāde   "worshipping"
      nəzel   "descend"   nzūl   "descending"
      ražaf   "tremble"   ražafān   "trembling"
      ʕəref   "know"   ʕərfān   "knowing"

Verbal nouns of many simple trilitteral verbs have singulatives derived from them:

(12) Verb   Verbal Noun   Singulative
      darab "hit, strike"   darb   "hitting"   darb-e "blow"
      dafaʕ "push"   dafʕ   "pushing"   dafʕ-a "a push"

Singulative nouns are denominal derivatives denoting an individual unit of what their base denotes collectively or generically. The derivational suffix is *-e*.

Collective		Singulative	
xass	"lettuce"	xass-e	"a head of lettuce"
baʔar	"cattle"	baʔar-a	"a cow"
naxl	"date palms"	naxl-e	" a date palm"

Many masculine nouns (denoting male beings) can be converted into feminine nouns (denoting female beings) by the same suffix *-e*:

(13) Masculine   Feminine

ʕamm	"(paternal) uncle"	ʕamm-e	"(paternal) aunt"
kalb	"dog"	kalb-e	"bitch"

Occupational nouns are mostly deverbal derivatives (there are also some denominal derivatives) formed on the pattern $C_1aC_2C_2\bar{a}C_3$. As the term suggests, only nouns denoting human beings belong here:

(14) Verb   Occupational Noun

raʔaṣ	"dance"	raʔʔāṣ	"dancer"
falaḥ	"cultivate"	fallāḥ	"peasant"

Noun

ḥadīd	"iron"	ḥaddād "blacksmith"
laḥm	"meat"	laḥḥām "butcher"

Instrumental nouns are deverbal derivatives formed on the patters: $C_1aC_2C_2\bar{a}C_3e$, $m\partial C_1C_2\bar{a}C_3(e)$, and $maC_1C_2aC_3(e)$:

(15) Verb   Instrumental Noun

ṭār	"fly" (root ṬYR)	ṭayyāra	"airplane"
fataḥ	"open"	məftāḥ	"key"
ḍarab	"hit"	mɔdṛāb	"bat"

Locative nouns are mostly deverbal derivatives formed on the following patterns: $maC_1C_2aC_3(e)$ and $maC_1C_2eC_3$:

(16) Verb
?aʕad "sit"
daras "study"
žalas "sit"

Locative Noun
maʔʕad "seat"
madrase "school"
mažles "session room"

Noun
ktāb "book"

maktabe "library"

So-called **hypostatic nouns** are deverbal derivatives formed on the patterns listed for (15), (16) and several others; they denote an abstract result or object of the activity denoted by their derivational base:

(17) Verb
?aṣad "intend, aim at"
nām "sleep" (root NWM)

Hypostatatic Noun
maʔṣad "intent, goal"
manām "dream"

Diminutives are denominal derivatives formed on the pattern C_1C_2 ayy(eC_3):

(18) Noun
zġīr "child"
?əbn "son"

Diminutive
zġayyer "little one"
bnayy "little son"

So-called **elatives** are mostly deadjectival derivatives formed on the pattern ?aC_1C_2aC_3. The meaning of elative corresponds to both comparative and superlative of English, cf. 1.4.

(19) Adjective
sahl "easy"
ṭawīl "long"
Noun
šōb "hot weather"
rəžžāl "man"

Elative
?ashal "easier, easiest"
?aṭwal "longer, longest"

?ašwab "hotter, hottest weather"
?aržal "more of a man, most manly"

RECOMMENDED READINGS

Anderson, Stephen R. 1985. "Typological distinctions in word formation". *Language Typology and Syntactic Description*. Volume 3 ed. by T. Shopen, 3–56. Cambridge: Cambridge University Press.

Aronoff, Mark. 1976. *Word Formation in Generative Grammar*. Cambridge, Mass.: MIT Press.

Bloomfield, Leonard. 1935. *Language*. London: Allen and Unwin.

Brekle, Herbert E. 1978. "Reflections on the conditions for the coining, use and understanding of nominal compounds". *Proceedings of the XII*th *ICL* (Vienna, 1977). Innsbruck.

Chomsky, Noam. 1970. "Remarks on nominalizations". *Readings in English Transformational Grammar* ed. by R. Jacobs & P. Rosenbaum, 184–229. Waltham, Mass.: Ginn.

___ & Maurice Halle. 1968. *Sound Pattern of English*. New York: Harper & Row.

Cowell, Mark W. 1964. *A Reference Grammar of Syrian Arabic*. Washington, D. C.: Georgetown University Press.

Dressler, Wolfgang U. 1978. "Elements of a polycentristic theory of word formation". *Proceedings of the XII*th *ICL* (Vienna, 1977). Innsbruck.

Erben, Johannes. 1975. *Einführung in die deutsche Wortbildungslehere*. Berlin: Schmidt.

Fleischer, W. 1975. *Wortbildung der deutschen Gegenwartssprache*. Tübingen: Niemeyer.

Halle, Maurice. 1973. "Prolegomena to a theory of word formation". *Linguistic Inquiry* IV.3–16.

Jespersen, Otto. 1942. *A Modern English Grammar on Historical Principles*. Part VI. *Morphology*. London: Allen and Unwin.

Koziol, Herbert. 1937. *Handbuch der Englischen Wortbildungslehre*. Heidelberg.

Lees, Robert B. 1963. *The Grammar of English Nominalizations*. Bloomington/The Hague: Indiana University Press. (2nd Printing.)

Lipka, Leonhard 1975. "Prolegomena to 'Prolegomena' to a theory of word formation". *The Transformational-Generative Paradigm and Modern Linguistic Theory* ed. by E. F. K. Körner. Amsterdam: Benjamins.

Macdonell, Arthur A. 1916. *A Vedic Grammar for Students*. Oxford: Oxford University Press.

Marchand, Hans. 1969. *The Categories and Types of Present-Day English Word Formation*. 2nd Edition. Munich: Beck.

Rohrer, Christopher. 1974. "Some problems of word formation". *Linguistische Arbeiten* 14. Tübingen: Niemeyer.

Rosén, Haiim B. 1977. *Contemporary Hebrew*. The Hague: Mouton. (Chapter 6).

Zandvoort, Reinard W. 1966. *A Handbook of English Grammar*. Englewood Cliffs: Longmans.

EXERCISES

1. Traditionally, the area of word formation was treated as consisting of derivation and compounding. If we want to keep the term derivative only to derivatives formed by suffixation we have to introduce a new term expansion. Explain and exemplify.

2. In the analysis of compounds it became customary to set up several groups such as coordinate, determinative, descriptive, possessive and syntactic compounds. Define them and give some good examples for each.

3. Comment on the appropriateness of terms for compounds coined by Hindu grammarians (*dvandva, karmadhāraya, bahuvrīhi, tatpuruṣa*).

4. Below are a group of French words containing derivational suffixes. Compile a list of them, and classify them according to (a) the word classes they attach to (b) and the word classes they form. Add to this list any additional suffixes you can think of.

(1)	interrogation	(17)	maisonnette	(33)	divisible
(2)	éclairage	(18)	ourson	(34)	courageux
(3)	commencement	(19)	travailleur	(35)	porteur
(4)	dépendance	(20)	connaisseuse	(36)	Genevois
(5)	largeur	(21)	horloger	(37)	chimiste
(6)	gentillesse	(22)	pompier	(38)	sucrier
(7)	bonté	(23)	marxiste	(39)	compteuse
(8)	exactitude	(24)	Hongrois	(40)	négrillon
(9)	marxisme	(25)	respiratoire	(41)	trentaine
(10)	canonnade	(26)	dépensier	(42)	limaille
(11)	soirée	(27)	enfantin	(43)	apprentissage
(12)	plumage	(28)	théorique	(44)	cuillerée
(13)	pierraille	(29)	sportif	(45)	glissade
(14)	vingtaine	(30)	pointu	(46)	difficulté
(15)	finesse	(31)	connaissance	(47)	refroidissement
(16)	traduction	(32)	guérison	(48)	exposition

5. Compile a similar list of words containing derivational suffixes in a language you know or study and classify them according to (a) the word classes they attach to (b) and the word classes they form.

6. Provide two examples for each of the following:

I.   Compound nouns
    (a)   noun + noun
    (b)   verb + noun
    (c)   noun + verb
    (d)   verb + verb
    (e)   adjective + noun
    (f)   particle + noun
    (g)   verb + particle

II. Compound verbs
    (h)   noun + verb
    (i)   verb + noun
    (j)   verb + verb
    (k)   adjective + verb
    (l)   particle + noun
    (m) noun + noun

III. Compound adjectives
    (n)   noun + adjective
    (o)   verb + adjective
    (p)   adjective + adjective
    (q)   adverb + adjective
    (r)   noun + noun
    (s)   verb + noun
    (t)   adjective + noun
    (u)   particle + noun
    (v)   verb + verb
    (w) adjective/adverb + verb
    (x)   verb + particle

CHAPTER TEN
THEORETICAL MODELS OF MORPHOLOGY

10.1 *Morphology and Formal Syntax*

One of the promises made by the generativists was to come up with a formal analysis of tense and aspect. In their *Beginning English Grammar* (1976:358) J. Keyser and P. Postal suggested that "a natural way to treat tense in the present grammar is to assume that present and past, like the 'future' *will*, are verbs in initial structure". This assumption resulted in monstrous 'initial' structures for very simple sentences such *Joan has been singing*, reproduced here from Keyser & Postal (1976: 359), as shown in Figure 10.1.

This represents a rather extravagant proposal (with six clauses and seven verbs) for the structure containing one tense (present) and two aspects (perfect and progressive; perfective is a misnomer), cf. 6.3.3. Nevertheless, the authors maintain that "it is not hard to develop a formal analysis of tense and aspect along the lines of this note ... but this lies beyond the scope of an introductory work".

Fourteen years later, to judge by Haegeman's *Introduction to Government & Binding Theory* (1991), the contemporary formal syntax still makes no provision for the study of grammatical and lexical aspect. As far as tense is concerned, it is assumed that the tense specification of the sentence is separate from VP and it is associated with the AUX node; the latter node is the site on which tense is realized. In all sentences, with or without overt auxiliaries, tense is located under a separate node, labelled INFL. Sentences are viewed as possessing INFL as their head; INFL takes a VP category as its complement and an NP (the subject) as its specifier. Given the fact that an actual word such as the modal auxiliary can appear in the INFL position the label AUX is dispensed with. Under this analysis the sentences *John saw the boss* and *John will see the boss* possess identical structures. This is shown in Figures 10.2 and 10.3.

In view of the long-established morphological practice to label the bound morpheme *-ed* **inflectional suffix**, to use the label INFL for the modal auxiliaries such as *will* is most regrettable and misleading. Furthermore, as the label **Inflectional Phrase** (for Sentence) suggests, INFL is a node which is taken to dominate all verbal inflection including person and number. The latter two categories are taken as **agreement markers** which may be very restricted as, for instance, in English. Haegeman (1991:102) claims that there is always **abstract agreement** which is often not morphologically realized (the difference between English and Latin would be to assume that the abstract AGR has fewer morphological realizations in English than Latin, i.e. not that English lacks AGR). Under the assumption that INFL dominates not only the tense feature of the verb but also its agreement properties (AGR), the above two sentences would be represented as Fig. 10.4.

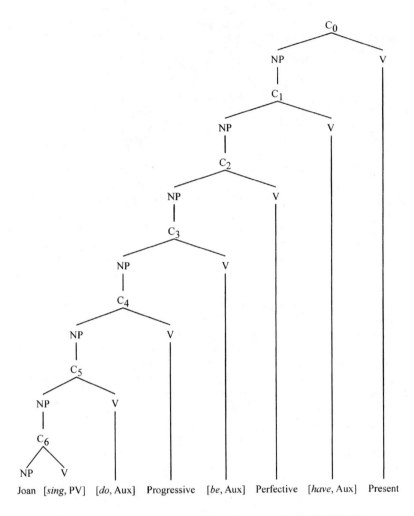

Joan [*sing*, PV] [*do*, Aux] Progressive [*be*, Aux] Perfective [*have*, Aux] Present

Fig. 10.1 Tense and aspect according to Keyser & Postal (1976:359)

A propos aspect, Haegeman (1991:106) mentions that the aspectual and modal auxiliaries of English often correspond to inflectional affixes in other languages (Latin *amābō* "I shall love", *amāvī* "I have loved") but no complex aspectual forms are analyzed in the formal apparatus proposed above. The inflectional matrix with two features allows for four combinations: [+Tense +AGR] is found in tensed clauses; infinitives lack both tense and agreement [-Tense -AGR]; and the other two options [-tense +AGR] and [+tense -AGR] are claimed to illustrate certain infinitivals in Portuguese and English, respectively. Whatever the typological merits of this proposal, one

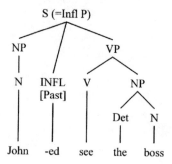

Fig. 10.2 John saw the boss

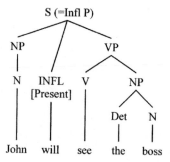

Fig. 10.3 John will see the boss

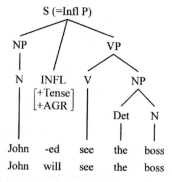

Fig. 10.4 Tense and aspect according to Haegeman (1991)

can object that it is based on the confusion of relationship (agreement) with entity (tense). And it certainly does not take us anywhere with respect to the analysis of lexical and grammatical aspect which cannot be accomplished without due attention to their semantics. Given the current emancipation of morphology in generative circles, one has to read monographs on formal syntax concurrently with those on morphology, such as Spencer (1991). The synthesis of morphology and syntax is yet to come.

10.2 *Morphology and Generative Phonology*

It was only fairly recently that generative phonology acknowledged the existence of morphology (in the sixties and seventies morphology was either ignored or taken for granted or even denied). It is of special interest to note that the rise of the more concrete type of phonology (so-called **Natural Generative Phonology**, Hooper 1976) has been to a large degree a return to traditional pre-generative notions in phonology accompanied by emancipation of morphology. One of the cardinal mistakes of the orthodox line of abstract generative phonology was the 'morpheme-invariance hypothesis' (versus traditional concept of variants in paradigmatic arrangements). In other words, orthodox generative phonology considered 'surface variants' only as a by-product of the all-important deep processes operating on abstract invariant morphemes; consequently, it was not interested in looking for true generalizations about surface forms (for instance, the so-called exceptions which are explained in traditional models in terms of morphology and semantics, have to be explained by cumbersome machinery of reordered phonological rules). We will elucidate these important theoretical points by analyzing certain morphophonemic phenomena of **accent**. As is well-known, accent belongs to both phonology and morphology. To the former by its nature (accent as an interplay of phonetic features of loudness, tone and length), to the latter by its inherent properties (word-accent, which may be a matter of stress or tone or both). Let us examine the accent pattern of Spanish verbal forms. The paradigms below represent the complete set of simple forms with the stress indicated by the acute:

(1)

			Present Indicative	Present Subjunctive
Nonfinite "to love"				
amár	Sg	1	ámo	áme
amándo		2	ámas	ámes
amádo		3	áma	áme
	Pl	1	amámos	amémos
		2	amáis	améis
		3	áman	ámen

		Preterit	Imperfect Indicative	Imperfect Subjunctive
Sg	1	amé	amába	amára
	2	amáste	amábas	amáras
	3	amó	amába	amára

Pl	1	amámos	amábamos	amáramos
	2	amásteis	amábais	amárais
	3	amáron	amában	amáran

		Future	Conditional
Sg	1	amaré	amaría
	2	amarás	amarías
	3	amará	amaría
Pl	1	amarémos	amaríamos
	2	amaréis	amaríais
	3	amarán	amarían

J. W. Harris (1969) proposed to account for this accent pattern in the framework of generative phonology by a rule that stresses the penultimate syllable of all verb forms except the 1st and 2nd Pl of the Impf 2nd and Subj:

$$V \rightarrow [1\text{stress}]/ — (([-\text{perf}])C_oV)C_o\#]_{verb}$$

This rule has three expansions:

(i) the first expansion applies only to the 1st and 2nd Pl of the imperfect and places the stress one syllable before the imperfect morphemes -ba and -ra;

(ii) the second expansion /-$C_oVC_o\#]_{verb}$ assigns stress to all penultimate vowels;

(iii) the third expansion /-$C_o\#]_{verb}$ assigns stress to monosyllabic forms.

In other words, according to this rule all verb forms, except 1st and 2nd Pl Impf, are stressed on the penultimate syllable. The forms which are accented on the last syllable (Infinitive *amár* 1st Sg Pret *amé*, 3rd Sg Pret *amó*, Sg Fut *amaré, amarás, amará*), are derived by Harris from more abstract underlying representations which have penultimate stress. Thus the infinitive *amár* has a final vowel -*e* in the underlying form, which is deleted after stress assignment; the preterite forms *amé* and *amó* are derived from /am + a + I/ and /am + a + U/, respectively. The penultimate vowel is stressed by the general rule, then altered, and the final vowel is deleted (notice that the deletion rule must be **extrinsically** ordered after the stress rule). The future and conditional forms are derived by Harris from the combination of two separate words: infinitive and auxiliary. Stress is assigned to both words: [[amare]a]. The infinitive is stressed on the penult, and stress is assigned to the single syllable of the auxiliary. Later a general rule removes all but the rightmost stress, leaving stress on the auxiliary: *amará*.

Obviously, Harris's abstract analysis is not a true generalization about surface forms and he has to rely on rule ordering to give a systematic account of exceptions. As pointed out by

Hooper (1976:26) in *An Introduction to Natural Generative Phonology* one cannot claim that *amár, amé, amó, amaré* and *amará* receive stress by a penultimate stress rule. Whereas Harris counts syllables from the end in order to assign stress to individual verb forms, Hooper prefers to look at the whole paradigmatic display and makes a simple observation that the most striking point about stress in the verb forms is not the fact that the majority of forms have penultimate stress, but that for each tense (except present) all persons have stress on the same syllable in relation to the stem. In the imperfect, the 1st and 2nd Pl forms are not exceptional because they do not have penultimate stress. Rather their antepenultimate stress makes them regular in that the stress falls on the same vowel (thematic vowel) as in all other persons. Thus a seeming irregularity (exception) in phonology turns out to be a morphological regularity. Of course, it means that we have to recognize that stress has a morphological function in language and make place for traditional morphological notions such as thematic vowel in our descriptions. It is fairly well-known that stress in Spanish is actually one of the markers of tense and mood, i.e., that stress is an important morphophonemic category; witness the minimal pairs such as *ámo* "I love" vs. *amó* "he loved" (Pret), *áme* "that I/he love" (Subj) vs. *amé* "I loved" (Pret). (In Generative Phonology, these forms would be considered only as accidental products of abstract derivation). It may be noticed that even if we work with more concrete phonology and morphological notions we still do not do away with exceptions. That is, if we claim that in Spanish each tense stresses a certain vowel in all persons, we still have to say that the 1st and the 2nd Pl Pres are exceptional (as shown above, forms such as *ámo ~ amámos*, etc. furnished the best evidence for the abstract penultimate rule). However, we may be interested in looking at Spanish dialects which abandoned the penultimate rule in favor of a rule that stresses the stem vowel in all persons. For instance, in Andalusian Spanish the subjunctive forms of the second and third conjugations stress the stem vowel in all persons (*cóma, cómamos, cómais, cóman*). It is of interest to note that historically the same happened in the imperfect when a penultimate rule of Latin was given up in favor of a rule that stressed the thematic vowel:

(2)		Latin	Spanish
Sg	1	amābam	amába
	2	amābās	amábas
	3	amābat	amába
Pl	1	amābāmus	amábamos
	2	amābātis	amábais
	3	amābant	amában

Stress on the 1st and 2nd Pl was retracted and the result was a regular paradigm. What does all this tell us about the internalized grammar of native speakers? One of the conclusions is that native speakers do not make use of the rule order and abstract underlying forms. When the phonological analysis becomes too abstract the speakers obviously prefer the morphological analysis. In the case above, when vowel length stopped functioning distinctively at a certain point in the history of Spanish the penultimate rule 'accent the heavy penult' had to give way to a more transparent rule such as 'stress the thematic vowel'. In other words, the original phonological rule of Latin has been morphologized in Spanish. As mentioned above, dialectal evidence points in the same direction. Native speakers simply prefer to consider phonological variations meaningful rather than meaningless (and phonologically predictable). Summing up, we cannot do abstract phonology as camouflaged morphology. Morphology has to be studied in its own rights and side by side with concrete phonology.

10.3 *Morphology in Functional Grammar*

In **Functional Grammar** (Dik 1980, 1989) morphology is dealt with by using the expression rules. These determine the way in which functionally specified underlying predications are mapped onto the linguistic expressions by means of which they can be realized. The following sorts of expression devices are distinguished:

(i)   the form in which terms are realized
   (a)   case marking
   (b)   adpositions (prepositions and postpositions)
(ii)   the form in which the predicate is realized
   (a)   voice differences in the verb
   (b)   auxiliary elements
(iii) the order of the constituents
(iv)   stress and intonation.

The **expression rules** are sensitive to the functional specification of constituents. **Semantic functions** (Agent, Goal, Recipient, Beneficiary, Instrument, etc.) will most usually be expressed through **case marking** (5.2.3) or **adpositions**, or a combination of these. Terms with only a semantic function are normally not strongly tied to specific positions in the clause (2.1.3). **Syntactic functions** (Subject, Object) are also expressed through case marking and/or adpositions. Typically, the cases used for subject and object are the most unmarked cases of the language (cf. the situation in Turkish and Finnish under 5.2.3). Different assignments of Subject and Object will usually be coded in the verb in terms of voice distinctions. For a ditransitive verb, such as *give*, different assignments of Subject function will result in the use of the passive voice:

(3)   Agent   Goal   Recipient
   a.   Subject   Object
   b.   Subject
   c.   Subject

a.   John (Ag Subject) gave the book (Go Object) to the friend (Rec)
b.   The book (Go Subject) was given to the friend (Rec) by John (Ag)
c.   The friend (Rec Subject) was given the book (Go) by John (Ag)

Subject and Object terms are typically tied to specific positions in the clause; thus in English the Subject is typically the leftmost term, whereas in languages with a rich case marking system the Subject may appear in any position in the clause. In Latin, sentences (a) and (b) allow for 24 permutations, since the semantic functions are unambiguously specified by case markers. Here are some possible translations of (a):

(4)   i.   Ioannēs(Ag)   librum(Go)   amīcō(Rec)   dedit.
      ii.   Ioannēs(Ag)   amīcō(Rec)   librum(Go)   dedit.
      iii.   Librum(Go)   Ioannēs(Ag)   amīcō(Rec)   dedit.
      iv.   Librum(Go)   amīcō(Rec)   Ioannēs(Ag)   dedit.

Sentences (i) – (iv) are *not* equivalent pragmatically: (i) may be taken as representing the normal state of affairs; (ii), (iii) and (iv) put the Goal, Recipient, and Agent in the focus, respectively. **Pragmatic functions** constitute a third layer of functional specification of the constituents of predications in Functional Grammar. Two pairs of pragmatic functions are distinguished, namely Theme and Tail, and Topic and Focus. The former two characterize material outside the predication (Theme is assigned to constituents which precede, and Tail to constituents which follow the predication). Topic and Focus are assigned to constituents of the predication proper. They are defined as follows:

(5)   Topic: The Topic presents the entity about which the predication predicates something in the given setting.

      Focus: The Focus presents what is relatively the most important or salient information in the given setting.

Pragmatic functions mark the informational status of the constituents and they have their consequences for the form in which a given underlying predication is to be expressed. Certain languages (e.g. Japanese) have special markers for constituents with given pragmatic functions, and probably all languages use special ordering and prosodic patterns for expressing pragmatic functions. The Topic is typically unstressed, whereas the Focus usually carries sentential stress. The Topic often favors the initial, the Focus the later (or the final) position in the clause. In our Latin sentences (ii) – (iv) the most salient pieces of information are the Goal, Recipient and Agent, respectively. The assignment of pragmatic functions yields the following representation:

(6)   ii.   Ioannēs (Ag Top) amīcō (Rec) librum (Go Foc) dedit.
      iii.   Librum (Go Top) Ioannēs (Ag) amīcō (Rec Foc) dedit.
      iv.   Librum (Go Top) amīcō (Rec) Ioannēs (Ag Foc) dedit.

Their English equivalents:

(7)   ii.   John gave the friend a BOOK (i.e., *not* a knife).
      iii.   John gave the book to a FRIEND (i.e., *not* to his brother).
      iv.   The book was given to the friend by JOHN (i.e., *not* by Fred).

It will be observed that in Latin (and other inflectional languages) Topic and Focus expression neutralize the expression differences connected with the syntactic functions of a given term. Thus in Latin it is impossible to define the Subject and Object purely positionally (as in English). In Latin, it is impossible to assign Subject function to the Recipient as in English *The friend was given the book by John: Amīcō* (Rec) *liber* (Go) *datus est ā Ioanne* (Ag), but not **Amīcus liber datus est ā Ioanne*.

On the other hand, in English if some term has both a semantic and a syntactic function it is usually the case that the expression for the syntactic function overrides that for the semantic function. This can be demonstrated by means of the following schema (Dik 1980:18):

(8) | *Ag* | *Go* | *Rec* | *Ben* |
|---------|---------|----------|----------|
| by John | John | to John | for John |
| by him | him | to him | for him |

Ag Subj	*Go Subj*	*Rec Subj*	*Ben Subj*
John	John	John	John
he	he	he	he

	Go Obj	*Rec Obj*	*Ben Obj*
	John	John	John
	him	him	him

The terms with only a semantic function (as in Latin) are always distinct form each other in form, whereas terms which have also Subject function and terms which have also Object function are identical in forms and are only distinguished from each other in the case of pronominal terms. This sort of situation is typical for the effect of Subject and Object assignment on the formal expression of terms.

10.4 *Natural Morphology*

Natural Morphology is an approach to morphology developed in Germany and Austria during the 1980s by W. Dressler, W. Mayerthaler and W. Wurzel. Its name was adopted in imitation of the title **Natural Phonology**, coined by D. Stampe for his approach to phonology (Donegan and Stampe 1979).

The Natural Morphologists operate with several explanatory principles: **universals, typology, system-dependence, paradigmatic structure** and **naturalness**.

10.4.1 *Universals*

Under **universals** the main concern is the relationship between expression and meaning (in their terminology, the relationship between *signantia* and *signata* corresponding to Saussure's *signifiants* and *signifiés*). In the eighties (Mayerthaler) naturalness was understood as the inverse of an all-pervasive notion of markedness. Markedness applies essentially to morphological symbolization (or coding), i.e. to the relationship of the *signans* (*signifiant*) to its *signatum* (*signifié*). An unmarked, or natural, symbolization for a pair of signata of which one is more marked is such that the signans of the marked one is also more **markerful** (the latter term, calqued on German *merkmalhaft*, is somewhat unfortunate because in the English speaking world the term marked is used for both **marked** (*markiert*) and **markerful** (*merkmalhaft*). This type of coding is claimed to be **constructionally iconic**; it is the type which is met most frequently when dealing with inflectional morphologies of various languages. But as we saw in 3.3, it is not always the case that the marked formed is phonologically more substantial (or 'markerful') than its unmarked counterpart.

For instance, the marked plural forms are quite commonly markerful (i.e. formed by suffixes) but they may also be markerless when morphological processes such as umlaut (*man → men*) are used. Even less natural plural formation process would be to remove the singular suffix (e.g. in Syrian Arabic *zalam-e* "man" → *zəlm* "men"); in Natural Morphologists' terminology, the plural formation by umlaut is **non-iconic**, that by subtraction **counter-iconic**:

(9)		"man"	Plural	Marked	
	Latin	(vir)	vir-ī	+	iconic
	English	(man)	men	+	non-iconic
	Arabic	(zalam-e)	zəlm	+	counter-iconic

Another famous example of counter-iconicity is the genitive plural form of feminine nouns in Russian. This one is suffixless (markerless) in spite of being double-marked vis-à-vis its nominative singular counterpart. Contrast the following Russian forms with their Latin equivalents which are constructionally iconic:

(10)	Latin	Russian
Sg Nom	schol-a	škol-a
Sg Gen	-ae	-y
Pl Nom	-ae	-y
Pl Gen	-ārum	-Ø

Both languages treat the Gen Sg and Nom Pl as marked categories (marked corresponds to markerful) but the Russian Gen Pl is anomalous in being markerless in spite of being double-marked (for number and case as shown nicely by the disyllabic Latin suffix -*ārum*).

10.4.2 *Typology*

According to Dressler (1985) linguistic types mediate between universal principles and language-particular issues. Setting aside the difficulty of defining clearly the five morphological types (**isolating, fusional, introflexive, agglutinative, polysynthetic**) the Natural Morphologists are faced with several typological dilemmas. One of them is why the **fusional type** should exist at all given the optimality of one-to-one relationship between morphology and semantics. Dressler compares the Latin and Turkish ablative plural forms "from our islands" in this respect:

(11) i. insul-īs   nostr-īs   (Latin)
          island-ABL/PL   our-ABL/PL

      ii. ada-lar-ımız-dan   (Turkish)
           island-PL-our-ABL

The Turkish version in (ii) is perfectly **diagrammatic** in displaying a one-to-one relationship between the signifiers and signifieds (-*lar* - PL, -*ımız* - "our", -*dan* - ABL), whereas in Latin the ablative and plural are realized by a single polysemous suffix -*īs*. In addition the same suffix -*īs* encodes also the dative plural (vs. Turkish -*lar-a* = -PL-DAT), and two other functions with other lexical items (accusative plural with *i*-stems, *cīv-īs* "citizens", and 2nd Sg with verbs, *aud-īs* "you hear"). Hence the legitimate question why the fusional type is so wide-spread (esp. in the Indo-European phylum of language) and diachronically so persistent. Dressler maintains that this is so by two other criteria of naturalness, namely, **word-size** and **indexicality**. As far as the average length of words is concerned, Dressler (1985) claims that it is between two and three syllables (notice that this figure coincides with the optimal size of a prosodic foot in phonology). This being so the Latin example in (11.i) is 'more natural' than the Turkish one in (11.ii). In general terms one can say that the cumulative and fusional exponence is more economical than the agglutinative which results typically in four- and five-syllable words. On the dimension of indexicality, Latin also scores better than Turkish in that its polysemous suffix -*īs* locates precisely the root *insul-* in the sense that no other formative may intervene between these two.

In Turkish, on the other hand, the ablative suffix *-dan* locates its nominal root very vaguely in that other formatives (such as the plural or the possessive suffix) could intervene (*ada-lar-dan* "from islands", *ada-mɪz-dan* "from our island").

10.4.3 *System-Dependence*

In addition to typology, there is another mediating factor between universals and language-specific phenomena, namely **system-dependent naturalness**. In simple terms, two languages may differ as to which is the dominant pattern for each language. As an example we may mention the plural formation in Arabic and English with both languages exhibiting internal and external inflection (cf. 2.2.2 and 4.3):

(12)	Arabic		English	
	Singular	Plural	Singular	Plural
Internal	RaǰuL	RiǰāL	MaN	MeN
External	FaLLāH̦	FaLLāH̦īn	peasant	peasants

But as we found out, most Arabic nouns exhibit internal inflection, whereas nearly all English nouns exhibit external inflection in their plural formation. External inflection therefore constitutes a system-defining structural property of English; its internal counterpart, not being **system congruent**, is open to elimination (we know from the history of English that there were many more internal plurals, such as *bōc* "book" - *bēc* "books", which were replaced by external ones). It is the other way in Arabic where external plurals are vulnerable to erosion (e.g. in Gulf Arabic one forms plurals of occupational nouns on the pattern *xabbāz* "baker" - *xababīz* "bakers, *sammāk* "fisherman" - *samamīč* "fishermen", vs. external plurals of literary Arabic *xabbāz-īn, sammāk-īn*).

10.4.4 *Paradigmatic structure*

One of the salient features of the languages with fusional and cumulative exponence is the existence of **inflection classes** (traditional conjugations and declensions). Their very existence is somewhat embarrassing for universal principles of Natural Morphology in that it implies lack of uniformity in morphological expressions. Not all the instances of polymorphy (such as English *-s* or *-en* for Nom Pl; Latin *-ī* or *-is* for Gen Sg) are rationalizable synchronically; but some are at least partly motivated by **extramorphological factors** (phonological, lexical or semantic). To stay with nouns, their referential animacy with its lexically and semantically determined characteristics may be used to rationalize polymorphous realizations of Case-Number aggregates. For instance, in Slavic languages the accusative singular (of masculine nouns) may be realized by either *-a* or *-Ø*, with *-a* being appropriate with animate nouns and *-Ø* with inanimate nouns (in addition both *-a* and *-Ø* are polysemous in that *-a* marks also the Gen Sg and *-Ø* the Masc Sg), as shown in Figure 10.5.

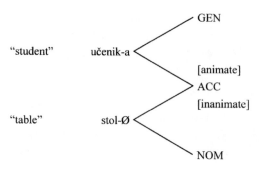

Fig. 10.5 Animacy and Case in Slavic languages

Another concern of the Natural Morphologists is what constitutes the **unmarked inflection class** and its **complementary relationship** to other inflection classes. To use Wurzel's examples, German nouns ending in vowels (other than schwa) are pluralized differently, i.e. belong to different complementary classes: *Auto* "car", *Autos*; *Cello* "cello" *Celli*; *Schema* "schema", *Schemata*; *Firma* "firm", *Firmen*. The class with *Auto* is the unmarked one because of the existence of alternative plural forms *Cellos, Schemas, Firmas*.

Another concern is the 'size' of paradigms, handled by what is called **paradigm economy**, and the existence of **macroparadigms**. For instance, we saw in Chapter Four (4.3) that it is possible to a certain degree to reduce the five (or six) Latin declensions to two **macroparadigms** (one for thematic nouns, I & II, and one for athematic nouns, III–V) if one operates with notions such as short and long thematic vowel, zero suffix and morphophonemic rules. In more general terms, one has to shift the emphasis from the Word and Paradigm (WP) model to the Item and Process (IP) model (cf. 2.5).

10.4.5 *Morphological and Phonological Naturalness*

One of the major dilemmas of the Natural Morphologists are the **intercomponential conflicts**; the achievement of naturalness in phonology may obstruct the achievement of naturalness in morphology, and vice versa. This issue was studied by Dressler (1985) who placed the phonological, morphonological and morphological rules on the cline of naturalness. For instance, the morphonological rule producing an alternation *electri[k]* ~ *electri[s]ity* is claimed to be more natural than the rule producing fusion as in *conclu[d]* ~ *conclu[ž]n;* or the 'weak' suppletion seen in *child* ~ *children* is more natural than its 'strong' counterpart in *Glasgow* ~ *Glaswegian* or *Halifax* ~ *Haligonian*.

A famous intercomponential naturalness conflict is the Germanic **umlaut** which loses its phonological motivation and results in irregular (unnatural) morphology. For instance, in the following set of German verb forms umlaut correlates neither with number nor with person:

(13)   Umlaut
   Sg 1   geb-e
       2   gib-st
       3   gib-t
   Pl 1   geb-en
       2   geb-et
       3   geb-en

Morphological regularity (naturalness), however, may be restored by **proportional analogy** producing the 1st Sg form *gib*; then the allomorphs acquire semantic values: /gɪb/ - Sg, /geːb/ - Pl.

RECOMMENDED READINGS

Carstairs-McCarthy, Andrew. 1992. *Current Morphology*. London: Routledge.

Dik, Simon C. 1980. *Studies in Functional Grammar*. London: Academic Press.

_____. 1989. *The Theory of Functional Grammar*. Dordrecht: Foris.

Donegan, Patricia J. & David Stampe 1979. "The study of Natural Phonology". *Current Approaches to Phonological Theory* ed. by D. A. Dinsen, 126–173. Bloomington: Indiana University Press.

Dressler. Wolfgang U. 1985. *Morphonology: The Dynamics of Derivation*. Ann Arbor: Karoma Publishers.

___, W. Mayerthaler, O. Panagl, & W. U. Wurzel, eds. 1987. *Leitmotifs in Natural Morphology*. Amsterdam: Benjamins.

Harris, James W. 1969. *Spanish Phonology*. Cambridge, Mass.: MIT Press.

___. 1975. "Morphology in generative grammar: Vowel alternations in Spanish verb forms". *El español y la linguistica generativo-transformacional* ed. by J. Guitart & J. Roy. Barcelona: Ediciones 62, Peninsula.

Haegeman, Liliane. 1991. *Introduction to Government & Binding Theory*. Oxford: Blackwell.

Hooper, Joan B. 1976. *An Introduction to Natural Generative Phonology*. New York: Academic Press.

Hudson, R. A. 1976. *Arguments for a Non-Transformational Grammar*. Chicago: University of Chicago Press.

Itkonen, Esa. 1976. "The use and misuse of the principle of axiomatics in linguistics". *Lingua* 38.185–220.

Keyser, Samuel J. & Paul M. Postal. 1976. *Beginning English Grammar*. New York: Harper & Row.

Kiparsky, Paul. 1968. "Tense and mood in Indo-European syntax". *Foundations of Language* 4.30–57.

Li, Charles N. 1976. *Subject and Topic*. New York: Academic Press.

Lightfoot, David. 1975. *Natural Logic and the Greek Moods*. The Hague: Mouton.

Spencer, Andrew. 1991. *Morphological Theory: An Introduction to Word Structure in Generative Grammar*. Oxford: Blackwell.

Steinberg, Dany D. 1975. "Chomsky: From formalism to mentalism and psychological invalidity". *Glossa* 9.83–117.

Stockwell, Robert P. 1977. *Foundations of Syntactic Theory*. Englewood Cliffs: Prentice-Hall.

REFERENCES AND SELECT BIBLIOGRAPHY

Anderson, John M. 1971. *The Grammar of Case*. Cambridge: Cambridge University Press.

Anderson, Stephen R. 1985. "Typological distinctions in word formation". *Language Typology and Syntactic Description*. Volume 3 ed. by T. Shopen, 3–56. Cambridge: Cambridge University Press.

———. 1985. "Inflectional morphology". *Language Typology and Syntactic Description*. Volume 3 ed. by T. Shopen, 150–201. Cambridge: Cambridge University Press.

———. 1985. *Phonology in the Twentieth Century*. Chicago: University of Chicago Press.

Applegate, Joseph R. 1958. *An Outline of the Structure of Shilḥa*. New York: American Council of Learned Societies.

Aronoff, Mark. 1976. *Word Formation in Generative Grammar*. Cambridge, Mass.: MIT Press.

———. 1993. *Morphology by Itself: Stems and Inflexional Classes*. Cambridge, Mass.: MIT Press.

Bach, Emmon W. & Robert T. Harms, ed. 1968. *Universals in Linguistic Theory*. New York: Holt, Rinehart and Winston.

Bauer, Laurie. 1988. *Introducing Linguistic Morphology*. Edinburgh: Edinburgh University Press.

Bazell, Charles E. 1966. "Linguistic typology". *Five Inaugural Lectures* ed. by P. D. Strevens, 29–49. London: Oxford University Press.

Bloomfield, Leonard. 1935. *Language*. London: Allen and Unwin. (Revised edition.)

Brekle, Herbert E. 1972. *Semantik. Eine Einführung in die sprachwissenschaftliche Bedeutungslehre*. München: Fink.

———. 1978. "Reflections on the conditions for the coining, use and understanding of nominal compounds". *Proceedings of the XIIth ICL* (Vienna, 1977). Innsbruck.

Bybee, Joan. 1985. *Morphology: A Study of the Relation Between Meaning and Form*. Amsterdam: Benjamins.

Campbell, A. 1959. *Old English Grammar*. Oxford: Clarendon Press.

Carstairs-McCarthy, Andrew. 1992. *Current Morphology*. London: Routledge.

Chomsky, Noam. 1970. "Remarks on nominalizations". *Readings in English Transformational Grammar* ed. by R. Jacobs & P. Rosenbaum, 184–229. Waltham, Mass.: Ginn.

——— & Maurice Halle. 1968. *Sound Pattern of English*. New York: Harper & Row.

Comrie, Bernard. 1976. *Aspect: An Introduction to the Study of Verbal Aspect*. Cambridge: Cambridge University Press.

———. 1985. *Tense*. Cambridge: Cambridge University Press.

Cowell, Mark W. 1964. *A Reference Grammar of Syrian Arabic*. Washington, D.C.: Georgetown University Press.

Curme, George O. 1960. *A Grammar of the German Language*. New York: Frederick Ungar.

Diakonoff, Igor M. 1988. *Afrasian Languages*. Moscow: Nauka.

Dik, Simon C. 1980. *Studies in Functional Grammar*. London: Academic Press.

——. 1989. *The Theory of Functional Grammar*. Dordrecht: Foris.

Donegan, Patricia J. & David Stampe 1979. "The study of Natural Phonology". *Current Approaches to Phonological Theory* ed. by D.A. Dinsen, 126–173. Bloomington: Indiana University Press.

Dressler, Wolfgang U. 1978. "Elements of a polycentristic theory of word formation". *Proceedings of the XIIth ICL* (Vienna, 1977). Innsbruck.

——. 1985. *Morphonology: The Dynamics of Derivation*. Ann Arbor: Karoma Publishers.

——, W. Mayerthaler, O. Panagl & W. U. Wurzel, eds. 1987. *Leitmotifs in Natural Morphology*. Amsterdam: Benjamins.

Erben, Johannes. 1975. *Einführung in die deutsche Wortbildungslehre*. Berlin: Schmidt.

Falkenstein, Adam. 1949. *Grammatik der Sprache Gudeas von Lagaš*. Roma: Pontificium Institutum Biblicum.

Fillmore, Charles J. 1968. "The case for case". Bach & Harms 1968.1–88.

Fleischer, W. 1975. *Wortbildung der deutschen Gegenwartssprache*. Tübingen: Niemeyer.

Fodor, I. 1959. "The origin of grammatical gender". *Lingua* 7.1–41, 186–214.

Fromkin, Victoria & Robert Rodman. 1974. *An Introduction to Language*. New York: Holt, Rinehart and Winston.

Gleason, Henry A. 1961. *An Introduction to Descriptive Linguistic*. New York: Holt, Rinehart and Winston. (Revised edition.)

Goodwin, William W. 1894/1965. *A Greek Grammar*. London: Macmillan.

Greenberg, Joseph. 1966. *Language Universals with Special Reference to Feature Hierarchies*. The Hague: Mouton.

Haegeman, Liliane. 1991. *Introduction to Government & Binding Theory*. Oxford: Blackwell.

Halle, Maurice. 1973. "Prolegomena to a theory of word formation". *Linguistic Inquiry* IV.3–16.

Halliday, Michael A. K. 1967. "Notes on transitivity and theme in English, Part I". *Journal of Linguistics* 3.37–81.

Harrell, Richard S. 1965. *A Short Reference Grammar of Moroccan Arabic*. Washington, D.C.: Georgetown University Press.

Harris, Alice C. & Lyle Campbell. 1995. *Historical Syntax in Cross-Linguistic Perspective*. Cambridge: Cambridge University Press.

Harris, James W. 1969. *Spanish Phonology*. Cambridge, Mass.: MIT Press.

——. 1975. "Morphology in generative grammar: Vowel alternations in Spanish verb forms". *El español y la linguistica generativo-transformacional* ed. by J. Guitart & J. Roy. Barcelona: Ediciones 62, Peninsula.

Harris, Zelig S. 1951. *Methods in Structural Linguistics*. Chicago: University of Chicago Press.

Havránek, Bohuslav & Alois Jedlička. 1963. *Česká mluvnice*. Praha: Státní pedagogické nakladatelstvi.

Hewson, John & Vit Bubenik. 1997. *Tense and Aspect in Indo-European Languages: Theory, Typology, Diachrony*. Amsterdam: Benjamins.

Hirtle, Walter H. 1975. *Time, Aspect and the Verb*. Québec: Presses de l'Université Laval.

Hjelmslev, Louis. 1935. *La catégorie des cas. Etude de grammaire générale. Acta Jutlandica* VII.1.xij–184 and IX.2.viij–78.

Hockett, Charles F. 1954. "Two models of grammatical description". *Word* 10.210–231.

——. 1958. *A Course in Modern Linguistics*. New York: The Macmillan Company.

Hooper, Joan B. 1976. *An Introduction to Natural Generative Phonology*. New York: Academic Press.

Hudson, R. A. 1976. *Arguments for a Non-Transformational Grammar*. Chicago: University of Chicago Press.

Hyman, Larry M. 1975. *Phonology: Theory and Analysis*. New York: Holt, Rinehart and Winston.

Itkonen, Esa. 1976. "The use and misuse of the principle of axiomatics in linguistics". *Lingua* 38.185–220.

Jakobson, Roman. 1936. "Beitrag zur allgemeinen Kasuslehre". *Selected Writings* II, 23–71. The Hague: Mouton.

——. 1957. *Shifters, Verbal Categories and the Russian Verb*. Cambridge, Mass.: Harvard University Press.

Jensen, J. 1990. *Morphology*. Amsterdam: Benjamins.

Jespersen, Otto. 1929. *The Philosophy of Grammar*. London: Allen and Unwin.

——. 1942. *A Modern English Grammar on Historical Principles*. Part VI. *Morphology*. London: Allen and Unwin.

Joly, André. 1975. "Toward a theory of gender in Modern English". *Studies in English Grammar* ed. by André Joly, 229–287. Lille: Presses de l'Université de Lille.

Katz, Jerrold J. 1966. *The Philosophy of Language*. New York: Harper and Row.

Keenan, Edrward L. 1985. "Passive in the world's languages". *Language Typology and Syntactic Description* ed. by T. Shopen, 243–281. Cambridge: Cambridge University Press.

Keyser, Samuel J. & Paul M. Postal. 1976. *Beginning English Grammar*. New York: Harper & Row.

Kiparsky, Paul. 1968. "Tense and mood in Indo-European syntax". *Foundations of Language* 4.30–57.

Klavans, Judy. 1985. "The independence of syntax and phonology in cliticization". *Language* 61.95–120.

Koziol, Herbert. 1937. *Handbuch der Englischen Wortbildungslehre*. Heidelberg.

Krámský, Jiří. 1969. *The Word as a Linguistic Unit*. The Hague: Mouton.

Kuryłowicz, Jerzy. 1964. *Inflectional Categories of Indo-European*. Heidelberg: Carl Winter.

Ladefoged, Peter. 1975. *A Course in Phonetics*. New York: Harcourt Brace Jovanovich.

Lees, Robert B. 1963. *The Grammar of English Nominalizations*. Bloomington/The Hague: Indiana University Press. (2nd Printing.)

Lewis, Geoffrey L. 1967. *Turkish Grammar*. Oxford: Clarendon Press.

Lewis, M. B. 1968. *Malay*. London: The English Universities Press.

Li, Charles N. 1976. *Subject and Topic*. New York: Academic Press.

Lightfoot, David. 1975. *Natural Logic and the Greek Moods*. The Hague: Mouton.

Lipka, Leonhard 1975. "Prolegomena to 'Prolegomena' to a theory of word formation". *The Transformational-Generative Paradigm and Modern Linguistic Theory* ed. by E. F. K. Körner. Amsterdam: Benjamins.

Lyons, John. 1968. *Introduction to Theoretical Linguistics*. Cambridge: Cambridge University Press.

——. 1977. *Semantics*. Volumes 1 and 2. Cambridge: Cambridge University Press.

Macdonell, Arthur A. 1916. *A Vedic Grammar for Students*. Oxford: Oxford University Press.

Marchand, Hans. 1969. *The Categories and Types of Present-Day English Word Formation*. 2nd Edition. Munich: Beck.

Martinet, André. 1965. "De la morphonologie". *La linguistique* 1.16–31.

Matthews, Peter H. 1972. *Inflectional Morphology: A Theoretical Study Based on Aspects of Latin Verb Conjugation*. Cambridge: Cambridge University Press.

——. 1974. *Morphology: An Introduction to the Theory of Word-Structure*. Cambridge: Cambridge University Press.

Meillet, Antoine & Joseph Vendryes. 1948. *Traité de grammaire comparée des langues classiques*. Paris: Champion.

Mitchell, Terence F. 1962. *Colloquial Arabic*. London: The English Universities Press.

Moreland, Floyd L. & Rita M. Fleischer. 1973. *Latin: An Intensive Course*. Berkeley: University of California Press.

Nida, Eugene A. 1949. *Morphology: A Descriptive Analysis of Words*. 2nd Edition. Ann Arbor, Mich.: University of Michigan Press.

Ogden, Charles K. & I. A. Richards. 1946. *The Meaning of Meaning*. 8th Edition. London: Routledge & Kegan Paul. (First edition 1923.)

Palmer, Frank R. 1965. *A Linguistic Study of the English Verb*. London: Longmans.

Peirce, Charles S. 1955. *Philosophical Writings of Peirce* ed. by Justus Buchler. New York: Dover.

Robins, Robert H. 1959. "In defense of WP". *Transactions of the Philological Society* 57.116–144.

——. 1967. *A Short History of Linguistics*. London: Longmans.

Rohrer, Christopher. 1974. "Some problems of word formation". *Linguistische Arbeiten* 14. Tübingen: Niemeyer.

Rosén, Haiim B. 1977. *Contemporary Hebrew*. The Hague: Mouton.

de Saussure, Ferdinand. 1955. *Cours de linguistique générale*. 5th Edition. Paris: Payot. (English translation by Wade Baskin, *Course in General Linguistics*. New York: Philosophical Library, 1959.)

Schachter, Paul. 1985. "Parts-of-speech systems". *Language Typology and Syntactic Description*. Volume 1 ed. by T. Shopen, 3–61. Cambridge: Cambridge University Press.

Schwyzer, Eduard. 1959. *Griechische Grammatik*. München: Beck.

Spencer, Andrew. 1991. *Morphological Theory: An Introduction to Word Structure in Generative Grammar*. Oxford: Blackwell.

Steinberg, Dany D. 1975. "Chomsky: From formalism to mentalism and psychological invalidity". *Glossa* 9.83–117.

Stevenson, C. H. 1970. *The Spanish Language Today*. London: Hutchinson.

Stockwell, Robert P. 1977. *Foundations of Syntactic Theory*. Englewood Cliffs: Prentice-Hall.

Tesnière, Lucien. 1959. *Éléments de syntaxe structurale*. Paris: Klincksieck.

Trubetzkoy, Nikolai S. 1929. "Sur la morphologie". *Travaux du cercle linguistique de Prague*. 1.85–85.

_____. 1934. "Das morphonologische System der russichen Sprache". *Travaux du cercle linguistique de Prague*. Volume 5, Part 2.

_____. 1939. *Grundzüge der Phonologie. Travaux du cercle linguistique de Prague* 7. (English translation by C. A. M. Baltaxe, Berkeley/Los Angeles: University of California Press, 1969).

Tzermias, Paul. 1969. *Neugriechische Grammatik*. Bern/München: Francke.

Wardhaugh, Ronald. 1972. *Introduction to Linguistics*. New York: McGraw-Hill.

Wright, W. 1896–1898. *A Grammar of the Arabic Language*. Volumes 1 and 2. Cambridge: Cambridge University Press.

Zandvoort, Reinard W. 1966. *A Handbook of English Grammar*. Englewood Cliffs: Longmans.

INDEX OF LANGUAGES

GENERAL INDEX

Languages of the World/Materials
LINCOM's Descriptive Grammar series

* = already published

208 **Embera** (Chocó) Daniel Aguirre*
209 **Hiligaynon / Ilonggo** Walter L. Spitz
210 **Lobire** Moses Kwado-Kambou
211 **Fering** (Northfrisian, Germanic) Karen Ebert
212 **Udmurt (Finno-Ugric)** Erberhard Winkler
213 **Ancient Greek** Silvia Luraghi
214 **Chiwere Siouan** N. Louanna Furbee & Jill D. Davidson
215 **Chuckchee** (Paleosiberian) Alexander Volodin
216 **Chiriguano** Wolf Dietrich
217 **Latvian** Nicole Nau*
222 **Tyvan** Gregory Anderson
225 **Slovenian** Ch. Gribble
227 **Malayalam** Rodney Moag
242 **Modern Scots** Alexander T. Bergs
251 **Xakas** Gregory Anderson*
252 **Old Saxon**   James E. Cathey
254 **Saho** (East Cushitic) Giorgio Banti
255 **Udeghe** (Tungus-Manchu) Albina H.Girfanova
256 **Newari/Newar** E. Austin Hale
257 **Tyvan (Turkic)** Gregory Anderson
258 **Biri (Pama-Nyungan)** Angela Terrill*
260 **Ostyak (Uralic)** Irina Nikolaeva
261 **Lingala** Michael Meeuwis*
262 **Klallam** Timothy Montler
263 **Manchu** Carsten Naeher
266 **Chuj** Judith Maxwell
267 **Kaqchikel** Judith Maxwell
268 **Urak Lawoi'** David Hogan*
273 **Bubbure** Andrew Haruna
274 **Romanian** Cynthia M. Vakareliyska
275 **Aragonés** Carlos Inchaurralde
276 **Chagatay** A. Bodrogligeti
277 **Turkish** A. Bodrogligeti
278 **Isleño Spanish** Felice Coles
298 **Gheg** Pandeli Pani
300 **Nuu-chah-nulth (Nootka)** T. Nakayama
301 **Oneida** C. Abbott
302 **Sapuan** P. Jacq & P. Sidwell*
303 **Oi** P. Jacq & P. Sidwell
304 **Talieng** P. Jacq & P. Sidwell
305 **Ostyak** I. Nikolaeva
306 **Ottoman** A. Bodrogligeti
307 **Faetar** Naomi Nagy
308 **Choctow** P. Kwatchka
311 **Juang** Manideepa Patnaik
312 **Karitiana** L. Raccanello Storto
320 **Kawesqar** Oscar Aguilar F.
321 **Turkish** A. Bodrogligeti
322 **Shanghai** Sean Zhu
323 **Santali** Lukas Neukom
324 **Karaj** K. David Harrison
325 **Pileni** Åshild Næss
326 **Echie** Ozo-Mekuri Ndimele
327 **Judeo-Arabic** Benjamin Hary

328 **Tobelo** Gary Holton
329 **Ogbronuagum** E. Kari
330 **Old Nubian** Gerald M. Browne
331 **Taiwanese** Lilly L. Chen
332 **Kiswahili** Sakari B. Salone
333 **Wolof** Fallou Ngom
334 **Karao** Sherri Brainard
335 **Japanese** Yoshihiko Ikegami
336 **East Friesland** Yaron Matras & Gertrud Reershemius
337 **Selayarese** Hasan Basri
338 **Old Church Slavonic** Boris Gasparov
339 **Malagasy** Charles Randria-masimanana

Languages of the World/Text Collections:

01 **Even- Texts** Andrej Malchukov
05 **Palestinian Texts** Kimary N. Shahin
07 **Tariana Texts** (North Arawak) Alexandra Aikhenvald*
08 **Chinook Jargon** Zvjezdana Vrzic
09 **Western Apache Texts** W.de Reuse
11 **Camling -Texts** Karen Ebert
12 **Itelmen - Texts** Jonathan David Bobaljik
14 **A Collection of Laz Spoken Texts (+CD-ROM)** Silvia Kutscher & Nuran Sevim Genç*
15 **Saho Texts** Giorgo Banti
16 **Mbay Texts** John M. Keegan
17 **Der Ostfränkische Basisdialekt von Hetzles** Klaus Geyer

Languages of the World/Text Library:

01 **Minhe Mangghuer Folktales** Zhu Yongzhong, Wang Xianzheng, Keith Slater & Kevin Stuart
02 **Xunhua Salar Folklore** Ma Wie, Ma Jianzhong & Kevin Stuart
03 **Huzhu Mongghul Folklore** Limusishiden & Kevin Stuart
04 **Huzhu Folklore Selections** Limusishiden & Kevin Stuart (eds.)
05 **Die udischen Evangelien der Gebrüder Be)anov (1893)** Wolfgang Schulze
06 **Anthology of Menominee Sayings** Timothy Guile
07 **Kawesqar Texts** Oscar Aguilar F.

Languages of the World/Dictionaries:

01 **Minhe Mangghuer - English Dictionary** Wang Xianzheng (*Qinghai Medical College*), Zhu Yongzhong (*Zhongchuan Junior Middle School*), Keith Slater (*Qinghai Junior Teachers' College*), & Kevin Stuart (*University of California, Santa Barbara*)
03 **Dictionary of Mbay** John Keegan*
05 **Dictionary of Sango** Bradford & Bradford
06 **A Dictionary of Negerhollands** Robin Sabino & Anne-Katrin Gramberg
07 **Degema - English Dictionary** Ethelbert Kari
08 **Eudeve Dictionary** David Shaul
09 **A Short Bonan-English Dictionary** Chen Nai-Xiong
10 **A Short Dongsiang-English Dictionary** Chen Nai-Xiong
11 **A Short Mongour-English Dictionary** Chen Nai-Xiong
12 **A Short East Yugour-English Dictionary** Chen Nai-Xiong
13 **A Short Dagour-English Dictionary** Chen Nai-Xiong
14 **Tyvan dictionary** Gregory Anderson
15 **Xakas dictionary** Gregory Anderson
16 **Nhaheun - French - English Lexicon** Michel Ferlus (ed. by P. Jacq & P. Sidwell)
21 **Comparative West Bahnaric Dictionary** P. Jacq & P. Sidwell
22 **Palestinian Arabic-English / English-Palestinian Arabic Dictionary** Kimary Shahin
23 **Loven (Jruq) Consolidated Lexicon** Pascale Jacq & Paul Sidwell

An Introduction to the Study of Morphology
VIT BUBENIK
Memorial University of Newfoundland

Each chapter (with the exception of the last one) is provided with pertinent exercices. Its data are taken from languags the author has been researching over the last twenty years (Latin, Greek, Turkish, Arabic, Hebrew, Sanskrit, Russian). Its argumentation is built around the major turning points in the history of morphology linked with scholars such as Hockett (1954), Matthews (1974), Bybee (1985), Dressler (1985), Bauer (1988), Spencer (1991), Carstairs-McCarthy (1992) and Aronoff (1993). In the last chapter the author explicates a cognitively conceived subdiscipline of Morphology in its relation to Formal Syntax, Generative Phonology, Functional Grammar, so-called Natural Morphology, Universal Grammar, and Typology.

Contents: Introduction, Grammatical Units, Paradigmatic and Syntagmatic Relations, Inflectional and Derivational Morphology, Inflectional Categories Associated with Nominal Elements, Inflectional Categories Associated with Verbal Elements, Morphosyntactic Properties and their Exponents, Morpheme and Allomorph, Derivational Morphology, Theoretical Models of Morphology, References.

ISBN 3 89586 570 2.
LINCOM Coursebooks in Linguistics 07.
Ca. 220 pp. USD 48 / DM 72 / £ 28.

Structure and Interpretation in Natural Language
MARC AUTHIER & LISA REED
The Pennsylvania State University

The central objective of this book is to present an integrated theory of the syntax-semantics interface, one which combines the most recent advances in the generative framework with the basic tenets of model-theoretic semantics. The three opening chapters develop, in a step-by-step and highly accessible fashion, an approach to structure and meaning in these terms.

The remaining chapters show how this approach sheds light on three long-standing issues in formal grammar: the treatment of "syntactically-triggered" presuppositions, the treatment of some notable exceptions to the generative binding conditions, and the issue of the relative autonomy of syntax and semantics. With respect to the first issue, it is argued that a compositional treatment of syntactically-triggered presuppositions can be formulated as a condition which ties presuppositional triggers to a specific class of syntactic configurations definable in terms of devices found in Minimalist syntax. A subsequent chapter demonstrates that the empirical coverage of so-called Bare-Output Conditions in generative syntax can be increased if such conditions are made sensitive to the two types of semantic information which have sometimes been recognized in model-theoretic semantics; that is, extension expressions and implicature expressions. Finally, empirical evidence is adduced which supports the view that there are two distinct types of semantic constraints and that those which make reference to features of tree geometry can, under specific circumstances defined by representational Economy conditions, override those which do not.

Audience: Linguists, philosophers, computational and psycho-linguists, cognitive scientists; advanced undergraduates, graduate students and researchers in these fields.

ISBN 3 89586 603 2.
LINCOM Studies in Theoretical Linguistics 14.
210pp. USD 70 / DM 112 / £ 42.

Introduction to Linguistic Field Methods

BERT VAUX & JUSTIN COOPER
Harvard University

The present volume addresses the need for an up-to-date, accessible, and comprehensive introduction to the elicitation of linguistic data from native speaker informants. The material, following an introductory chapter surveying the general enterprise of field research, is organized into eight major areas of current linguistic and anthropological interest: Phonetics, Phonology, Morphology, Syntax, Semantics, Sociolinguistics/ Dialectology, Lexicography, and Folklore. The chapters are designed to be covered at a rate of one per week, based on a sixteen-week semester. Each chapter presents basic structures to be elicited, and provides cautionary tales drawn from the experiences of seasoned field workers who have attempted to elicit these structures. These, in turn, are followed by suggested readings and illustrative exercises for each chapter. Emphasis is placed not on developing a theory of field work, but rather on providing enlightening suggestions and entertaining anecdotes designed to guide students down their own personal path to linguistic discovery.

ISBN 3 89586 198 7.
LINCOM Coursebooks in Linguistics 01.
Ca. 240 pp. USD 48 / DM 72 / £ 28.

Coursebook in Feature Geometry

JOHN NEWMAN
Massey University

The *Coursebook in Feature Geometry* is an undergraduate course introducing students to current phonology through a sustained use of the Feature Geometry framework. It is written as a coherent, accessible, and well-illustrated introduction to the key ideas of Feature Geometry, focusing on rules of assimilation. In its 20 units and 40 exercises, it takes the reader step-by-step through the representational devices of Feature Geometry. The *Coursebook* attempts to present the core ideas of Feature Geometry in a unified way, rather than attempting to incorporate the (considerable) debate concerning almost every aspect of the theory. The version of Feature Geometry underlying the *Coursebook* is basically that found in Sagey's The *Representation of features in non-linear phonology* (1990), revised in accordance with the claims of Lahiri and Evans' 1991 article on *Palatalization and coronality*.

The author is Senior Lecturer in the Department of Linguistics and Second Language Teaching, *Massey University*, New Zealand. The author has a PhD in linguistics from the University of California at San Diego.

ISBN 3 89586 102 2.
LINCOM Coursebooks in Linguistics 02.
160pp. USD 38 / DM 62 / £ 25.

Course discounts available!

LINCOM Coursebooks in Linguistics

in this series: